AROUND
MADAGASCAR
ON MY KAYAK

MADAGASCAR

AFRICA

Madagascar

Cap d'Ambre

Antsiranana
(Diego Suarez)

Mitsio
Archipelago

Cap Saint Sébastien

Nosy Bé

Sambava

Mozambique
Channel

Antalaha

Nosy Lava

Tanjona
Angontsy
(Cap Angotsy)

Maroantsetra

Mahajanga
Katsepy

Cap Masoala

Soalala

16°S

16°S

Besalampy

Soanierana-
Ivongo

Juan de
Nova*
Island

Ile Ste Marie

Maintrano

Start / Finish

Tsingy
Reserve

ANTANANARIVO
(Tananarive)

Toamasina
(Tamatave)

Vatomandry

Belo Tsiribihiri

Morondava

Belo sur Mer

21°S

21°S

Andranopasy

Mananjary

Morombe

Andavadoaka

Cap Tala

Manakara

Tsiandamba

Ifaty

Toliara (Tulear)

Farafangara

Anakao

Beheloka

Indian Ocean

Sainte-Luce

Lohatanjona
Fenambosy

Italy

Tolanaro

Star Bank

Ambovombe

Lavanono

Antaritarika

Cap Ste Marie
(Tanjona Vohimena)

Faux Cap (Betanty)

50   0   50   100 150 200 250 km

45°E

50°E

Canale des Pangalanes

AROUND
MADAGASCAR
ON MY KAYAK

RIAAN MANSER

JONATHAN BALL PUBLISHERS
JOHANNESBURG & CAPE TOWN

Published in 2010 in trade paperback by
JONATHAN BALL PUBLISHERS (PTY) LTD
PO Box 33977
Jeppestown
2043

Reprinted once in 2011

This paperback edition published once in 2012 by Jonathan Ball Publishers

ISBN 978-1-86842-537-2
Also available as an ebook 978-1-86842-433-7

PHOTOGRAPHIC ACKNOWLEDGEMENTS
Every effort has been taken to credit the correct copyright holder
for the pictures in the three picture sections. In the event of
any error or omission, please contact the publishers so that
it can be remedied in the event of a reprint.
The majority of the photographs in all three sections
© 2010 – Round the Outside Media
First section – page 12 – Red Sunset © Harriet João

Edited by Willem Steenkamp and Frances Perryer
Cover design and reproduction by
MR Design, Cape Town
Text design by Triple M Design
Set in 11.25/15.5pt ITC Legacy Serif
Printed and bound by CTP Book Printers, Cape

Twitter: www.twitter.com/JonathanBallPub
Facebook: www.facebook.com/pages/Jonathan-Ball-Publishers/298034457992
Blog: http://jonathanball.bookslive.co.za/

CONTENTS

PREFACE

My name is Riaan Manser. In 2004 and 2005 I became the first man in the world to circumnavigate Africa on a bicycle. The story of my adventures was published in 2007 under the title of *Around Africa on My Bicycle*, and for the next year I stumbled around in a daze, bombarded with questions, mostly from strangers, about what had happened in my life after returning from my bicycle trip.

'What happened to your girlfriend?', and 'What happened to your dogs?', and 'What happened to you?' and so on and so on. I answered them all quite comfortably, over and over, although I began to hope that the barrage of all-too-familiar questions would eventually dry up.

But the fact was that when the story of my epic adventure was published I had unknowingly roped many people into my life, my dreams and aspirations. Going around Africa on my bicycle had changed my life and many people who had lived that journey vicariously with and through me wanted more.

And so did I. And so here is the story of the second step I took in the process of turning my life around.

CHAPTER 1

AN END AND A BEGINNING

*I was home, alive, and bound by the non-negotiable promise
I had made to Vasti never even to entertain a thought of
another lengthy (and dangerous) journey ...*

My kayak trip around Madagascar grew directly out of my long slog around Africa's coasts on my bicycle in 2004 and 2005, and so it is worthwhile starting this story by describing the end of my circumnavigation and how it led me to the dangerous and exciting coasts of the greatest of Africa's islands.

The crowds had gathered in force at the Cape Town Waterfront that Friday afternoon in late November 2005. Many were there to welcome me back, because thousands of newspaper readers had followed my progress around Africa through the newspaper columns I had sent back at various points. But I'm sure a sizeable number of the spectators were there mainly to see for themselves whether I actually existed.

I would even venture to say that some came along to see not myself but the bicycle on which I had pedalled 40 000 km through 33 countries, including some of Africa's toughest and most dangerous ...

I fell into the clutches of the TV crews the second I had crossed the finish line and the Africa trip had become history. What I really wanted to do, first and foremost, was wrap my arms around my long-suffering girlfriend, Vasti, who had taken every step along with me in spirit, but what I got was a camera crew and an interviewer's microphone in my face as soon as I came to a halt. This was *their* moment, not mine.

Things were a little less hectic at the media conference my main sponsor, Windhoek Lager Light, had laid on in the adjacent Nelson Mandela Gateway restaurant, lubricated by generous stocks of their famous beer. This sort of media attention was new to me, and while I might have looked comfortable with it all, it was a different story inside myself. I even remember worrying – a bit selfishly, perhaps – whether Windhoek Light would consider it worthwhile to sponsor me on a future project. But it wasn't long before I was mentally pinching myself every five minutes or so to confirm the reality: I was home!

Earlier I had made a conscious decision not to be over-emotional about the end of my two-year journey, because I did not believe the moment deserved that sort of attention. After all, any journey has to end sooner or later, and almost every one of the 808 days of my travels through Africa had served up its adventure, some of which were fun and others much less so.

The bottom line right then was that I was home, alive, and bound by the non-negotiable promise I had made to Vasti never even to entertain a thought of another lengthy (and dangerous) journey like this again, ever.

We had been offered free accommodation for the night in an ultra-luxurious Waterfront hotel, but I declined. Of course I declined! I had not slept in my own bed for over two years, and simply could not wait to get back home to our house on the Gordon's Bay mountainside with its majestic views of False Bay.

My homecoming was both sad and sweet. One of my dogs,

Murphy, had died while I was away, but my Boxer, Jester, my first-ever pet – grey-muzzled now, half blind and totally deaf – was waiting for me. She probably didn't know who the hell I was, but that didn't matter. I knew who *she* was.

What was the first thing I did when I got home? That's my business ... but actually time was blurred for a few days, although I will say we spent it at home, for the simple reason that Vasti and I had no money for going out.

The scary fact of the matter was that we had no idea where the next month's rent would come from. The monthly allowance from Windhoek Lager had ended that very month, my bank account was empty and Vasti was still doing her articles at a firm of attorneys. Yet we were not in serious panic mode, although we were certainly concerned.

I reminded Vasti of my long-standing conviction that opportunity would always be there if only we took hold of it, and that somehow I would always be able to feed my family – even if it meant, in my best friend Troy's colourful phrase, 'shovelling shit'. And to be truthful, the need for some energetic shit-shovelling was looking and smelling more and more like a certainty.

My life has always been a mixture of good and bad fortune, and just then good fortune struck in no uncertain terms. My clothing suppliers for the Africa trip, First Ascent, surprised me with a R5 000 bonus, which – thank heavens – not only took care of the rent but sucked the desperation out of me when I had to negotiate with three large South African publishing houses about producing my story in book form. Desperation is not a good companion when you are negotiating – let's face it, even with a bad cold most of us can smell it a nautical mile away.

The temporary lack of desperation gave me some control over my life as I sat in a seaside coffee shop talking details with a constantly smoking Joe Cocker look-alike whom almost any writer would recognise instantly as the renowned Mr Jonathan Ball, of Jonathan Ball Publishers.

Thanks to that respite, I was able to turn down Jonathan's offer of some immediate financial relief in exchange for the manuscript I had just presented to him. It wasn't easy saying 'I'm OK' when I wasn't really OK. But I had changed so much in the time I had spent away from reality that the last thing I wanted was to fall easy prey to one of the bigger of the seven deadly sins, greed. And so the following week I signed up with Jonathan – a decision which I am happy to have made.

As if I did not have enough dream stuff on my plate, there was more to come, additional evidence that dreams do come true; that thoughts you scoff at in jest because they seem too much like fairy tales might be only a whisker away from coming true. Ask me – I know.

While I had been cycling through Senegal I had made contact with the Nelson Mandela Children's Fund to investigate the possibility (yes, I can hear you scoffing already) of meeting with Mr Mandela on my return to South Africa. I had only completed about 12 000 km at that stage, so I wasn't too surprised when Zelda, Mr Mandela's PA, came back to say that he had taken the difficult decision to step out of public life and dedicate his time to his wife, Graça (whom he had married in 1998), and his children.

Of course I understood, although I was very disappointed. So you can imagine how I felt one evening when I got a call to say that Mr Mandela had expressed the wish to meet me. Jeez, I was floored!

I was at a friend's house to watch the short TV documentary piece about my bike trip, and just after it finished I started receiving call after call from people I knew, congratulating me on my effort. There were so many calls that I missed plenty of them, but I was sure that most were from friends who would most likely call back later or the next day. Then suddenly Vasti's phone began to ring and she immediately interrupted me to say I needed to end my current call and take the one she had received.

It was Seamus, producer of the documentary we had been watching, and he didn't waste any time on greetings or how-are-yous. 'Where have you been?' he wanted to know.

'I've been here, watching the story on TV,' I replied, not adding the top question in my sub-conscious, namely: 'Why do you ask?'

'Mr Mandela just watched your story on TV,' Seamus blurted, 'and wants to meet with you. When are you next in Joburg?'

'Don't joke with me, Seamus,' I replied, then had second thoughts. 'Are you serious?'

'Of course I'm serious, don't I sound serious?'

Now I realised that Seamus was telling the truth, and there were tears in my eyes. Nelson Mandela wasn't just a legendary political figure, he was the man who, above all, instilled in us the belief that we could do what we had always been convinced we couldn't do, that we could share our awesome land and live together in peace. My initial reaction was that I didn't deserve to spend time with this great man. Compared to him, what had I done, really?

'When?' I asked when I had found my voice again. 'Where? How?' Not that I had the money to fly to Johannesburg. But I knew I would find a solution somehow. And I knew for sure that I would not be going to see Mr Mandela without Vasti. I wanted her to see and experience at first hand what it felt like when one of my amazing dreams came true. And after all, she deserved the honour as much as I did.

That Monday morning, while sitting in Jonathan Ball's office, I asked him if he would be willing to fly Vasti and me up to meet Mr Mandela. He agreed without hesitation, and next thing we were on the plane to meet Madiba in real life. Unreal!

That wasn't all. EuropCar had heard about the meeting through the grapevine, and when we went to collect our hire car we were gently ushered in the opposite direction, to the limousine service area, and then we were being driven to Mr Mandela's Houghton address in the luxury of a Mercedes 500 with a driver named James (yes, that really was his name) ... that's about all I remember – it was just too much to absorb all at once.

Some prominent people don't live up to their public image when you meet them face to face, but in real life Madiba was every ounce the legendary figure depicted in the world media. Waiting in the foyer for him to welcome me, I was stunned when he called out: 'Where is that boy, where is that boy and his bicycle?'

I smiled so broadly that I remember it was difficult even to speak clearly as I stood alongside this most adored South African statesman and heard him tell me I was great and also (and most notably as far as I was concerned) that I did not realise what I had accomplished. When we parted, his last words – which I know will come to fruition one day – were: 'You have done something that will inspire the youth of our continent.'

I'd been back home less than a week and already I was ticking dream boxes I had not even considered options up to then. But there was no honeymoon period – things were happening very quickly. Apart from the Mandela visit, there were TV and radio interviews with the very same people who had scoffed at my departure two years before now queuing up to get some insight into how my mind worked.

What I could not help thinking about was what was probably in many other people's minds. It's not true, many of them must have said at dinner tables, there has to be a catch. He probably had a big support crew, he probably carried a gun for safety and a Garmin for navigation. He probably skipped the countries that were at war and took a doctor along to look after his health. What the heck, he's probably only a fictional character anyway.

Fortunately I had a platform from which to dispel the notion that I was a lunatic – and fortunately, too, enough opportunities arose for me to relieve our current dire financial situation, because corporates were now booking me to tell their staff members my story in a conference setting. It was a far cry from the pitiable level of luxury I had had in the past two years.

I was constantly being asked: 'What's next?', and I would confess that I had zero desire to set off again any time soon. Home was exactly what the cliché said it should be … sweet.

But who was I fooling? Maybe others, but not myself. In my innermost being I knew that something else was on the cards, although I didn't know what at that stage. It wasn't my doing. If ever Lady Destiny was calling the shots, this had to be it. She knew what she had in store for me, and was now sitting patiently back while I slowly unwrapped the surprise she had planted inside my head.

So there I was, pretending to myself that the bicycle trip had been enough. My original goal had been to try to circumnavigate Africa, and, if I failed, at least to come back with stories of grand adventure with which to entertain my grandchildren one day! But the other half of me knew all too well that I was in denial, and that the next life-changing 20 seconds of decision-making were not too far off. The truth of the matter is straightforward. Once I had promised myself that I was going to tackle the next big one, all that remained was to deal with the details and set a departure date.

I had conquered Africa – in so far as *anyone* can conquer Africa – but every time I glanced at a map which traced my progress around the continent I could not help but notice that I had missed out a humungous chunk of earth named Madagascar off the east coast. So in fact I had not come near to conquering Africa, as I had been claiming. That, it was glaringly obvious, would take a little more effort.

So the decisive 20 seconds kicked in. And Destiny smiled.

'Just add water' – we've all heard that phrase at one time or another. Well, that was exactly what I was about to do. Or rather add myself to the water. And not a teeny weeny bit, either – a hell of a lot. Madagascar was the world's fourth-largest island, and I was going to be the first person ever to circumnavigate her by kayak. Alone and unaided once again, just as I had been on my bike. I found I didn't care that professionals had tried to do it already, failed and nearly died, even with assistance. It was something I had to do, and mentally I began packing.

CHAPTER 2

GETTING READY TO ROLL

I needed two categories of sponsors: one for equipment and the other for finance ...

Research gave me exactly the same overall answer as I got for my African cycle trip. Every statistic shouted the same message: *Why even bother? You'll never make it!* What the gloomy stats couldn't drag down with them, though, was that I would be off to the most beautiful and unique island on the planet, with indigenous fauna and flora that represented a large percentage of the world's diversity. Seventy-five per cent of its animals were found nowhere else in the world, and the same applied to an enormous number of its myriad plant species. Incredible! It began feeling like a dream again, a fine idea that would never come to fruition.

I also discovered how little the world knew about Madagascar. As far as I could see, most people thought it was only the name of a cartoon documentary! Yet the basic figures were there for anyone to see. The most important ones for me were all to do with its size – a massive 581 540 square kilometres, sparsely populated by only 18.5 million French- and Malagasy-speaking people – and the length of the coastline ... all of 4 828 kilometres.

The most important thing of all, however, was the fact that the Madagascar trip would mean reneging on my earlier promise to Vasti that I would never leave her alone again as I had on my two-year trip around Africa. Before embarking on my preparations we had to talk this through very thoroughly, to clear up any confusion or misunderstanding and to let me explain to her why my career as an adventurer had a second chapter that needed to be written. Her unwavering support would be crucial.

I had learnt some lessons in this regard, and this time a chunk of my budget would be dedicated to making it possible for us to see one another more regularly at various stages of my journey, and having the resources to communicate more effectively. It was asking a great deal of her: my time-estimate was 12 months at worst and eight months at best. At the same time, however, I knew that my time estimates were notoriously inaccurate (I had thought the circumnavigation of Africa would take a year!).

With Vasti fully on board, I started collecting the best equipment and rounding up the potential partners/sponsors I would need to turn my idea into reality. I had set mid-May 2008 as my departure date, which gave me about six months to prepare. That was not much time to do everything I needed to do, but I thrive under pressure and did not see it as a negative. Get out there and get things together. No excuses.

Which sponsor to approach first was a no-brainer as far as I was concerned. I had been loyal to those who had been loyal to me, and obviously I should approach them before anyone else. Loyalty, I hear you scoff, the business world knows nothing about loyalty! But naivety had been my major ally thus far, and I was banking on it once more. Personally I don't think it was only the African cycle trip that taught me to be loyal. Not being the social person that most people perceive me to be, I had actually avoided building a network of relationships and instead had focused on quality above quantity. Maybe it was always an issue of trust that had now filtered into my socialising skills.

Anyway, I needed two categories of sponsors: one for equipment and the other for finance.

The most important item of equipment was obviously a kayak. The first kayak company I approached was aware of my African trip and its management wanted to chat about the possibility of a sponsorship. But although they were very eager initially, this approach ultimately came to nothing. The African trip had had me tagging along like a fool after the 'wrong' people, but this time I was much more experienced at spotting delaying signals.

So while they were umming and aahing about the benefits to them I made contact with Johan Loots, the owner-builder of PaddleYak kayaks. Johan was a man I'd heard many stories about, and the good stories came mostly from people who knew him personally and had used his kayaks – no better referrals, in my mind.

I visited Johan and his partner Teresa in his Hout Bay home and had an answer from him before we had even started on the second cup of tea. His concern, though, was that I should adhere to safety regulations. I was surprised. Was he serious? I was heading for some of the world's most dangerous waters and an exposed shoreline, going where no other person in a kayak had ever gone, so what sort of safety precautions did he expect would apply?

We agreed though that wearing a life-jacket *full-time* was non-negotiable, and that my GPS and satellite phone would always be safely stored and available in case anything went wrong. Naturally I agreed with his terms, although as yet I had neither GPS nor satphone!

The arrangement we reached was that Johan would supply training kayaks, and then, nearer the departure date, we would design and build a boat that we believed could see me around Madagascar. After this meeting it felt as though the journey was already under way. The very next day I was on the water, training away furiously in a new Paddleyak Swift – a special sea-going 'sit inside, sit on top' type very similar to the custom-made one I would be using.

Johan and his team had won numerous design awards for this specific craft. What made it unique among kayak designs was that it incorporated the surf-ski shell design into the respected traditional kayak design. It felt ideal. It felt right. Not just the kayak, but also my association with Johan.

Now, of course, I needed a GPS and a satphone as soon as possible to honour the terms of my agreement with Johan. I approached Garmin, which did not hesitate to supply me with equipment and also to become an assistant sponsor. For their cash support the assistant sponsor company would, apart from product use and placement, get branding on my vessel for the duration of the journey.

I still needed a headline sponsor (my fingers were still tightly crossed regarding Windhoek Lager) and two co-sponsors – although I had no one in mind at this stage, with only a few months to go. Craaaaazzzzzzzzy!

The satphone negotiations followed more or less the same course I had travelled in the run-up to my cycle trip, with tests and 'agreements' which went nowhere. Then I got on to a cellular company called Cellucity, and accepted immediately when they agreed to supply me with a loan unit for a year.

I had hoped to organise some airtime too, but settled for getting just the phone, which as far as I was concerned was a bonus by itself, since I couldn't afford to spend about $3 000 US buying one. I felt afterwards that I should have been more patient in looking for other offers, but needed another 'yes' to keep my organisational momentum up to speed. So Cellucity were going be my communications HQ, so to speak, at least in emergencies.

My search for the best high-definition video equipment that would be able to survive the journey ahead brought a bigger breakthrough than I had expected. I had to do better than the previous time, on several levels. I needed about 100 times more – and better-footage for the planned visual story this time, plus someone back home (*not* Vasti) to manage what I was doing in terms of the audio-visual stuff, as well as running a communications link with the South African and world media.

And my search brought me to the best man to help me with both requirements: Seamus Reynolds, the producer of two popular TV pieces on my African trip. He and I had stayed in touch, mostly because I had needed his advice during the turbulent media time I enjoyed since my first return to South Africa.

Seamus understood the nature of the media beast, I knew, and would be able to give me constant advice to keep me pointed in the right direction. Since my return he had made a big career move by leaving the famous Carte Blanche TV crew to set up his own production company (with the coolest of names – AFRICANBORN Media).

So I asked him to join me in the negotiations with a few companies that had shown interest in assisting me. Sony were first on the schedule, and Seamus was particularly excited at the thought of this option because of Sony's good name in his industry, as well as the compact construction of their new HD cameras.

Sony were well aware of the fact that I had used their equipment on the African trip, and, what was even more fortunate for me, were looking for an avenue by which to promote their new range of underwater housings. Perfect! Perfect!

Seamus and I chatted at length about Sony's offer of two HD hard-drive cameras, two still cameras, a small, compact laptop on which to download the footage, and waterproof housings for each piece of equipment. Seamus was especially pleased with Sony's commitment to back me through my entire never-been-done-before journey; he had seen many a shoot go pear-shaped because of equipment failure.

There was no doubt about the fact that this journey was going to be a few levels up from the norm; with Seamus's clear interest in my journey, I felt it would be madness not to approach him to assist me on a more permanent basis. I floated the idea of his managing the basics of my trip with a special focus on the two of us producing a documentary afterwards; I suggested he mull over the fundamentals of my offer for a week and then I'd bring him to Cape Town, where, I hoped, we could iron out details. In the meantime I kept my fingers crossed. I badly needed someone, and he was perfect!

There was no doubt about the fact that in Sony we had landed a big fish, which got me to thinking about exactly that – catching real big fish. If I wanted to survive in the most isolated parts of the Madagascan coastline I'd have to provide for myself, namely by harvesting the fruits of the sea.

Once again, there was no doubt about another fact, that the lures used the world over all fell under the intimidating shadow of the Rapala brand, and I intended to troll these plastic fish lookalikes almost full time while I was in the Madagascan seas so that I wouldn't go hungry. They were not cheap, however, and I anticipated going through quite a few during my projected 10 or so months on the water, so I needed a decent supply, and also the best reels and line on the market.

Shimano had sponsored me during my cycle trip, and I trusted they would be willing to assist again, but this time with survival equipment in the form of fishing gear. In South Africa Shimano has two separate divisions – cycling and fishing – and so I was referred to Mark Pledger, who, with his father and brother, runs Rapala VMC, which owns the Shimano fishing gear brand.

The Pledgers are people who don't really believe they are working to make a living so much as making a living from their hobby and passion. They were fans of what I had done on my previous adventure, and without much fuss generously supplied everything I needed.

They even put me in contact with some of their other sponsorees, Durban-based kayak fishermen, for information and advice. These

Durban fishermen were old hands at the game, and without even physically going out fishing with them I learnt loads by just picking their brains about their successes and failures. The best advice I received came from the one who said: 'If you want to catch a fish, you have to think like a fish, even if it feels weird.'

Then there were what I call the 'stationary' expenses of any adventure trip – items such as the tents, sleeping bags, knives, torches, dry bags and so on and on and on. This category is an unmanageable creature with a dynamic of its own, because it is a sort of never-ending list that mutates as time passes and the departure date draws nearer.

This time I homed in on the Trapper's Trading outdoor equipment chain, which had helped me in the past, and it took literally one call to brothers Grant and Mark Ponting to secure their involvement again. They understood that the demands – both mine and those of the journey itself – would be greater than last time, but it didn't worry them. 'We'll be glad to get involved again,' Grant said. 'Get to our Fourways Mall store and take whatever you need.' The details could be sorted out later.

So much for the support sponsors. But finance was needed to make the journey possible, and I had to act fast now. Pam Golding Properties had assisted me the year before in getting to New York to speak at the famous Explorers' Club, whose past and present members included astronaut Buzz Aldrin, the first man on Everest, Sir Edmund Hillary, and Antarctic adventurer Robert Scott.

The event had been a huge success, with rave reviews from all who attended my talk. Later, Pam Golding's son Peter had used me a few times to address his staff, and he was happy to have his company become one of the assistant sponsors.

I also had fleeting discussions with both the Mugg & Bean coffee-shop chain and my long-standing clothing sponsor, First Ascent, which I was extremely chuffed to have as partner again. Apart from the fact that their clothing is beyond question as regards quality, they also seemed to be thinking along the same longer-term lines as I was: I wanted to establish a clothing range and saw them as ideal in partnering this dream.

But now I needed to speak seriously and quickly to Windhoek Lager, a potential main sponsor, and also target a co-sponsor. The best one I could think of was Shoprite Checkers, a famous South African and African supermarket chain with strong representation in Madagascar.

Although I had targeted other retail chains, I had no doubt that Shoprite's influence on the mysterious island was more valuable than I could measure right now. And without wishing to seem naive once more, the guys I negotiated with were good people; it felt right, and it felt even better knowing I'd secured a co-sponsor with only two months to go. Cutting it fine!

Windhoek Lager remained. They had responded to my e-mails, but the people who signed the cheques, so to speak, were not in the loop. I was concerned; this was exactly the situation I had hoped to avoid. So I stopped sending e-mails and instead called incessantly in an effort to speak directly to the person who was in charge of the brand – Brendon Nash, the busiest man on the planet.

A week later the game of phone tag was over and we were speaking to each other face to face over a late-afternoon lunch. Brendon was aware of what I intended to achieve in Madagascar, but I felt he was holding back on telling me something. However, I shared the Madagascar budget with him – it was a very reasonable one, if I say so myself – hoping that when they had backed another successful world first featuring myself it would become almost a habit for both of us in the future, whatever that might bring.

I wanted also to be realistic about my financial future, and in any case Windhoek Lager was exactly up my alley as regards the brand image I was trying to build. Windhoek Lager's slogan was 'Keeping it real', and I was actually living it. So I was confident that Brendon and his upper hierarchy would see this, too, and not even hesitate in backing my 'reasonable' offer.

My heart dropped, though, towards the end of the meeting when he leaned back in his chair, holding up the budget's paperwork and using it as part of his gesturing as he shared with me what he had planned all along.

'Honestly, Riaan, this Madagascar journey looks interesting,' he said, then paused and followed up with the word no person in my position ever wants to hear – 'but' – and went on: 'It's just not up to the grandeur you reached with the Africa trip.'

Man alive, I thought to myself, *with a month and a bit to go I really don't need a search for a replacement main sponsor in my life ...* I heard myself shouting loudly but silently: *Riaan , you should have taken the offers made to you by the opposition. Stupid, stupid, stupid!'*

'But' – there was that word again, yet this time it sounded ever so soothing – 'I'm sure you'll surprise us all again, just as before. I'll speak to the powers that be and have an answer for you in a few days, OK?'

Of course it was OK. But a few nervous moments at the meeting were one thing, and several nervous days in a real-life adventure limbo were something else altogether. The waiting was very painful, but I made it bearable by consoling myself with the thought that either way I would find a solution. After all, I had done it before, and I would do it again. Call me a crazy optimist, if you like, but I believe those positive thoughts played a role in influencing Windhoek Lager to come back to me sooner than expected to confirm their involvement.

By now the sporadic training and the stress of watching my departure date rushing ever closer – in fact, it was almost upon me – had got me to the stage where I can't remember much about the last few weeks before I left. As I reached the point of more than mere nervousness, at times doubt would creep in. I would catch myself slipping in a negative thought like: 'You don't actually know what you're doing!'

The sort of thought I could do without.

Was I ready? Really, *really* ready?

CHAPTER 3

PRACTICE MAKES PERFECT

*I decided I was going to face my fear head-on, so I made a pact
with myself that every time I fell out of the kayak I would
count (slowly) to five (slowly) and then (again slowly) tell
myself: 'You can get back into the kayak now.'*

The business of getting physically prepared was what everyone
wanted to know about, but it took just one of my training sessions
at Gordon's Bay to drive home to me how important my mental
preparedness was going to be.

Gordon's Bay had been my training area for the last six months,
and if a session was scheduled I would head out to sea regardless
of the conditions. Some days the kayak would be blown out of my
grasp while I was walking down to the water, and you can imagine
what wind of that strength could do to the sea surface.

Training sessions could not be described as comfortable by any
stretch of the imagination – I learnt the sea's lessons the hard way,
and I was always wet and usually freezing cold. That was how it
went, day in and day out. I had evolved some unique methods of
training myself, and two moments remain fixed in my memory.

The first is of a beautiful late afternoon, with the sun turning everything in Gordon's Bay a rich crimson. Conditions were ideal for paddling, so that there were many accomplished kayakers out on the water. I had just finished a 20 km session and decided to do what Johan Loots had suggested, namely practise my balance in the kayak and learn to get back into it from the water.

I was not long into my self-designed wobble and stabilising exercise when I heard people shouting some distance from me. I turned to see three paddlers making a serious effort to get to me as quickly as possible – I recognised one of them as a fellow rugby-player named JP. Now JP recognised me as well, and his look of concern changed into a big smile, though I noticed that the other two paddlers still had a confused look on their faces: '*Wat maak jy, Riaan? Is jy OK?*' (What you doing, Riaan? Are you OK?).

'No, man, I'm OK. Just practising stabilising in difficult seas,' I replied as convincingly as possible. As I rambled on about how the paddle should be the most important balancing tool, even if you'd tipped over 90 degrees either way, JP reassured his friends with the information that I was the Africa bicycle guy. I can only imagine what the three of them must have been telling friends and family afterwards. 'We all thought that Manser was a nut-case; now we can confirm he really is. Jeez, the guy was shaking and splashing around on the water as if he was having a grand mal epileptic fit! *And* he wants to paddle round *Madagascar*!

The exercise made sense to me, though, especially the part about remounting out at sea. If you have fallen out of the boat in diffi-cult conditions (which even the best of the best sometimes do) you need to be able to remount without effort – and, which was essen-tial, without panicking. I had a particularly strong motivation for practising remounting. False Bay is world-famous for its abundant population of giant great white sharks, and I believed it would be crazy to tempt them with a snack that splashed and wriggled tanta-lisingly alongside a capsized kayak.

My first few unplanned fall-outs were scary because they took place far from land, in dirty, churned-up water, and I was not cool-headed about applying the maximum effort to get out of the sea and back into the kayak. Eventually, having given the matter some thought, I decided I was going to face my fear head-on, so I made a pact with myself that every time I fell out of the kayak I would count (slowly) to five (slowly) and then (again slowly) tell myself: 'You can get back into the kayak now.' After which, my negotiations with myself having been concluded, I was free to splash and act as crazy as I wanted to.

I was amazed to find out how much more control I had, right from the word go. Even my breathing seemed to settle down during those 10 long seconds, and remounting became easy, even in the worst of seas.

How did I know I was training in the worst of seas? Easy. One Saturday Vasti and I planned to watch the Super 14 rugby games on TV that afternoon, so I needed to squeeze in a two-hour paddling session before starting the braai fires. So off I went, heading out to the beach and the rough, choppy seas I had seen from our mountainside home.

At the beach I managed, with difficulty, to untie my kayak from the car's roof without having it blow away, noticing from the corner of my eye that about 30 people were standing at the water's edge in a haze of sea-mist and swirling sand. I figured it must have something to do with the helicopters we had earlier noticed flying along the coast and circling a few kilometres out to sea, because this part of the coast is notorious for emergencies involving small fishing boats. Maybe a boat had capsized?

I was wrong. As I neared the water's edge one of the people in the crowd came towards me, a guy I knew called Jaco.

'Riaan,' he said earnestly, 'I'm asking you very, very nicely to turn around now and go home. The sea is too dangerous. My dad has been missing for more than two hours, and conditions are getting even worse. They don't know if they will find him. Rather go home. It's too dangerous.'

The tension and anxiety in his voice and face were so intense that I stopped, put the kayak down and walked the last few metres to the foaming water with him. Jaco explained to me that his dad had disappeared while taking part in a popular surf-ski race from Monwabisi beach to Gordon's Bay's main beach.

I was impressed. The surf-ski crowd I had got to know at Gordon's Bay were a tough but careful bunch who were not sissies about tackling a dangerous day on the sea. And this was a bad one. The wind direction was down-wind, but the swell was big and, combined with the powerful gusts – gale force at times – made balance almost impossible.

Jaco's heartfelt plea almost convinced me, but not altogether. I went into the water, but stayed closer to shore than usual, which helped a little. Yet my stubbornness paid off, because to my surprise I never once felt I wasn't in control of the kayak and the general situation. This perplexed me until I realised that I had been out in even tougher conditions and had managed to survive. I might have been below peak physical condition, but what I lacked in this aspect I made up for with my trademark attitude and my ever-growing experience, which in turn provided me with the self-confidence I needed.

The point of all this is that any paddler will attest to the great truth that you don't learn how to handle yourself by reading about it, you learn from actual experience, and that is what will save you.

Jaco's dad, Kasper, is a case in point. Not too long after I met up with Jaco on the beach the incredible people of the National Sea Rescue Institute plucked him out of the raging seas *seven nautical miles* offshore. He had lost his paddle, but had adhered to another golden rule: Never let go of your boat! And it had saved his life.

Johan and I got together a few more times at his factory to decide on a couple of design alterations. We had decided on a boat which was essentially the same as my training kayak, but slightly longer. I found the seat uncomfortably deep, however, especially when punching through the surf, which I expected would be a regular feature of my Madagascar trip. Johan wanted me to stay with the deep seat, stressing the value of a lower centre of gravity and a more balanced ride.

I accepted his opinion, since he knew much more about the matter than I did, but I was just not happy with it. Johan was ultra-patient about this, but eventually suggested another option: an out-and-out sea-going kayak – an extreme shape and design for extreme seas. To show how naive I was, I literally judged this beautifully shaped craft by appearance alone, so that I was sold on her before I had even tried her out.

But luck was with me, and when I did get her into the water I knew she was the boat for me. Johan wasn't so sure, but agreed with me that she would survive the roughest seas, at least a bit longer than other sea kayaks would.

A new problem now presented itself: Johan needed more time to do some extra work on this new-model boat, at a time when his factory had many international orders literally on the tables, so that all the modification work to my kayak had to be squeezed into gaps in the production line.

But the factory staffers were eager to be involved, even though they were already under heavy pressure from the jobs on hand. Overtime and out-of-the-ordinary demands didn't throw them out of step, they just kept smilingly at it. Strange how a company can inherit an attitude, isn't it? Johan had impressed me from day one, and his staff turned out to be no different from their boss.

Even so, though, the completion date had to be extended by two weeks, meaning a delayed departure. In the meantime the media were eager to see me set off and continually enquired about the final departure date so that they could schedule appropriate 'good-bye' interviews.

To my joy my African trip arrangement to send periodical despatches to the *Cape Argus* newspaper was renewed for Madagascar without any fuss or lengthy negotiations. It took just one brisk conversation with the editor, Chris Whitfield, who had been a big supporter of my African journey and had personally enjoyed my contributions to his columns. It went like this:

'Hi, Chris , How are you?'

'Fine. When you leaving?'

'Soon, the boat's nearly ready. That's actually why I was calling –'

'Will you write for us again?'

'Huh? Ja, I'd love to –'

A seasoned journalist, Chris wasted no more time: 'We'll pay you this time, don't worry. I'll get my PA to call you and finalise the details, how's that?'

'Hey, thanks, Chris,' I spluttered. 'Thank you!'

'Good luck, and remember that we're all behind you. Be safe.'

And that was it.

It's experience that tells you what really is going on. Chris is a champion at what he does and every day he is expected to churn out a first-class edition, otherwise he and his business would be in trouble. Time is valuable, I remember thinking – and (an immediate afterthought) so is space, as I recalled how drastically my Africa articles had been shortened. Note to self: *Chris doesn't want long-winded stuff.*

By comparison, TV and radio were flexible and generous with their allocation of airtime, especially those we had built a relationship with since the African journey. Seamus was going to be instrumental in managing all this – if he took the bait, that is, and decided to go whole-hog into this new 'crazy' journey.

Flying Seamus down to Cape Town to get the pre-departure footage and interviews we needed was more than worth it, and he also confirmed his desire to be involved on a broader scale, acting as my go-to man while I was away, working through any problems with my sponsors and handling expected media requests for information.

Seamus saw the bigger picture and was willing to commit his time (outside of his day job) to managing the journey. Any business, no matter what it is, survives because of partnerships – official or not. Seamus knew what level of commitment I was willing to invest. He knew I was literally willing to give up my life. It was clear to him that he didn't have a partner who was unequally yoked.

A few pleasant surprises awaited us when we went to collect the kayak, with the media in tow. One was the colour of the boat, a bright shocking green that everyone agreed would make spotting me out at sea a simple task. The other was something I had mentioned to Johan, a trolley-wheel for the kayak to help me move it around over longer distances ashore. The wheel was specially designed to fit into a casing at the rear of the kayak, and was extremely easy to put on and take off.

Huh, I thought, *my own customised kayak – very nice!*

Johan and his team had also taken note of an earlier request and done away with the normal 250 mm screw-lid hatch entrance and replaced it with a much larger modified hatch with a neoprene cover and fibreglass lid. This meant that I would be able to remove and replace the larger of my dry bags quite comfortably.

Johan's only concern as far as this modification was concerned was that if the boat remained capsized for an extended period it would fill up and probably sink, and so to counter this possibility he had had foam pumped into both the nose and the tail. This used up some valuable space, but it was a potential life-saver.

Further safety features were that the front hatch was separated from the rear one, which took up about two-thirds of the interior space, and something the production team and I had collectively agreed on, namely triple reinforcing of the seams (the top and bottom deck joins) as well as areas that would take constant pressure, such as the seat and its surrounding area. If a boat pops, this is the most common area in which it will happen.

The boat probably doubled in weight because of all this, and now clocked in at a bulky 40 kilos – and that was without any luggage, or 105 kg of me! The lateral shape of the boat as she would lie in the water, known also as the rocker, now looked even more pronounced in her bright new colour. She looked beautiful. Considering all boats are traditionally regarded as women, I was pleased to announce that I was utterly besotted with her.

The following week I had her gently wrapped in the most luxurious bubblewrap money could buy, adorned with far too many 'Fragile' stickers, and obtained a cross-my-heart guarantee from the cargo manager at Johannesburg's OR Tambo International Airport that she would be flying first class to Madagascar. All this came with a hefty price tag, R12 000 ($1 715 US). *One way*! My *return* ticket only cost R8 000 ($1 142 US). As they would say in French, the language of Madagascar: Ooh la la!

Now there were only two weeks left before my estimated date of departure. My kayak was on her way, I had collected all the equipment I believed was essential for returning alive from Madagascar, and the space for my bum on an airline seat had been paid for. It was just about time to roll.

While we were in Johannesburg preparing the kayak for the flight to Madagascar and checking my heaps and heaps of baggage, Vasti and I became ever more uncomfortably aware of the fact that time constraints had had me so firmly in their vice-like grip that I had not yet had the opportunity to do what anyone – paddler or non-paddler – would have believed to be plain, non-negotiable common sense: pack everything in at least once before you go to see if it fits!

So there I was, with a small mountain of baggage which might or might not fit in, and of course I had never paddled the kayak with any considerable weight on board. Shades of last time, when we had had to get everything on to my bike somehow!

Now, as we did the final preparation work on the kayak – which was now carrying very impressive sponsor branding – we laughed, myself with the greater degree of nervousness, as we made wagers about whether all my equipment would actually fit in. There was no chance of taking the loaded kayak for a paddle, but we did the best we could by laying everything out on the lawn of Seamus's friend, Mike Yelseth.

Mike was another great mind Seamus had managed to rope in to assist me, and was famous for his successful work in leading the film crews of many of the US 'Survivor' and 'Amazing Race' series. Numerous Emmy nominations adorn his office wall – although, as I found out, accolades were not the reason he was involved in extreme film work.

Mike enjoyed outdoors and adventure, and his talent for cinematography allowed him to make a living out of his passion. He impressed me most with his unwavering attention to organisation (among other things making me label every cable and charger!) and most of all with his willingness to share his years of experience.

For example, the alternative energy company Flexopower had supplied me with solar charging equipment. I was familiar in theory with this wonderful gear, but actually putting it into use was another matter. Mike picked up on my cautious approach and proceeded to ease my concern with a story from his own experience.

He was shooting an 'Amazing Race' series in South America, he recalled, and on one leg his film crew had to trek across a mountain range. They had no electricity, of course, but this was no problem for Mike. He bought a solar blanket very similar to the one I was taking along, altered a few cable connectors/voltage converters and then proceeded to tie the solar panel to the back of a donkey with all the batteries now happily charging on either side of its belly as they walked along. I felt easier then about my future charging activities.

Although everything had been packaged and labelled at the end of those two days, I still hadn't actually packed everything *into* the kayak. Looking back as I write this, the only word that wants to come out of my mouth is 'stupid!'

To give you an idea of my packing problem, let me detail the luggage that had to be fitted in somehow.

Waterproof bags: Three 25-litre bags; two 15-litre bags (transparent so that I could see what was in them); three 5-litre transparent bags and one 20-litre bag with a transparent window for day-bag clothing and so forth.

Accommodation: One 'bicycle tent' (small and compact, the same general shape and size as a coffin!). One First Ascent sleeping bag with the +5 degrees Celsius summer rating and synthetic fibres.

Clothing from the First Ascent clothing range: Two button-up, long-sleeved Expedition shirts which had large collars and were 100 per cent UV resistant. One set of REEF wet-suit longs. A Dundee hat. A waterproof jacket for warmth and a light compact windbreaker jacket (135 grams of parachute material). One First Ascent polypropylene thermal long-sleeved top. Two sets of underwear, a pair of slip-slops, a pair of Salomon Amphibian trail-runner shoes, and a pair of long trousers which could be turned into shorts by unzipping the legs.

Medical kit: Broad-spectrum gastro, skin and cardio-effective antibiotics. Plasters, including 50 mm waterproof/breathable) Elastoplast. Two rolls of bandages (50 mm and 25 mm). Gauze patches. Antiseptic swabs. Two tubes of anti-bacterial cream,

Savlon antiseptic lotion, anti-inflammatory tablets and cream – Dioclofenac and Ibuprofen. Pain tablets (aspirin/paracetamol), and nausea and diarrhoea tablets, eye-drops and foil sachets of re-hydration mixture. A rubber tourniquet, Ciplamed multivitamin capsules, Factor 40 sunscreen, a foil-wrapped mobile test and post-positive treatment kit for malaria, stainless steel scissors, two disposable razors and two factor 50 sunscreen roll-ons for daily use.

Survival bag: A Leatherman, an extra knife, rehydration sachets. Two litres of water, a First Ascent thermal long-sleeve top, a Superlite absorbent towel, multivitamin tablets and a small spare cell phone.

Repair equipment: Fibreglass sheets, polyester resin, hardener, ready-to-use fibreglass patches (sun/UV ray-cured), stainless steel replacement screws and plastic external fittings. A spare rudder, spare elastic webbing (for the deck), two rolls of 75 mm duct tape. Three rolls of electrical tape, a screwdriver (butt handle), cable ties and two large tubes of marine silicone.

Video equipment: Two Sony HD 40G hard drive Handycams, two standard long-life batteries with 14 hours of endurance, a wide-angle lens, a charger and cables for the Handycams. A Sony underwater (5 m) video camera housing, a Sony Cybershot (8.1 megapixel), and two standard batteries, a charger and cables. A Sony Cybershot underwater housing. A Sony Alpha still camera (14 megapixels), and two lenses (18–70 and 50–200).

Solar charging equipment: 1 X Powerflex 5W, a flexible panel about half a metre square, a medium lead-cell battery pack, about the size of a motorcycle battery, for storage of power, as well as extensions, splitters and different connectors and a portable 5W Powerflex charger, about the size of a shoebox.

Food: 10 energy bars, 100 glucose sweets, 5 sachets of salt, 10 sachets of effervescent energy tonic (I planned to catch my own fish and rely on the local population for fruit and vegetables).

Water: Eight to 10 litres (including my survival supply).

Beer: Windhoek didn't do business in Madagascar at the time.

Yip, there was a heck of a lot of stuff, and no one on our planet knew if it all would fit in ... not even the guy who would be paddling it around Madagascar.

Probably the most special of the items I would take with me was Seamus's farewell gift. His reasoning was that while I had the obvious items everyone expected me to have for the trip, I was lacking one that all old-time explorers took along – a captain's logbook!

So Seamus had a customised logbook made up for me. It was bound in burgundy-coloured leather, and on the front cover embossed gold letters announced:

ROUND THE OUTSIDE
MADAGASCAR 2008/09
Riaan Manser
LOG BOOK

Inside Seamus had written:

> *Riaan, Wishing you the best of luck going 'Round The Outside'.*
> *Enjoy every minute. Remember, there's no such thing as*
> *a bad experience, just an experience!*
> *BON VOYAGE*
> *Seamus*

The logbook was designed for jotting down all the information that would later be valuable for documenting a historical first-ever journey: daily GPS co-ordinates, wind and swell conditions, descriptions of all special encounters, and so on.

The first two pages were for personal particulars and my thoughts about my objectives, answering some of the questions that had me thinking deeper at times, together with a description of my journey and the route I was taking.

It set me to pondering anew about my intended circumnavigation of Madagascar, and it struck me again just how confidently I was approaching what seemed a truly inconceivable task. Under 'Vessel Description' I wrote 'Small Sea-Going'. For my three South African emergency contacts I wrote down the names of Vasti, Seamus himself and my best friend's father, Vernon (without his permission, I must add).

The logbook added that final authentic touch. *I am an adventurer, a genuine adventurer*. In days to come it was to help me, amid all the gadgets, materialism and self-pity we wallow in daily, to identify again, even if only for me, *exactly* what I do as a life-choice. No queen would await me on my return with a reward or a knighthood, but I didn't want that sort of fleeting accolade. Just authentic adventure, discovery and memories.

CHAPTER 4

MADAGASCAR, HERE I COME!

*This is when the biggest challenge of doing something first rears
its ugly head. No one has gone before you, so no one can really
advise you from previous experience. Ouch!*

Vasti was the only one to see me off at the airport in Johannesburg
on the afternoon of 13 July 2008. That was our choice, to let us
enjoy a last bit of quality time. We spent some of it conjuring up
visions of what it would be like when I reached the finish line, although she was scheduled to meet up with me at several places
along the route as well.

But we both knew that many things could happen before then,
and Vasti understood the dangers better than most people. She
had spent long hours with me at our kitchen table, looking at the
Google Earth maps of Madagascar's coastline, with its jagged cliffs,
hundreds of metres high, that reared straight up into the sky and
sometimes (particularly in the south) ran for hundreds of kilometres without any obvious landing places, even for something as
small as a kayak. When I'm nervous I tend to smile, and I smiled
plenty that afternoon.

Then I went through, and spent the time awaiting the boarding call in further reflection, because as soon as I had said goodbye to Vasti I was filled with a growing uneasiness. I was very conscious of the overwhelming support I enjoyed, and I simply could not rid myself of an insistent nausea every time I thought about all those supporters. What if I let them down?

My following had grown very considerably, and had made me popular and successful back home. But the down-side was that this time it wasn't just me heading out on my own on a personal adventure. Now I would be carrying the hopes of so many others with me, and for the first time I realised how heavily the weight of their expectations was pressing down on me.

I had been lauded as a hero before I had even breathed Madagascan air, or put a foot into her warm Indian Ocean waters. Nobody believed I could fail – in fact Windhoek Lager, my major sponsor, believed this would be a walk in the park for me, compared to the African trip.

It was not flattering; it was downright scary. Expectations surely have to be the major reason why so many talented sporting youngsters fail, and here I was getting a full dose of their side-effects. I was on the brink of doing something that I enjoyed, yet the possibility of ignominious failure hung over me like a wet duvet.

When I boarded, the airliner gave me something different to think about. You know you're going somewhere exotic when you step on to the Antananarivo-bound flight. French is clearly discernable, but the melodic rhythm of the Malagasy language strikes you when you hear it for the first time. I snuggled into my window seat, trying to take in as much as possible of whatever was coming my way. But do you think I can recall any of it now?

I do remember seeing the wide expanse of the Mozambique Channel that separates Madagascar from the African mainland, and imagining myself in it. I remember, too, the sheer size of Madagascar. From 30 000 feet up, there is no way you can tell that it is an island. You would need to be looking down from a satellite space station to see it in its entirety, because all that is visible from an aircraft is a coastline that runs forever and rolling land as far as the eye can see!

Still, it was a good start, although misfortune struck almost as soon as we landed at Antananarivo, when my cell phone was stolen off the counter right next to me while I was filling in my customs form. Then things got a little worse when it turned out that my baggage had been lost. But I stayed in good spirits. The cell phone was just a cell phone (even though this one had all my numbers in it!), and my nervousness about getting a visa at the airport proved unnecessary.

I felt less easy about my missing baggage, but I kept cool and looked forward to receiving confirmation that it had been re-discovered. That was a bridge I would cross when I came to it. So I enjoyed my excitement as I walked through the terminal, armed with my cabin bags – one with all my expensive electronic equipment and a smaller one with all my documents – taking in my surroundings; everything new, everything fresh.

I negotiated with the Air Madagascar staff to find nearby accommodation until my baggage was recovered and set about getting a cheap replacement cell phone, which was no problem, since there was a Zain kiosk just about five metres away. To the disappointment of the enthusiastic salesman behind the counter I took the cheapest deal, a phone with a simcard included for $30 US. I paid with large sums of the Malagasy currency (the ariary) I had just drawn from the newly installed ATM at the international side of the terminal.

While I was doing all this Cyril, the owner of Riverside Lodge, came to collect me in his green Renault Cango. Fortunately he spoke English relatively well, although I was prepared to wrestle through any conversation in my long-disused French. The vehicle wasn't as green as many of my readers might think – creaky and smoky, with a suspension that was definitely in need of a service, but it got us safely to the hotel half an hour later.

My room, which cost a whopping 50 000 Malagasy ariary (that sounds dreadful but is actually the equivalent of $25 US), looked out over the paddy-fields and was very comfortable and clean. I would later find that I had a room-mate, a little mouse, but I did not share that info with Cyril: a proud former Air Madagascar pilot, he was even prouder of his retirement business.

Cyril was a good host and put himself out to look after me. By the time I was up he had already called the airline to check up on the whereabouts of my baggage (they were still looking for it) and arranged my first trek into the Antananarivo city centre. He drew maps, taught me my first few Malagasy words – *misoatra* (thank you), *azahafadi* (please/pardon me), and so on – and wrote out messages in Malagasy for me to carry around in case I got lost in the public transport system.

Hospitality aside, however, Cyril did me a vital favour by pointing my expedition in the right direction, both figuratively and literally, thereby saving me from the worst mistake I could possibly have made.

As an inhabitant and a retired pilot, Cyril knew a lot about Madagascar's wind and weather conditions, and he immediately spotted a potentially fatal flaw in my plans. Discussions back in South Africa had convinced me that I should paddle clockwise around the island, but Cyril told me in no uncertain terms that this would be totally wrong.

The worst thing a paddler can encounter on a long-distance journey is a headwind; the tides and direction of the currents are also relevant, but nothing is as taxing as a continuous headwind. Cyril pointed out that a year-round east-to-south-easterly wind blew along Madagascar's east coast, whereas the dominant winds on the western side varied considerably according to the season: on-shore easterlies to regular south-easterlies would be what I could expect to encounter. Off the cuff, he would say it was six of one and half a dozen of the other.

There might be something to say in favour of the clockwise route, considering the west coast was nearly double the length of the east, but – a big 'but' here – the hugely differing sea conditions and opportunities for sheltering on land from the wind now convinced me that the anti-clockwise route was the only one to take. The western side of Madagascar was supposedly calm all year round and almost totally protected from dangerous Indian Ocean swells, with an S-shaped shoreline contour which, theoretically, anyway, resulted in large wind-protected bays.

I asked myself how the hell I could be thinking of changing my plans at such a late stage, literally on my first day in Madagascar. But I was relieved to know that I had avoided a major pitfall, although at the same time I couldn't help but wonder if, in my ignorance, I had made other gross errors of judgement in my planning. This is when the biggest challenge of doing something first rears its ugly head. No one has gone before you, so no one can really advise you from previous experience. Ouch! But that is the uncomfortable reality which faces all pioneers.

I didn't see anything obviously wrong with the rest of my planning, though, so while I waited for my lost baggage to arrive I absorbed some of the local sights and atmosphere. The people were intriguingly different from those I had met on my African journey. I had been told that Malagasy were very south-east Asian in appearance, and that was definitely the truth. Although the country is regarded as part of Africa, you do not see many people (at least not immediately) who look like the average African. Some were very dark-skinned, I noticed, and others very Chinese in appearance, while others looked mainly like Filipinos. But one thing was very noticeable: everyone was shorter than me. I felt like Gulliver in Lilliput.

The city centre was like many of the numerous African cities I'd been to, filled with a continuous hustle and bustle, with the architecture probably the biggest giveaway as to who had been the colonial power. The impressive French gables on the façade of the railway station at the lower end of Independence Avenue were a regal reminder of days gone by, although the station itself was now derelict and unused.

The broad double-lane avenue heading from the station into the hills high above the city was lined with square buildings of four or five storeys, mostly in a dull, faded cream colour. For me the dead giveaway about the former French presence, though, was the ant-like activity of the petite, beige-coloured Citroën and Renault taxis.

One thing that was totally familiar, thinking of the Africa trip, was the fact that – being a white-skinned foreigner – I was assailed by eager mobile vendors: my skin-colour spelled money, and would have even if I had been in tatters and loudly pleading poverty.

Ducking away from this never-ending attention was easy enough, however, because there were coffee shops and bakeries on the ground floor of nearly every building along the avenue. I felt at home there, because the French and now the Malagasy people love bread, coffee and cheese, and so do I.

Vasti and I had particularly liked what we'd seen of Antananarivo on the 'Amazing Race' series on TV. Madagascar's capital is set among steep slopes that are covered by an assortment of houses with equally steep stairways in between, and I sent her an excited SMS when I stumbled onto a place we had both seen on the small screen.

This was the famous stairway called Tsiafakantitra, translating as 'old folks can't make it', which is about right, since it climbs up the mountainside for about 200 metres. At the top you can go one way to the 'Rova' (Royal Fort), which is now a museum dedicated to the long-gone kings and queens of Madagascar, or go in the opposite direction to Lake Anosy. In the centre of this lake, thrusting up

10 metres or so into the air, is a memorial topped by a large statue of an angel – the 'Black Angel', although it has never actually been black – a famous landmark which honours the Madagascans who died fighting for France in World War I.

Standing in front of the Black Angel, you get a great view of Antananarivo's Hollywood-style sign, which is sprayed along the mountainside. I've always thought signs like this a bit tacky and Las Vegas-ish, but somehow it went fairly well with the city's dramatic setting. The Rova sits elegantly perched on the mountain to the right of the sign, while elsewhere a few church steeples, probably French-built, pierce the blue skyline.

The way the red-brick houses on the mountainside fitted seamlessly together and were joined almost entirely by cobbled streets amazed me; I had never seen anything like it except in paintings or postcards of places like Prague. Not bad, I thought, not bad. Then there was a complete contrast when I spent 45 minutes on the 20-hour-a-day public bus service (total cost: 400 ariary, about 30 US cents) for a quick trip through the flat outer areas, made up of endless rice-paddies populated by cattle and labourers.

Fascinating though it was, however, I didn't forget why I was in Madagascar. I needed to get to sea. After all, I wasn't a tourist but an adventurer with an adventure to get on with!

Getting to sea proved to be more difficult than I had thought. Within minutes of being told the good news that my luggage had been successfully tracked down, I got a bigger dose of bad news – now my kayak was missing!

As I understood it, the kayak had not even left South Africa yet because of a cargo hold space issue. The airline couldn't transport items longer than 3.13 metres, and my kayak – though it measured only 45 cm at its deepest and 56 cm at its widest – was 5.8 metres in length, so it was clearly outside the parameters.

Why I had not been told this before I left was one of those great unanswered questions. Not that I didn't believe it. Johan Loots of PaddleYak had told me that when he visited Mauritius a few years earlier he had run into the same problem and had had to cut his kayak into two, then rejoin the halves after his arrival.

This was something I was not willing to contemplate. *Ai, man,* I thought, *give me a break! I should have rather paddled it over.* There was nothing to be done except return to Johannesburg and sort things out there. Cyril helped me to collect my recovered luggage from customs, dropped it off at his hotel and then immediately drove me back to the airport so that I could jump on to the late-afternoon flight to Johannesburg. What a waste of time and money! But thanks to Windhoek Lager's sponsorship I had enough in my budget for two emergency flights.

Back in Johannesburg, I went to the South African Airways cargo warehouse next morning, only to discover that the staff there knew nothing either of my kayak's whereabouts or of the manager's. I fought down the temptation to become worried and/or frustrated, because panic wasn't going to help the situation, and we set about searching the huge warehouse.

Forty minutes of searching the nine-metre-high shelves by the warehouse staff brought no results – and then it turned out that the searchers had no idea what a kayak was! I decided to take matters into my own hands and got permission from the manager (who had rolled up in the meantime) to search for her myself.

And there she lay, tucked away at the back of the building, high up on the second level of shelving among some other lonely-looking boxes. I rescued her, checked her for damage and then went off to arm-wrestle one cargo agent after another, unwilling to accept 'no' for an answer, because there was no way I was going to cut her in half. So I just kept asking the question most bureaucrats don't like to hear: 'Why not?'

Eventually I met a guy who knew about my previous travels and seemed more eager than the rest to help me. A few calls and some string-pulling later we got Air Mauritius to agree to take my kayak to Antananarivo via Port Louis in Mauritius. I was a little sceptical by this stage. Would these promises come to fruition, or should I wait around to actually see the kayak on to the plane?

I decided to wait until the kayak was actually airborne and then to get going right away, so it was possible for me to board the next flight back to Madagascar with my mind slightly more at ease. I felt as though I already had my first Madagascan adventure under my belt. *Sjoe!* as South Africans say when they have survived a narrow squeak. The great Madagascan adventure production was rolling at last. Everybody stand by ... lights ... camera ... action. Take two!

CHAPTER 5

TAKE TWO

With the date set, all that was still lacking was a traditional 'rum farewell', which, he promised, would put hair on my chest, like a pirate. What followed was a tasting marathon of all his favoured Madagascan rum brands, so strong that I thought they were more likely to take my chest hair off.

'Determined' is the right word for my frame of mind. I wasn't prepared simply to sit around and wait, so the people at the Air Mauritius office at Antananarivo's Ivato airport soon got used to seeing me at the crack of dawn every day, even if they had told me the previous afternoon that my kayak had not yet arrived.

After four long days I was finally told that my kayak had been offloaded at Port Louis and that the airline was just waiting for suitable space to become available in the hold of a passing Boeing 747 – the only aircraft, they said, that could take it.

The wait was frustrating but not wasted, because I used the extra time to deal with some other important things, like introducing myself to the South African Ambassador, Mr Mokgethi Sam Monaisa. It was wonderful to finally meet him face to face – when

I had passed through Gabon's capital, Libreville, on my bicycle trip he had arranged VIP treatment for me.

Mr Monaisa was a jovial, bright-eyed man with many stories to tell about South African adventurers he had dealt with, including Mike Horn on his circumnavigation of the globe along the equator, and he handed me over to two of his staffers, a South African named Roy Badenhorst and a wonderfully trilingual lady, Ms Langotiana, to assist me with translation and negotiations.

The offices of my co-sponsor, Shoprite, were less than a kilometre from the embassy, and I went along to do some basic shopping and arrange for the staff to be my go-to people in the event of an emergency medevac. There I met Thabiso Khotane. He had not been very well-briefed on what I planned to do, but did not let that dampen his enthusiasm in offering help.

Thabiso, who was married to a local woman, could speak French and some Malagasy, and had travelled by road to most parts of the country, so that he probably understood better than many the real challenges involved in getting someone out in a hurry. In my case, this meant setting off as soon as my kayak arrived, heading down to the east-coast port town of Tamatave (Toamasina), my new starting and finishing point instead of my original choice of Mahajanga on the west coast.

Shoprite had agreed to arrange the departure and arrival festivities, and Thabiso was keen to have my expedition's estimated date of departure so that he could begin mobilising his staff. I was just as keen. I had budgeted to spend a month in Madagascar on settling in and finally getting on to the water, and by now I was borderline on this estimate. This meant in turn that other problems were beginning to sneak up on me.

One such problem was feeding Chris Whitfield and his editorial team at the *Cape Argus*. Along with the other daily papers, the *Cape Argus* had made a splash of my departure and had promised their readers a weekly contribution from me. The trouble was that

I had nothing to tell them so far ... or did I? After the first panic had subsided I realised that of course I had something to tell: after all, circumnavigating Madagascar alone and unaided had many challenges besides those awaiting me out at sea. So the first article I sent back was entitled 'Easier said than done', which could not have been more appropriate.

Seamus, too, wanted to get the ball rolling as regards filming and needed to book a local film crew to interview me in my departure state as well as document the actual send-off. This was a thornier problem, since I had not been able to specify a firm departure date yet – thanks to a new set of frustrating delays.

Firstly, my kayak did not arrive on the flight that was supposed to bring it to Antananarivo because, so Air Mauritius informed me, the cargo manager at Port Louis had queried the validity of the paperwork and therefore had not loaded it. This meant another nail-biting week's delay. I was now way over budget, as regards both time and finance, and had not done any paddling for nearly two months. Push-ups and sit-ups were keeping me strong, but I could feel the cardio-fitness ebbing out of me with every passing day.

Then I got word that the kayak had finally arrived. I had a 4x4 pick-up and a driver named Andry booked and on standby, so I wasted no time in calling him to pick me up on the way to the airport, so that we could hit the road for Tamatave, seven hours away. Needless to say, it turned out not to be as simple as that.

I don't do well in bribe situations and fail miserably even when my logical inner person tries to convince me that slipping someone something under the table will save me a day or two of lost time. So it took lots of self-discipline to sit tight and persevere through every ridiculous demand made by the customs people – they even wanted the kayak's registration papers, as if I were importing a vehicle!

I spent the whole morning running back and forth from office to office, chasing ghosts. All the customs people knew that I needed the kayak desperately and that I had had a frustrating month in Madagascar already, but took great and highly visible pleasure in making me suffer after hearing that I was not willing to pay them off. This was not only a case of frustration – hiring the 4x4 was very expensive, so that even one more day's delay would have a significant effect on my budget.

And then, after all that, the customs officials closed for lunch. *Two hours* of lunch.

I decided to trade on the sympathy I had generated within the Air Mauritius staff contingent during the weeks of waiting, and implored them to intervene on my behalf. They agreed. But even that was not a simple matter.

The Malagasy gendarmes were awaiting the arrival of one of their number who had fallen ill and died in a hospital in Paris. Now the entire cargo area of the airport was cordoned off in preparation for the arrival of his remains. It was, as could be expected, an emotional affair. His comrades were neatly lined up, a band was playing appropriately funereal music and his extended family huddled to one side, weeping.

The soldier's arrival at the airport and his departure to the cemetery took all of two hours. Andry and I sat more or less patiently in the pick-up and watched while the proceedings dragged through to their end. I consoled myself by considering what the real problems in my life could be; the fact was that no matter what happens to you, someone, somewhere, is always worse off than you are. But that didn't change the fact that my plan to head straight off to Tamatave was a dead duck. I was not going to get the kayak out of official clutches before day's end.

Eventually I was physically ushered out of the airport terminal by the customs officials, who by now were speaking only to the Air Mauritius official – probably also out of disappointment, although for a different reason. The official assured me I would have the kayak by mid-morning next day, adding that 'you need one more document' as he stood there, clutching the basketful of paperwork I had accumulated, which seemed by now to include everything except a rabies vaccination certificate for my kayak.

Next morning Andry and I were the first people on the scene. We were about to enter the terminal building to hunt down that final document when we were confronted by yet another tout (unofficial this time), actually holding the precious piece of paper and demanding a reward. What he nearly got from me was a knuckle sandwich, but Andry wisely intervened, and soon we were wending our way out of Antananarivo and heading into the majestic countryside.

To my surprise I saw now that Antananarivo was much bigger than I had thought. It reminded me of my first impressions of Luanda, the Angolan capital, which has a small city centre but sprawls out into a succession of suburbs that house about 13 million people. Tana, as inhabitants call it, was just a few notches up in the beauty stakes. Looking back at the city from a distance I was amazed at how every square inch of even the steepest slopes of the crowded city suburbs were utilised either for housing (double storeys only!) or farming.

The kayak, still in its bubble wrap, sat on the roof of our double-cab and dwarfed the ever-present Citroën taxis that lined the roads as we headed out. It was all downhill, our surroundings dramatically beautiful but definitely not relaxing, since drivers moving in the opposite direction were not patient in overtaking the long lines of lorries crawling slowly up the steep and snaky passes.

Eight hours of stressful driving and conversation later we arrived in Tamatave at about 2.00 am. The town was dead on the outskirts, barring the brisk prostitute trade (unless, of course, they were just innocent, scantily dressed girls who enjoyed speaking to strangers while wobbling around the streets on extra-high heels at two o'clock in the morning).

Just finding a place to sleep was a small adventure in itself. Every hotel that fitted my requirements – cheapness and quietness – was booked up. Nor were we the only weary travellers looking for a resting-place; at one stage of the dreary hour we spent going from one booked-up lodging to another we crossed paths with three foreign girls who were in search of the same sort of accommodation.

Eventually Andry managed to find a place that looked suitable, named Hotel Tsik Tsik (Smile Smile), and he waited in the vehicle while I went inside to go through the well-worn routine of waking up the soundly sleeping receptionist and asking for a room. Just then a taxi with our three fellow-travellers on board came speeding down the road and pulled up next to the double-cab.

The five minutes I spent rousing the receptionist from his slumber gave the girls time to pour out of the taxi, sprint inside and line up alongside me. We were all tired and I could see that they were at their wits' end, so I greeted them and, by way of making conversation, asked if they had also been battling to find a place to stay.

Two of them greeted me back, but the third girl, a slightly larger, rather butch type, cut the conversation short by explaining to them in French (which I understood well enough to grasp what she was saying) that I was the opposition, the enemy of sorts. This shut them up and after that they ignored me.

At this stage the receptionist opened his glass doors and asked how he could help. Butchy-looking pushed her way to the counter in front of me and started speaking to him in French as if I did not exist. I asked her in French to let me inquire first, since I had obviously got there before them. She ignored me and carried on talking. Now I got mad. I took the receptionist by his shoulders, picked him up and turned him around to face me so that we could talk business.

The girl started shouting and swearing in a mixture of languages, telling me that I had no manners, otherwise I would stand aside for her and her friends. Nothing could calm her down. She kept on shouting, making such a commotion that Andry came in to see if I needed help, and eventually threatened to fight me. Her friends had to hold her arms down and lead her outside to calm down. It was a surreal business, and a sad example of women's lib at its worst.

While the other two girls were wrestling their leader out into the night air, I went about my business with the receptionist. There was only one small room left, and I took it without a qualm. In normal circumstances I might have offered it to the girls, but at that moment I did not give a shit where they slept or what happened to them. At the same time I felt sick at heart that I had had to build up such unnecessary aggression, especially against a woman. It was the first time in my life that I had felt this way; man, that was just not me.

South African men are chastised in our communities if we do not elevate woman to a higher plane. And don't forget about equal opportunities for education and in the workplace. Men with some intelligence are happy to see that happen, but not like this. The worst thing was that this girl was probably not even a women's-lib guerrilla fighter, *and* what was even worse was that I knew I would have given them the room ahead of me. I was angry and sad as I fell asleep that first night in Tamatave.

The next day Andry helped me to search for more comfortable accommodation. Just north of the town itself and right on the beach we found the ideal spot, a place called Darafifi ('Butterfly' in Malagasy) owned by a 60-year-old Indian woman who made it look easy to run a 20-chalet business which included a full-time restaurant.

Apart from the fact that my bungalow was quiet and secure enough for me to prepare my kayak in it, there was the added benefit that the sea was only 30 metres away from my front door. It was at times like this that my heart went out to all those poor suffering travel journalists who have to visit far-flung 'Third World' (tough luck!) countries to find stories and suffer hardships like having the breakers keep them awake at night, being forced to eat fresh seafood all the time, enduring over-friendly people – and being ripped off at the rate of $6 US a night. Poor souls.

After transferring my luggage into the bungalow I started with some trepidation to cut the layers of bubble wrap off the kayak. I had expected a bump and scratch here and there, but what was revealed was a battered boat that had clocked up serious voyager miles before even getting near the water.

The minor wear and tear wasn't of any concern, but I was seriously worried about two areas of major damage. There was a 10 cm crack 30 cm ahead of the rudder which could only have resulted from something very heavy being laid on top of the kayak – whatever it was had nearly snapped off the rudder area. Not good! Then there was the fibreglass splash cover frame that was designed to prevent 80 per cent of spray filling up the cockpit. It had been smashed in the centre – obviously also by something very heavy – so that the cover was now floppy and useless.

What worried me even more than all this visible damage, however, was the thought that there might be other damage which I could *not* see and thus would not repair before I left.

But good fortune smiled on me now. By sheer chance I met up with the best people in Tamatave to help me with getting the kayak back in shape. I started on the repairs by cleaning up the loose broken pieces from the damaged areas so that new layers of resin and possibly reinforcing fibreglass could be applied, then – having a passion for rugby, as my friends and acquaintances know well – took a couple of hours off to see the Springboks tackle the Aussies in a Tri-Nations test match.

I temporarily shrugged off my worries and with a spring in my step headed towards a well-known expat meeting place in Tamatave, a restaurant called the Bateau Ivre ('Drunken Boat' in French) which, according to the Darafifi staff, was the most likely establishment to have DSTV (South Africa's satellite channel).

Eager for a taste of home, I walked into the foyer area of the restaurant and approached two well-dressed woman who were chatting to each other. The one lady's accent I recognised immediately
as distinctly South African, although the other's was a mixture of
many varieties. The Bateau Ivre didn't have DSTV, they informed
me, but they would be happy to help me look for locally resident
South Africans who might be of assistance.

It worked. After a few calls Helen Fayd'Herbe (the wife of the
restaurant's owner) drove me over to the house of a friend called
Ansie. Helen had tried to call Ansie but had not succeeded, so this
was strictly an unannounced visit, but for the sake of scratching
my rugby itch I was willing to take the chance of a chilly welcome.

The upshot of this was that Ansie's husband, Riaan, ended up entertaining me for the afternoon. It turned out that the Springboks
were not playing after all, but my provincial team, the Sharks, were,
and Riaan and I watched part of the Sharks game. I didn't see the
end of the game because Riaan had something else to do, namely
attend a braai with his co-workers.

I was invited along to the braai, and at first I didn't really enjoy
myself, feeling that I had been asked along only because I was a
serial gate-crasher. But then Lady Fortune stepped in and had me
meet up with the most likeable of characters, Flippie van Vuuren
(lovely authentic Afrikaner nickname, that!).

Flippie was a mild-spoken, strongly built fellow who was on
contract at a Canadian nickel-mine construction project outside
the town, running the safety-training department for a sub-
contracted company called Training Management Africa. Flippie
was well-liked by most of the other contactors of all nationalities,
and with assistance from his boss, Sha Rampershad, was willing to
make enquiries on my behalf if I had problems with repairing my
kayak.

Which I did. One of the problems at Darafifi was that I had to
leave the kayak outside without cover, which meant that inquisitive

passers-by frequently satisfied their curiosity by fiddling with my newly completed repairs, and because I couldn't shelter it from the heavy afternoon showers the silicone would not set and the resin remained gooey.

So Flippie had my kayak and myself collected in a company vehicle and ferried to the project's workshop, where there were stands on which to place the boat and adequate overhead cover. I was very grateful for this: but for Flippie and Sha I would have continued repairing the kayak in the rain under the bushes of Darafifi in between swatting away the mosquitoes and flies. That wouldn't have been too unpleasant for a person who was not under stress and not trying to repair a kayak that had given him a month of headaches. But that person wasn't me.

Anyway, I managed to complete the repairs to my satisfaction and took the kayak out for her first sea-trials. It was a fiasco. I wasn't carrying any load, but I didn't even make it through the surf! The kayak immediately started taking in heaps of water. I couldn't make out where the leak was, although I was sure that it wasn't in the areas I had just repaired and then triple-checked and tested.

I contacted Johan back in South Africa. He didn't take offence at hearing that his kayak was leaking like a sieve, as some people might have done; he knew that it would be under severe stress en route, and that his factory had been so rushed to complete it on schedule that they had not had time to do the standard seaworthiness tests.

Johan started taking me through some tests by e-mail. A simple one, requiring some effort and assistance, plus lots of water, which was infallible for detecting even the smallest leaks, consisted of filling the cockpit in which I would be sitting, and then the actual interior of the kayak. If there was any hole, water would start leaking *out*.

I decided to do a complete overhaul of all the silicone areas that looked wet. This turned out to be severe test of my patience, since silicone not only needs to be neatly finished to ensure it lasts but ideally should be left for 36 hours before being tested in the water.

While I was doing this Flippie taught me a simple but effective way of smoothing silicone that I intend to pass on to my children one day. It goes like this: inject generous amounts of silicone into the area being repaired, then use your middle or index finger, even more generously coated in saliva (preferably your own) to smooth the silicone till it is flush with the surrounding surfaces. Easy as falling off a kayak! But believe me, it works.

The 36-hour wait now became my biggest personal issue because I was bored and very restless. But once again Flippie, Sha and another colleague named André made sure I was entertained. Flippie took me fishing, although the Afrikaans equivalent, *hengel*, is more appropriate. The difference between the two, he explained, is that when fishing you more or less presume that you are going to hook a fish and reel it in; *hengel* describes an outing where you put your line in the water and hope for the best. Flippie's version of the angling sport suited me fine, and I had a good time *hengel*ing, so to speak.

Rugby came to my rescue as well, helping to beef up my attitude towards all my never-ending delays. We had watched South Africa beat a determined Argentine outfit one Saturday, and the next weekend (yes, the kayak was still leaking) we saw the Kiwis give us a hiding.

I became deeply grateful for the way the Fayd'Herbe family of the Bateau Ivre restaurant looked after me during my time in Tamatave. Christiaan always made sure the beef curry was well prepped in anticipation of my daily visit, and I built up a wonderful friendship with his son, Marc.

Marc had had some tough luck as a result of (as he put it) some bad decisions he had made in his life. But unlike many others in the same boat Marc had realised what was going wrong and started again. Now he was enthusiastic about bringing his life on to the track he had originally envisioned.

In essence he was cut from the same cloth as his philanthropic father. It seemed as though everything Christiaan had touched in his 70 years had turned into gold, and he had had a colourful life which had left him rich in experience and life lessons. He had lived and worked on every continent of the planet, spoke four or five languages (including Malagasy) fluently and still harboured ambitions of achieving more. Bateau Ivre was a famous place because of him, not because of anything else.

I could clearly see all those qualities in Marc as well; the problem was just working out how he was going to harness and employ them. Among many other bright ideas he wanted to publish his experiences as a Brit serving in the Afrikaans-dominated South African military of the 1970s and 1980s.

Knowing how difficult it was for people to get published, I didn't mince my words when we discussed this scheme. His story would not be unique enough, I told him. He needed to find a fresh angle with which to entice a publisher. He wasn't too pleased with my honesty at first, but, as I explained to him, I could see he was serious and therefore didn't deserve sugar-coating something I had had some experience with.

He and I had a regular cheer-each-other-up lunchtime date throughout the three weeks I spent in Tamatave. I like characters and people with character, and I like people who are honest about themselves; and Marc was all three.

At the end of the three weeks my kayak was ready, or so I hoped. I had done some final 'do-or-die' repairs – 'do or die' because I had decided that when the silicone had cured I was going to leave, come hell or high water pouring in.

With the date set, Christiaan decided that all that was still lacking was a traditional 'rum farewell', which, he promised, would put hair on my chest, like a pirate. What followed was a tasting marathon of all his favoured Madagascan rum brands, so strong that I thought they were more likely to take my chest hair off.

The day after my final 'do or die' repairs we went off to the nickel mine's staff compound with two new friends, Gavin Steel Lombard, and his boss, Lionel. The compound housed the Aussies, Kiwis, Britons, Canadians and South Africans working at keeping the huge construction project on track, and I would recommend that any girl with self-esteem issues should spend just one evening in this camp – she will enjoy non-stop attention and compliments, and doubtless proposals of marriage from bachelors as well! Those guys were seriously home-sick and dying to get back for a visit to their loved ones. I felt for the catering manager, a charming and easy-on-the-eye Russian lady.

Now I was ready to leave, and I remember the telephone conversation I had with Seamus, which went something like this.

'Jeez, are you still stuck there? When are you going to leave?'

'You know what, Seamus, I leave on Monday, no matter what. Even if I have to buy a backpack and start *walking* around the island.'

Seamus thought I was joking, and chuckled. But when I spoke again he realised I wasn't.

'I've got a bag from Shoprite that will take enough water and survival equipment and my fishing gear, so initially it'll be uncomfortable, but I'll get 40 km a day under my belt, I think. So don't worry, I'll circumnavigate this place either way.'

Seamus digested what I had just said and started to laugh nervously: 'Nah, get the kayak sorted and then get going. Be patient.'

It was not that he was humouring me. He understood my frustration better than anyone else, because I had been communicating with him at every step of the repair process. He had made time commitments on my behalf which included the local TV crew, which was scheduled to arrive that day, and he didn't want this sort of negativity to seep into the early interviews.

That was why he instructed me rather to get into the kayak and then solve problems as they came up, which he knew I am famous at doing. So I gave in, but I really believed that after the first day's launch the kayak would never see dry land again.

I still had one misfortune to experience before I finally got away from Tamatave, and it was a bad one. Somehow I managed to delete all – yes, *ALL* – the footage I had shot to date. I was trying to format a drive on my laptop and couldn't call it up. When the video camera was plugged in an option for formatting popped up and I took it without confirming the contents. Stupid, stupid!

The dogs and cat and pig stuff in my garden at home, my battle to collect the kayak at the airport, my endless repair work, all gone for ever. I was fairly gutted, but what shocked me was the realisation of how afraid I was of what Seamus was going to say. I was afraid he would be furious and, God forbid, become as despondent as I was.

In that evening's entry in the beautiful logbook Seamus had given me I had what I described as my first little cry. Man, I felt so useless, useless beyond frustrated. But when I told Marc, it was his turn to administer a dose of brutal honesty. You dish it out; you have to take it, too. I was wallowing in self-pity, he said. 'Get on the sea and your world will change. This environment is not for you. Get out on the sea.'

And he was right, so come Monday morning, I did just that. Now my luck turned again. The 'do or die' repairs stemmed the leaks that had been plaguing me, and gave me the confidence to take on the choppy sea.

The Malagasy TV crew were enthusiastic but spoke no English, so our interpreter, Dina, had to play all sorts of additional roles, which at times included directing and producing. The filming was actually a lot easier than it might have been, thanks to the wholehearted support we got from yet another South African company contracting in Madagascar, B&W Instrumentals, which offered the services of some staffers and a six-metre rubber duck. Neels Minnie, the owner of the company – he was also a successful restaurateur who owned Dros steakhouse in the town of Secunda, north of Johannesburg – was another big, burly, warm-hearted South African who expected nothing in return for helping me to achieve what I had set out to do.

I paddled out of the harbour and turned to port. At my left was the rugged coast that would be my companion throughout my journey. Monday morning, 28 August, and my expedition around the outside of Madagascar had finally begun.

FOOLHARDINESS AT FOULE POINT

*I understood only too well that this was going to take some
old-fashioned testicular fortitude and a fat slice of luck, but
I believed I needed to show some character here, firstly by
making the decision and secondly by actually being brave
enough to act on it.*

The sea was choppy, with a medium-sized five-foot swell, but I
made steady progress as I drew away from Tamatave. I was keeping an eye open for whales, having seen some near the harbour's
entrance a few days earlier (when, incidentally, some unknown
big fish made off with my rod), hoping for some of the real close
deep-sea encounters that not many people ever have the chance to
experience.

This, by the way, was another reason why I had finally decided
on an anti-clockwise route starting at Tamatave. The Madagascar
humpback whales' migration would end in September, and with
the main migratory route passing up the east coast I was hoping
to be in one of the well-known calving areas, such as Sainte-Marie
Island, around mid-September – it would be a fiasco to miss out on

the chance of getting within touching distance of these giants of the sea.

And this first day delivered. I was about 10 km into the day's paddle and roughly 3 km from the land when I saw what looked like a large humpback cow and her calf only about 300 metres away and heading in my direction. I stopped paddling and waited, camera at the ready and my heart thudding away loudly, hoping (although not very hard, to be honest) that I would drift into their path.

They drew nearer and nearer, occasionally ducking out of sight under the bumpy sea-surface, and I waited, filled with nervous anticipation. Could they see me or sense me? Then, to my mingled surprise and shock, they popped up about 15 metres from me to take a rest. Now I could see them clearly; it was definitely a huge mother with her calf in tow. I found myself unconsciously holding my breath. The mother was gently pushing her calf, which was diagonal to her snout, in front of her. The calf was rolling slowly against her mother's barnacled forehead as if simultaneously fooling about and getting a back scratch.

Humpback cows are bigger than their male counterparts and can reach an incredible size – 17 metres long and weighing a whopping 40 tons. Their pectoral fins are the largest of any sea-going creature, sometimes six metres long, more than a third of their bodies! I decided that I really didn't need them to dive right now while we were at such close quarters.

Well, they didn't, but instead the cow decided to exhale. Simple enough, except that a whale, being very large, naturally exhales on a very large scale. Wow! She blew a five-metre-high cloud of spray and mist out of the blowhole on top of her head, and I gasped for breath as I realised for the first time just how close I really was to her. I remember thinking that it felt as if everything, even the minuscule particles of air around me, was shuddering in awe.

I realised now how small we humans really are in the world's scheme of things. We think we know everything and can do anything, and actually we know and can do very little by ourselves ...

The cow broke in on my self-revelation. With enormous strength she beat on the water with her tail, then sank down and swam away with her calf. The ripples from their departure sent waves washing over me and my kayak, two such frail, insignificant things in her world.

I paddled on, elated that I had experienced part of my dream on the very first day of the trip. I had decided not to undertake anything serious as far as distance went on this first day – not more than a little over 20 km, because I wanted to test a few things. I wanted to settle my concerns about the durability of the repairs to the kayak, and also to reassure myself about my lack of physical preparedness after not paddling hard and seriously for nearly three months. But the repairs stood up well enough, and so did my somewhat unused muscles, and about three and a half hours later – earlier than I had expected – I arrived at the hotel at Coco Beach, which was managed by Christiaan Fayd'Herbe and a business partner.

Actually getting ashore was another matter, though. Marc Fayd'Herbe had assured me that it would be easy for me to land my kayak on the 'beach' in front of the hotel. Well, if I hadn't known any better I would have thought that Marc wanted my account of my first day to be full of excitement.

The entire area in front of the hotel was crammed with slabs of rock and outcrops of jagged coral; in places the water sucked back to reveal unbroken stretches of reef. Where the hell would I be able to land without smashing into those forbidding walls of rock at headlong speed?

I circled a few times beyond the smashing surf (no less than eight orbits, according to my Garmin!), seeking ever more desperately for a landing-place where I would have the best chance of reaching shore without dying in the process. I recalled some valuable advice from one of South Africa's toughest men at sea, Dawid Mocke. He had said to me, after I had told him of the dangers I expected to face in Madagascar, that beaching your craft safely had less to do with skill than with patience.

Patience, he had told me, was the safest tactic to employ in what was probably going to be the most life-threatening aspect of my journey, because not all the beaches would be what one saw in the tourist brochures: 'If you're not sure, wait. If you're still not sure a few minutes later, wait a bit more, and then, if you're really desperate to land, wait a bit more.'

I circled again, following Dawid's advice as much out of raw fear as actual trust in his words. Then, as I had done in many other scary situations in my life, I went through my hyperventilating psyching-up routine, which consists of breathing rapidly and at the same time chanting a mantra of my own devising: *Balls to the wall, no chance for second chances here, balls to the wall, no chance for second chances here, balls to the wall, no chance for second chances here, balls to the wall, no chance for second chances here ...*

Luckily for me I was only chanting at 50 per cent intensity, and before following through with action some of the local village fishermen had spotted me, realised something was wrong and frantically waved me northwards. There was no mistaking their urgency and I didn't waste any time in taking their advice. Sure enough, about 300 metres northwards was a little basin, probably not more than five metres wide, into which they directed me.

There was no time for hesitation or second thought now. With a lump of fear blocking my throat I headed into the basin and finally – *finally* – reached dry land. And then for the first time I realised just how close to disaster I had come. If I had tried to land at the spot I had originally picked the jagged reef would have destroyed both my kayak and myself.

At the hotel the warm hospitality of Christiaan's sister Laurie and the staff untangled the knot in my stomach. Laurie's son,

Bernard Fayd'Herbe, happened to be the most famous jockey in South Africa at the time, a 52 kg ball of muscle who had pushed his horses to victories in both the Durban July and the J&B Met, the country's premier horse-racing events. In addition to making me feel at home his very proud mother also gave me a crash course on the esoteric world of the turf.

Laurie showed me the much-publicised photo finish draw of the 2008 Met. It rarely happens that there are two winners in a main race at one of the major racing events, but this was what happened at the Met – literally a whisker in line with the other whisker. Exciting stuff. She also told me an interesting story which graphically illustrated the sacrifices it took to become a top jockey. A week before the Met the two of them had shared a very unusual special dinner. Between every taste of vegetable Bernard would drink a glass of water, and when it came to the medium-rare steak he would chew every chunk to a pulp and then spit it out instead of swallowing it. That was when I grasped for the first time the harsh reality of just how tough and self-controlled a jockey has to be, even if he weighs only 52 kg.

It made me think of my grandfather, when I was a school-kid, explaining to me how strong even the smallest boxers were, so that 'they'd beat you up with one hand tied behind their backs'. Now I really understood what he had meant.

Next day I picked up a wonderful story which beautifully illustrated the marvellous variety of ethnic mixes in Madagascar when a visiting couple from the UK asked me about my kayak and my journey. The guy was pure British through and through, whereas the girl had that Malagasy look-of-many-nations about her. I was intrigued, and since one thing travelling had taught me was not to be embarrassed about asking people about themselves, I did just that. And what a story I heard!

This girl, who looked as if she might have some Indian blood, was the daughter of a Malagasy doctor who had been stationed at the Tamatave hospital in the early 1970s, with a number of Indian nurses working under him. One of the nurses was entirely devoured by a huge shark while out swimming one day, and the locum agency sent out a replacement, who – you've guessed it – ended up marrying her boss!

As the girl said, if the unfortunate nurse had not been eaten by the shark she herself would not be sitting there telling me about herself. A bittersweet story of tragedy and happiness, of the death of one young girl giving rise to the birth of another.

But my thoughts were concentrated on what lay ahead. The east coast of Madagascar is almost one straight line, except for the northern region I was heading into. There were plenty of sheltered bays and plenty of fishermen with dugout kayaks, and I would be able to make up some time in the calmer, flatter waters. My first destination goal was Sainte-Marie Island (also known as Nosy Boraha), where Seamus and Mike Yelseth, whom he had persuaded to come out as the cameraman, would do the first 'catch up' interview session with me, one of five we had planned for the journey.

Seamus and I were determined to make a serious effort regarding the quality of the story we would get out to the TV media. The Africa cycle trip had been about a guy who wanted to achieve something, but hadn't the advice and expertise to create a credible product (I still believe my fans would have wanted to see the *real* footage of my trip around Africa, though). Now that same guy had acquired the expertise he had lacked, and had also got plenty of expert advice. On top of that, Mike was a tier-one cameraman, not just in South Africa but worldwide, so it was an honour to have him heading out to cover me.

Launching from Coco Beach was almost as exciting as my landing there the day before. The whole village turned out to run their fingers over the kayak and watch my departure. As a result it was a real too-many-cooks-spoil-the-broth situation. I waited tensely in my ready-steady-go position in front of the smashing shore break, while four or five people screamed instructions from behind me.

The head fisherman would screech something, which was then re-layed in broken English to Laurie, who in turn repeated the instruc-tion – usually a simple 'go' or 'wait' – to me.

Eventually everyone was shouting over each other at once, and I became ever more confused. Should I listen to them or trust my in-stincts? After all, if I'd followed the advice of my little voice on my arrival I wouldn't be here, waiting for the doubtful privilege of tak-ing on another dangerous enterprise.

I decided to give my instincts the benefit of the doubt. Holding the kayak's bow by its handle I dragged it energetically over a wave which had just broken, then pushed it a few metres forward and swam after it, to a an area about 10 metres wide where the waves were not breaking, where I planned to scramble on board as fast as I could. Fortunately this worked out without any further drama, and off I went into Day Two. *This is huge,* I remember thinking, *I'm going to remember this day. It's going to be relevant.*

And as it turned out, it *was* relevant, although not because of any major incident – actually quite the opposite. The early-morning sea was as smooth as a mirror, only slowly turning choppy as the wind picked up. It was what I'd expected, a firm south-easter, slightly over my right shoulder. I soon had the Rapala out trolling enthu-siastically 15 metres behind me; although I had had no bites as yet, fishing was more of an entertainment activity than anything else at this stage, so I didn't take my failure as a hunter-gatherer to heart.

Essentially this day felt as new as Day One. Cigar-shaped fly-ing fish about 25 cm long were hyperactive in the first few hours, launching themselves out of the water without warning and then gliding in the wind to get as far away from me as they could – surely a good way to evade predators, because I regularly saw them glide for more than 50 metres before hitting the water again. All this ac-tivity led me to believe that the fish population beneath my kayak was extremely healthy, although I still didn't catch anything. As be-fore, I was unconcerned about my failure to harvest anything from the sea, because my destination for the evening was the town of Foule Point (Fenoarivo), a famous east-coast tourist attraction.

The early-morning paddling went very well, but as time passed the temperature rose steadily and I became tired, so that the small waves that hit the kayak at regular intervals began to feel like bigger ones, and at times it seemed that I was moving slower than a tortoise. Foule Point was still out of sight somewhere ahead when my muscles told me that enough was enough – and then I realised that I had arrived.

I had been sighting a growing number of fishermen in their pirogues, wooden dugout canoes varying in length from two to five metres, and fishermen at sea, I reckoned, were a sure sign of a nearby village or town. Before leaving South Africa I had read that Madagascar had over 1 250 fishing villages. No wonder fish with a helping of the island's abundant supply of rice was the first choice for hungry Malagasy.

And there it was, a hotel and other buildings right on the beach, which was swarming with what I presumed were holiday makers, mostly Malagasy people, swimming in the calm waters of the lagoon and sun-bathing. I revelled in the sight: it was just like the postcard picture the Fayd'Herbes had created in my mind's eye. Now the problem was to get over the reef protecting this little slice of paradise from the sea.

This was easier said than done. It was a formidable reef, clearly visible from a few kilometres out, and I could hear the sizeable surf crashing loudly against it. Obviously a life-threatening barrier to cross. But when I asked some fishermen for information about the safest place to land, they told me that the reef was only open on the northern side, 17 km away, and I simply did not have the energy to go that much further. So there was nothing for it but to head straight in through the thundering surf, reef or no reef.

I understood only too well that this was going to take some old-fashioned testicular fortitude and a fat slice of luck, but I believed I needed to show some character here, firstly by making the decision and secondly by actually being brave enough to act on it. But now, as I wallowed beyond the surf, waiting for exactly the right moment to dart in on the heels of the last big six-foot wave of a series, I began to realise how foolhardy my decision was. It would be the end of me if I ran at full force into one of the jagged pieces of coral that poked out of the water every now and then. And this was only Day Two!

It was too late to worry about that now, however. I circled, calculating my timing so that I would be able to head in right after the last of a series of swells. When it came swooping past me and smashed on the reef, I went in hot on its heels and literally paddled for my life. Vasti's boss, Daantjie Malan, had given me some valuable advice about this sort of situation. The impact zone of a breaking wave, he had said, was usually no more than 30 metres, if that, and so 'you have to paddle with everything you've got to get out of that danger area, and if you fall off, at least the foam should push you laterally'.

And that was exactly as it turned out. I paddled for dear life to get out of the impact zone and then tried to keep the kayak facing the shoreline as the next wave's foam hit me from behind. But it was too powerful and bucked me out of the cockpit and into the swirling foam and water around me. All I could think of doing was to keep heading towards the safety of the still water ahead.

Clutching hard to my kayak and paddle, I tried vainly to find a footing on the sharp, jagged rocks underneath me, but the next big surge of foam was approaching, and I knew I had to act quickly. I kicked against whatever surface I could find under me, every kick sending me lunging a little closer to safety. The reef sliced into the soft sole of my foot with every kick, but I had to keep going or die. So I kept kicking, the adrenalin storming through my arteries now and turning my earlier fatigue into merely a distant memory. Twenty metres further in and close now to safety, I got back on to my kayak and started paddling. Soon I was on dry land, all in one piece.

I checked into the Mandy Hotel (38 000 ariary, or about $20 US) with just two immediate priorities in mind: a big bowl of beefy spaghetti bolognaise and a snooze. I got both, the snooze fitting in nicely between the two giant servings of spaghetti!

By the evening I had recovered enough to go out and get a few insights into a cross-section of Malagasy culture I had not expected. Gambling! But gambling with a difference, very different from what most people imagine a casino is like. Instead of a big smoke-filled room full of old people who should have known better hunched over the one-armed bandits, this establishment was a strictly open-air variety. It was set up on the beach near the hotel and consisted of tables, crudely cobbled together and offering a variety of games of chance.

I decided to have a flutter on one that was clearly based on roulette. The wheel was a fully spoked bicycle wheel, mounted vertically on a wooden board (or even a tree, as I saw later on); instead of a ball there was a flexible rubber peg in the 12 o'clock position which flicked through the spokes as the wheel was spun. The spacing between each spoke was numbered and corresponded with its partner number on the table underneath the wheel. Wherever the rubber peg stopped after the wheel had stopped spinning would pay out five times the amount wagered on the corresponding partner number.

I didn't win anything, but I consoled myself with the thought that my little wager wouldn't disappear into some yawning coffer belonging to the government or a casino boss – instead it would be invested directly into the local community. So it wasn't really lost, just directed into a genuine good cause ... I suppose I had better stop right here before it begins to sound as if I am making a pathetic attempt to justify a gambling problem.

The next day was supposed to be a short day, but the radio interview times had changed, and I decided to stay over for another night to carry out some basic maintenance I had planned for later in the week and give the cuts on my foot some healing time. And yes, I let the restaurant's manager know that he could stock up on spaghetti and mince!

The radio interviews were very different from all those I'd done before about this Madagascar journey. Now I was actually on the way, not just talking about it.

I set off soon after first light next morning, under a paling sky with the rising sun streaking through the clouds on the horizon and the lamps of the evening fishermen still twinkling along the outer edge of the lagoon. I thought of how many places there were in the world where a local population depended on one main source for its prosperity, or even its very existence. Usually a source like this was some type of industry – the Toyota complex in Amanzimtoti, for example, or Volkswagen in Uitenhage, or Appletiser in Grabouw. Here it was the harvesting of the fruits of the sea by fishermen in small boats.

One of the local guards gave me a hand and we walked the 100 metres or so that took us to the water's edge, 70 kilos of kayak pressing down on our shoulders. I felt free as I splashed my face with water, shook hands with my helper and headed out to sea. Free as a bird; better still, free as an adventurer.

CHAPTER 7

RE-FIGHTING THE COLD WAR IN THE MIDDLE OF NOWHERE

The whales were very active, breaching, swirling and splashing about 200 metres from me. It took some courage to jump off the kayak and start fiddling around with my camera equipment.

I could see that the men in the pirogues I passed on my way to the lagoon's mouth were tired – they had probably been out on the sea for the entire night – but in spite of their fatigue many wanted to know who I was and where I intended to go in this little boat of mine. I pointed to the north and repeated '*Laba, laba*', meaning 'there, there'. No doubt this sounded pretty crazy to them, but my apparent foolishness seemed to give them a second wind.

For myself, I was full of energy. But if today was going to be like the previous two, I would be full of beans for the first 10 km or so, and then I would begin to run out of steam and seem to be more fatigued than I should be.

Now it happened again, and I couldn't understand why – there was no reason for me to feel so tired, because I had eaten enough and the conditions definitely were in my favour for those first three hours of paddling.

The only thing at this stage of my journey that I was unsure of was what my optimal paddling speed would be, taking into consideration the design and weight of my kayak, the sea conditions and temperatures, and – probably most important – the effects on my body of paddling marathon distances, day in, day out.

The sea was choppy and made the paddling hard work, but fortunately this leg was a short one, and I arrived at Mahambo Bay after only four hours. In spite of my second-stage fatigue I felt good as I rounded the point that my Garmin told me was the southern edge of the bay. Christiaan from Bateau Ivre had referred me to a friend of his who owned a new bungalow-style lodge called La Pirogue, and it wasn't too difficult to locate, because as I got closer in I could not help noticing a huge pirogue strung up on the facade of one of the few buildings on the beautiful stretch of rocky beach. It was a no-brainer.

And so it was, of course. Ten minutes after landing (no surf-and-reef battles this time) I was laying into a plate of – yep, you've guessed it – spaghetti bolognaise kindly supplied by the owners, Bernard and Dominique. Dominique and her son Jason lived half the year in the United States and so spoke English perfectly but Bernard, like many French people the world over, spoke only French and was very proud of it.

With my belly full of spaghetti and my body inside some dry clothes, I sat back while Dominique attended to the cuts on my foot, which had begun to fester. They were only two days old and in my opinion still looked OK – my foot was certainly sensitive to the touch, but I believed the exposure to salt water would ward off infection. Being colour-blind, however, I hadn't spotted the reddening that warned of an infection, something quite obvious to somebody with normal vision like Dominique.

Dominique's concern was actually more about my nonchalant

attitude towards what lay ahead than the immediate problem of my infected foot. Right now I was still in the touristy part of Madagascar's east coast and had a false sense of security, she warned. A few hundred kilometres on I might die, very painfully and very alone.

My foot attended to, I attended to some domestic jobs, namely, draining water out of the kayak from both hatches and unpacking baggage that had got wet to dry it in the late-afternoon sun and breeze. I didn't give routine maintenance a thought, or even check where the water had leaked in: I was well into my adventure, and the leaking problem was going to have to take care of itself, so to speak.

That evening I had dinner with Dominique and some of her guests, and something happened that I had noticed occurring more and more frequently over time: some white South Africans' lack of self-identity and a sense of belonging.

A group of young guys in their early twenties walked into the dining hall and greeted Dominique and the others. By their accents I could hear they were English-speaking South Africans. One of them sat down next to me and introduced himself – he knew who I was and wanted to chat to me about the Africa adventure. At this time a dark-haired guy in the group, who seemed new, was introducing himself to Dominique, and I couldn't help but notice this fellow white South African's way of introducing himself to his hosts.

Dominique asked: 'So, you're working with Anton and the other South Africans?'

'Yes,' he said. 'I'm working with them. I'll also be here for six months.'

'Then you're also South African?' she commented.

'No, no, no, no, no,' he said. 'I'm not South African, I'm Portuguese. No, definitely not South African!'

This, mind you, in the most South African of English accents that you could hope to find. It shocked me to hear how brazenly he was willing to renounce his country and heritage. I wondered if I was being over-sensitive and over-reactive, but it stuck with me, and when the alleged Portuguese sat down opposite me I thought: *Perfect, now I can ask a question or two to prove to myself whether my initial reaction was unfounded or not.*

'Where in Portugal do you live?' I started.

'Umm, I actually live in Durban, but my parents come from Portugal,' he replied.

'Do you speak Portuguese?'

'Yes, a little.'

'Do you have a South African ID?'

'Yes, I do.'

'Where were you born ... where did you go to school?'

'South Africa of course.' By this stage his tone had grown wary, as if he were girding his loins to counter my inquisitive banter.

I just could not stop myself from carrying on.

'Then why do you call yourself Portuguese if in fact you're a South African?' I asked. 'After all, everything about you, even your parents, ties you to South Africa. I mean a technicality could make you Portuguese on paper, but the bulk of real Portuguese people in Portugal would see you as nothing more than an immigrant.'

I half-expected him to put up a strong counter-argument, but he didn't, and listened in silence to my argument about taking ownership of our country, with all its failings. And I meant it, because that sort of attitude has infinitely more chance of success than the opposite tack of denouncing your country at every opportunity. The bottom line, though, is that I definitely over-reacted and should have kept my mouth shut. But I was missing South Africa and my people already. The thought of someone going to extreme lengths to distance himself from the country of his birth, the country that had given his family all the opportunities that it had had in life, was simply disgraceful, in my view.

The bungalows at La Pirogue were very naturally styled and varied in levels of luxury. My bedroom had an en-suite shower and toilet, the walls and roof being constructed of wood and grass on top of a smooth concrete floor. The salty sea-breeze that blew through the room during the night was fresh and invigorating, and in spite of the adrenalin-provoking dinner conversation I managed to catch the best night's sleep I was to have in Madagascar.

Dominique and her son Jason had the staff up at the crack of dawn to make me some coffee before I set off, and as we sipped the piping hot brew she and Bernard taught me another rule for inhabiting an earthly paradise that we humans have still not learnt to adhere to.

There was a rock shelf that ran out to sea at right angles to the beach, and I asked them why they hadn't built some sort of jetty along it; to my mind it would have rounded off the camp very nicely, allowing visiting ski-boats to dock without effort, and thereby boosting their visitor income.

Dominique explained: 'When Bernard and I stood here for the very first time we were in amazement. We looked at each other and said loudly: 'This is paradise, we have to own this.' So if this is the closest we'll ever get to paradise, then why should we change it? If we alter anything we automatically wouldn't have the original paradise any more.'

Fair enough. The bottom line is that paradise cannot be bettered, so don't waste your time and our planet trying to.

The coffee drunk and farewells said, I paddled away through the mystical silence of early morning, which always makes the world feel brand-new, and now I really felt the magic of the place.

What gradually brought me down to earth again, though, was the fact that my wrists began to hurt – any paddler's nightmare, especially one who can't afford to rest, the first remedy that is prescribed for tendon pain. For a paddler, tendonitis is the worst possible injury, because your wrists become so inflamed and painful that you wouldn't even be able to pick up your morning scone.

There are many opinions on the major reason why paddlers develop tendonitis – apart from too much paddling, of course – but most kayakers will tell you it has to do with your grip. When you paddle you actually push and pull simultaneously, with a special effort to keep all forces squarely on your wrists at all times. Essentially the 'push' action resembles a boxing punch, while the 'pull' requires a locked wrist, and the 20 000 or so strokes it takes to do 40 km a day will antagonise the tendons in even the toughest, most seasoned paddler's wrists if his grip is sub-standard.

Obviously my grip was inferior, and while it probably would have sufficed if I had been in an unloaded boat, the fact was that I was paddling one with lots of extra weight, and in the teeth of constant afternoon head winds. If things got no better there was no way that I would even see out the coming week. So I did the only thing possible: I eased off the strength aspect of each stroke and concentrated on paddling as naturally as was possible in the choppy seas.

It was a difficult and frustrating business, but one consolation was that the sea was bubbling with wildlife. Apart from hundreds of flying fish and numerous large schools of other fish I also saw six whales, all before midday! The whales were very active, breaching, swirling and splashing about 200 metres from me. It took some courage to jump off the kayak and start fiddling around with my camera equipment. Sony had kitted me out with their robust video-camera housings, and what better time to try them out than now, with whales all around me?

It proved to be more difficult than I had imagined. The suction mount underneath the camera needed a very smooth flat area to be able to attach properly, and while the kayak had plenty of smooth surfaces, it didn't have many flat ones. The biggest problem, though, turned out to be the humidity factor – so much condensation gathered on the interior part of the lens that all the footage I took was hazy.

Sony was aware of this problem, as I knew from several readings of the operating manual, and had specially shaped silicone strips neatly fitted into the camera housing to absorb the moisture. But for some reason the strips weren't working as well as expected, and I knew I needed to investigate the cause as soon as possible, or I wouldn't have any footage at the end of the journey. Gloomily I envisaged the prospect of a working title on the lines of 'A Gorilla in the Madagascan Mist'. And apart from anything else I was still committed to bringing back evidence for my grandchildren about what their old man (or gorilla, depending on the footage) had been up to in his salad days.

Eventually, sore wrists or no sore wrists, I reached the village town of Fenerive Est, about 20 km further, and looked up friends of Bernard's who had offered to house me that evening. They even tempted me with spaghetti bolognaise, which I thought was a bit of unintentional cruelty. Reluctantly I turned the offer down, for two reasons. The first was that the dates for Mike to arrive on Sainte-Marie had been set, and second, my weekly newspaper column was due in two days, and the only place I could see on the map that suggested civilisation (that is to say, an internet connection) was the ferry town of Soanierana-Ivongo. That meant I had to cover 75 km in the next two days to make my dates.

On my way again, for kilometres at a time the water was patchy – very dirty, then crystal-clear, then muddy and then clear again. This, I concluded, must provide an optimal fish-hunting environment, and I remember that when Seamus phoned me I asked with great nonchalance if he would mind calling me back later because I wanted to catch one of the bonito that were jumping up all around me, making a meal off hordes of tiny fish.

I didn't have much experience with bonito, but I could see that these were bigger than the ones on Hennie Papenfuss's fishing DVD that I had watched over and over before leaving home, and I knew that when these stocky, muscular, bright blue fellows (genetically they belong to the tuna family) go into a feeding frenzy, which was what they were engaged in at this moment, they don't see anything around them because all their attention is concentrated on gorging themselves. I felt a bit sorry for those little fish, which had a double problem. From below they were under attack by the bonito, and from above they were being harassed by squawking gannets and terns which were swooping down on them in kamikaze-style dives.

Anyway, I cast out a few spinners (small, shiny metal lures that are supposed to imitate tiny fish, for those who don't know) into the froth of the feeding frenzy, but perhaps the bonito weren't as distracted as I thought, and I drew another blank. But once again I wasn't too disappointed. I was on a high, and when you are on an adventure high anything short of a real catastrophe doesn't have any impact.

My target destination for the day was a village named Antakabola on the banks of the Antakabola River, which, my Garmin showed clearly, flowed into the sea at an acute angle. That sort of shape usually provides refuge from breaking waves, and I hoped this would be the case with Antakabola as well. Well, hope springeth eternal, but it isn't always realised, as I discovered once again when I actually got there.

The river did *not* flow into the sea, and so there was no sheltered area in which to paddle in. It was a crash-boom-bang effort to get to shore; I tried surfing in on one of the smaller waves, but I hit a returning swell that was travelling at such speed that I was flung from my seat, away from my kayak. Fortunately the kayak was seized by the waves of foam and deposited on the beach long before I was, because I was caught in a rip (the gulley of water that sucks back out to sea) for a while and had some washing machine-style abuse in several of the impact zones. I never felt threatened, though, just tired.

When I finally made it to shore my first priority was to drag my kayak up past the highest watermark and inspect it for damage, but there was none I could see. Good! I felt good, too, except that my wrists hurt. Now I could pay my intended visit to Antakabola and get hold of a meal and a well-earned rest.

Except that Antakabola wasn't where it was supposed to be. There was no sign of life for as far as the eye could see to either right or left – not even a footprint – although my Garmin was adamant that I was, in fact, standing right in the middle of the village. Eventually I gave up and decided to leave my kayak and go on foot to the river, simultaneously looking around for a sheltered spot where I could pitch the tent that I hadn't had to use so far.

The river's mouth was a few hundred metres wide and still a kilometre or two away, and with this in mind I decided to set up camp on a patch of grass I found which was littered with cow-dung, a sure sign that the elusive village was nearby, rather than try to find the village itself. Dragging the heavy kayak along the soft sand was sapping the remaining energy I had in me, and every 20 metres or so I paused to stretch my back and catch my breath.

Then I lost that last bit of breath when I was confronted by 20 or so huge cows, marching straight towards me, accompanied by a young herd-boy who was no older than about 15. The boy didn't notice me at first. Then he spotted me and reacted with all the urgency of a frog zapped by electricity. He froze in his tracks, dropped a stick he was holding, spun around and sprinted away in the opposite direction.

I was too tired now to play the fool and make scary noises, as I would do and have done in similar situations in the past; I just stood there while the cattle moved past on either side of me and my kayak, completely unfazed, unlike their caretaker, who had paused on a dune and was watching to see what I would do next. I went back to dragging my kayak, a few metres at a time, towards the patch of neat grass. Meanwhile the cattle kept heading southwards down the beach, mooing occasionally, perhaps out of boredom.

I carried on dragging the kayak towards my chosen camping spot. In the meantime the herd-boy had vanished, but as I was assessing the final onslaught up a steep dune about 20 minutes later he returned with a slightly older youth who didn't seem as scared of me as his companion and walked slowly up to me.

'*Bolatsara*,' I greeted him.

'*Bolatsara*,' he dutifully replied.

I leaned forward to shake his hand and inquired: '*Invovo?*' meaning 'what is news?' in Malagasy.

He didn't give the usual reply of 'there is no news', but signalled to me that the direction I was heading with my kayak was upsetting him. '*Fady, fady, cimetière, fady, sacrée,*' he kept repeating. This much I managed to understand. *Fady* meant more or less 'not allowed', and *cimetière* and *sacrée*, I deduced, referred to a sacred cemetery or graveyard of some kind.

Now I recalled the stories that Flippie had shared with me about the '*fady*' intrusions often committed by foreigners. Malagasy cemeteries are sacred places, and visitors, especially foreigners, are not allowed into the actual sites. This is such a serious matter that Madagascan women have to put up their hair in specific styles before they are allowed access. I shuddered. Just say the herd-boy hadn't spotted me and I had pitched my tent on top of Grandma's and Grandpa's graves?

The older boy was into sign-language again by now, indicating that I should head for the river mouth and then go up-river, which I guessed would get me to the actual village. I nodded, but subconsciously I shook my head. Dragging the kayak for another kilometre would just make this day too long; I wanted to eat something, and even though it was earlyish, I wanted to sleep.

But I didn't have much choice in the matter. The elder boy set off southwards after the cows, looking back occasionally to see if I was following. So, slowly and unenthusiastically, I followed with the kayak in tow. When we came to the river mouth I saw that it was silted up by some big dunes, but here and there were small, shallow pools of water which lightened my burden because I could slide the kayak through them, saving lots of my remaining energy.

The first thing I did when I got to the river itself was to wallow in the shallow fresh water for a few minutes – it's amazing how soft and soothing fresh water feels when you've been in salt water for any length of time. It also made my introduction to the village much simpler, because my wallowings had brought life to the river's banks. People, more children and women than men, called out to me and pointed to what I could now see looked like the docking area for most of the pirogues.

At the docking site were more men who now were coming to welcome me to their village. I struggled up the steep, muddy river bank, trying not to fall, and shook hands with what seemed to be a few hundred men and children, sharing smiles with the shy ones, mainly toddlers and women.

I informed them by sign language that I was tired, hungry and in need of sleep, having discovered right away that my fractured French was falling on deaf ears. Once again, Flippie and my other informants had been right. Outside the larger towns no one spoke French. The good news was that Madagascar had only one language. The bad news was that every 200 or 300 km they spoke a drastically different dialect of it. Great! I needed to learn more Malagasy, and very quickly at that, but which variety?

By now my kayak was riding high on the shoulders of some of the young fellows who were slipping and sliding up the bank with it. That suited me fine. I followed in their wake and was eventually delivered to the front door of a small hut on stilts, which I found belonged to the president. Yep, the president, but in Madagascar that did not necessarily mean the head of state. In this case it signified the head of the region, or, as they term it in Malagasy, a '*fokontany*'. So here I was, standing, smiling in front of the Chef de Fokontany de Antakabola. Believe it or not ...

Mr President was a short, grey-haired man whose wrinkled face bore a frown and a broad smile, all at the same time, which I took to indicate suspicion mixed with enthusiastic hospitality. He spoke some French, and wanted to know who and what I was. My idea of carrying my old business cards which had pictures showing me on my Africa travels, including a picture of me with Nelson Mandela, paid off nicely.

The president loved the pictures and studied them at length while I explained that the information on the card was how he and I could stay in touch in future. He formally introduced himself, by way of a neatly hand-written equivalent of my card, as Monsieur Demi Augustine, and told his wife to start clearing the house of loose things to make way for my bed. Right alongside theirs!

This was obviously a matter for utmost diplomacy, and so I explained as tactfully as I could that there was no need for them to make room for a bed for me and that I had a bed of my own and would be happy to place it outside his door. For a while it was touch and go, because (so I gathered) it was a bit like not burping after eating yourself silly with a tentful of Arabs, or refusing to break a plate or two at a Greek party.

I've always found that the best thing to defuse tension is a liberal dose of humour, and since I couldn't communicate properly – if at all – in English, French or Malagasy, I turned my focus to the children, who were now glued to me, becoming braver all the time, to the point where they were actually addressing me. Since I didn't know what they were saying, I decided to imitate each child's voice and words as best I could. The children loved every one of these renditions and shrieked with laughter each time I spoke.

Having mended any breach of diplomatic relations that I might have caused, I set up camp amid total chaos. Children would touch me, especially my hair, and then turn and sprint off as fast as they could, all this to the accompaniment of a chorus of shrieks and shrills. After an hour I was all set up next to the president's hut and explained to Monsieur Augustine that I was very tired and wanted to sleep, although what I actually wanted first of all was some quiet time.

He understood what I wanted, but not the kids. I had only set up the interior part of my tent, so they could stand up against it and stare at me through the mosquito-gauze, saying 'hallo, hallo, hallo' until they got a reply. I satisfied this game for about 40 minutes, but their enthusiasm showed no signs of diminishing, and I finally resorted to responding with a grumbling: 'Come on! Enough, now!'

This had just the opposite effect, and their enjoyment went up a notch rather than down. It illustrated the truth of the story we're all told in childhood, that if someone is teasing you it is only to get a reaction. That was exactly what was happening here, and after some more of this I felt myself going quietly insane. But then some parents came to my rescue and ordered the hysterically laughing children to go home, seeing it was nearly sunset.

I reflected on my experiences of the last couple of hours as I lay back on the flat clay ground, enjoying my long-delayed quiet time. How did people on the other side of the equation react when a visitor arrived and there was no way to communicate with him? Did they react like me and also feel uncomfortable when everyone had run out of things to laugh about out of pure politeness? Did they also think: *Get this guy as comfortable as possible, get some food in his stomach and then put him to bed as quickly as possible?* Or did they stand there thinking: *OK, let's keep staring at this guy for another hour or so and see if he can pull out another bout of laughter from us?* I ask this because the latter thought is what I believed a lot of the adults had in their heads as they stood there in the crowd which had surrounded me for over two hours.

I slept well, but when I woke just before sunrise I had a feeling I had been talking in my sleep – I know that if I can't recall a specific dream but remember activity in my sleep, it is normally a sign that I was guilty of some loud debates with myself while I was out cold.

In any case, I packed my gear and shared a cup of black coffee with the president and his cabinet before getting on my way.

But there was tension in the air now, signs of an issue that no one wanted to bring up, although what the cause of it was I didn't have any idea. At first I thought it was that they wanted money from me, but then it turned out that overnight my nationality had become an issue, one that dated from the Cold War and apartheid days, two decades earlier.

In the 1970s and 1980s the South African government had been obdurately opposed to the Soviet Union and the spread of communism, but many African countries had had resident populations of Soviet 'advisers', and the ones in Madagascar had convinced the Malagasy that they were firmly in the sights of those nasty South African white racists, who were bent on colonising their island. Now, 20 years later, both apartheid and the Russians were long gone, but the news did not seem to have reached this isolated little village, and the 'informed' section of the inhabitants was of the opinion that my kayak, my smile and I were highly suspicious. Something was going on, they just couldn't put their finger on exactly what it was that I was up to.

I didn't react to the pointing and gesturing, some of it distinctly unfriendly, since most of the people were still as amiable as they had been in the beginning. The president had become wary, though, and he asked to see my passport and asked me to travel with him to the police station in a nearby town. I didn't agree, and so I concentrated on joking and interacting with the friendly part of the early-morning crowd that had gathered around us now.

Then rescue came from a most unusual source. One of the villagers took me by my elbow and excitedly guided me to a small tree in which a huge chameleon was moving from branch to branch. As it happens, I love chameleons, and I decided to hold this one while one of the village youngsters filmed me. When the filming was over I made further use of this unexpected foot in the door and soon had the ad hoc cameraman and his friends, spurred on by the promise of some cash, carrying my kayak back to the river so I could set off.

The villagers were fully into the spirit of things now and gave the president and his cabinet no further opportunity to continue their interrogation. With great cheerfulness they accompanied me to the river, and some crammed into a few pirogues and followed me down to the mouth, where they stood on the banks like spectators at a soccer match to watch me bash my way through the crunching surf. I didn't disappoint them – I got knocked off the kayak and had to remount under pressure from the waves that followed. The crowd loved it, and their cheers followed me as I paddled my way out of the surf into flat water. Not a bad farewell for a suspected racist colonialist invader!

My goal for the day was the ferry town of Soanierana-Ivongo, 35 km away, from where I would do my first open-sea crossing to meet up with Mike Yelseth on Sainte-Marie Island. That would complete the first of the seven legs into which I had divided my journey. It would also be the first catch-up and status check to see how I felt about actually being in the adventure now. I reckoned I would be in a better way, by then, to answer the question of whether I had bitten off more than I could chew.

It was time for me to get serious about actually catching a fish, and I targeted reefs and muddy river mouths along the route, paddling harder than normal through these target areas to entice my first victim, and it worked.

The sea being very smooth in the morning, it was easy to spot where swells rose above the reefs, and I was about 200 metres into a hard push when the reel on my rod, which was behind my seat to the left, began to scream as line was taken out it at speed – the sound all fishermen dream about. I actually know of several guys who work for Rapala in South Africa whose cell-phone ring-tones are this exact sound! I wasn't so excited that I forgot the appropriate drill I had dinned into myself, though.

I took a few more strokes to set the hook in the fish's mouth and then stopped paddling to swing my legs over the side of the kayak for better balance, swivelled my torso towards the rod and swiftly lifted it out to keep the line taut, because a fish can easily free itself from the hook if the line goes slack. That was the scenario, anyway.

What actually happened was that I battled a bit to get the rod out, and by the time I eventually had it between my legs there was no tension on the line or signs of life at the end of it. Nevertheless, I reeled in with enthusiasm, just in case there *was* a fish attached. The immediate result of this was that, thanks to the fact that I had swivelled in the current, the line became tangled around the rudder.

I jumped out of my seat and swam to the rear of the kayak to untangle the line, sadly aware that I had lost what would have been my first fish. Well, there was nothing I could do about that, so I remounted and began to reel in the remaining line. Then, to my utter surprise, there was a forceful tug on the line, followed by a determined pull. The fish was still there! Remaining as calm as I could, bearing in mind that I was dreadfully excited, I kept cranking the reel, probably with much too much 'vooma', and 10 minutes later I was sitting with a fish weighing around 7 kg in my lap. I was feeling pretty satisfied. I had a lapful of dinner and I had videoed the episode as well. I felt so good that I even took out my cell phone, found I had reception and sent an SMS of my mini-adventure to as many people as I could.

I put my back into my paddling as the hours passed, although the sea became increasingly choppy in the afternoon, because I needed to speed up if I wanted to reach my destination before nightfall. I also received a few calls, specifically from the mayor of a town called Ampisimbe, who told me to report to him because the police now knew about me.

Know about me? What are you on about? I thought. More outdated Cold War-and-apartheid stuff? After giving the matter some consideration I decided to ignore his calls and threats, and focus on getting safely to Soanierana-Ivongo before darkness fell.

Paddle, paddle, paddle ... Only another five or six kilometres now, but my arms and back were preparing to go on strike. On the other hand, my Garmin showed that I was moving in the right direction. So if I kept doing what I was doing, no matter how tough it might be, I would get to Soanierana-Ivongo in time. And I did, although I was in fairly poor shape as I headed into the harbour with its high communication towers on top of the cliff heads that protected the entrance, like the famed Knysna Heads in my home province. My wrists, my lower back, my shoulders, my bum and my knees were all in pain, either from the continuous eight hours of effort and move-ment or the opposite; no movement at all.

Tomorrow, I thought, as I cruised in, I'll write my article for the *Cape Argus* and then prepare my boat for crossing 40 km of open sea. Yip, just like that.

CHAPTER 8

THE GREAT SOANIERANA
LEGAL TANGLE

*The police office was abuzz with excitement at my arrest and
the subsequent deliberations as to what to do with me. I agreed
with all the obvious allegations ... but not with either of two
solutions to my problem that they came up with,
both of which bordered on lunacy.*

By this time I arrived at Soanierana-Ivongo it was late afternoon
and on the default side of tranquillity, but it didn't take long for a
small crowd to gather around me. I could see this becoming a regular thing ... not that I was complaining.

The people were friendly, smiling and laughing while I tried to
steady myself. I had been at sea for so long that it felt distinctly
odd to be standing on my feet in traditional *Homo sapiens* style. As I
say, the people got much amusement out of my wobbly stance, but
there was another reason why I wasn't complaining – as with previous welcoming crowds, there were a couple who wanted to help me
carry my craft with its load of baggage and water to a safe sleeping-
place up the beach.

So there I was, walking unsteadily along behind my admirers, who had my kayak and baggage on their shoulders. They were taking me, I was given to understand by some sign language, to a much better sleeping-place than a patch of beach.

We zigzagged through a straggle of decaying squarish white houses till we came to the local hostelry, 'Chez Nat and Fred', a tired-looking building with a restaurant on the porch and a few cubicle-style rooms on the side – usually let by the hour, I later discovered. I had stayed in fancier places in my life, but I was so tired and hungry that I didn't care one morsel about where I was going to lay my head for the night.

Now it was time to say goodbye to my new friends and give them something for their trouble. They made it clear that my fish, which still hung proudly at my side, would do very well. But this was not just any old fish – I had wrested it from the sea with my own hands! Instead I handed over some ariary notes from a small stash in my shirt-pocket. The notes were a little slimy (strange how paper money goes slimy when it's wet – I wonder why?) but this didn't bother the locals.

I was welcomed by Natasha, the proprietor of Chez Nat and Fred. She disappointed me a little when she said the fish would take a bit too long to prepare, but asked if had a second choice. Which, of course, I did ... and yes, both helpings of the spaghetti bolognaise I crammed down my throat were delicious.

When I awoke next morning after a solid night's sleep I felt as if I was in a different village altogether. I had been so tired when I arrived that I had seen everything through a haze. Now all the colours were brighter, and I could actually make out people's faces. I had some fish for breakfast (free, of course) and started the hunt for an internet connection with the help of a trilingual local named Alex, whom I met at the restaurant and who had told me he hailed from Réunion Island.

With Alex at my side we went on a door-to-door search involving everyone he knew who might have an internet connection. No luck – the people were either out and about or they had the facilities but the connection was down. After two hours of fruitless search we decided to try the Roman Catholic mission in the centre of the village.

Yes, the Mother Superior replied to our hopeful inquiry, the mission not only had access but the connection was up. Then without further ado she led us upstairs to an office and told me that I had the use of the computer for one hour only (I didn't quite understand this restriction, seeing I had bought my own airtime, but who was going to argue in a situation like that?). So I sat down and logged on under the eyes of a hyperactive priest the Mother Superior had detailed to keep an eye on us.

I got my article written and sent well within the deadline, in spite of the distraction from the priest, who was patrolling up and down behind me, grumbling away about how much important work he still had to do. I went to say goodbye to the Mother Superior, and when I left I saw our grumbling preacher again ... lounging on the sofa in the foyer, idly thumbing through a magazine. Maybe he was just a cyber-nanny in a dog-collar?

This done, Alex and I headed back to Chez Nat and Fred for our second appointment of the morning. While we were searching for an internet connection I had telephoned the town's mayor – Soanierana-Ivongo was a major centre in this east coast province – and I reckoned that it wouldn't hurt to meet him and establish a friendly relationship: after all, if I landed in trouble it would be good to have someone of local stature to appeal to.

Alex had translated my overtures to the mayor in some detail, suggesting that we all meet for breakfast at Chez Nat when I had finished using the internet. He seemed extremely eager to meet with me, Alex said. The mayor probably couldn't wait to meet this 'famous' (Alex's description) adventurer, I thought, which could only be a good sign.

I was excited as we sat and waited in the restaurant – I was getting off on the right foot! I had decided to give him a South African flag sticker as a token of my thanks for the time he was giving us. But we waited and waited, and nothing happened. Eventually I decided to call him again, and he said he would not be long, we must just be patient. So we waited some more ... and waited.

Eventually, when each of us had had two breakfasts and enough coffee to last us for a long time, Alex had to go about his business. He suggested that if I spotted the mayor on his scooter I should approach him myself. I agreed, waved goodbye and started looking out for the mayoral scooter.

After a while I spotted him at the town circle, chatting to some of the town police and members of the military. I jumped up, asked Natasha to look after my bag and sprinted down the road to where they were standing. There I stood at a polite distance from their roadside conference, catching my breath and waiting for an invitation to interrupt.

Eventually my turn came. The mayor looked at me and nodded. '*Oui*,' he said.

'*Bolotsara ... Bonjour, Monsieur Mayor*,' I said in a croaky mix of broken French and even more broken Malagasy. '*Moi appelle Riaan Manser. Sud Africain le tourist, tour Madagascar avec le bateau*,' all this while smiling broadly and holding out my hand, the other hand clutching my forearm in customary South African style as a sign of respect. He looked like a really good man.

'*Où est le bateau?*' he blurted out, making half an attempt to shake my hand. '*Où est le bateau?*' In other words, where was my 'boat'?

'*Moi bateau le petit kayak*, no *grande bateau*,' I said. '*Laba avec* security Nat and Fred,' I continued. But the mayor clearly didn't know what a kayak was.

'*Viens avec moi, s'il vous plaît, regarde le bateau. Viens s'il vous plaît*,' I invited, sure that when he saw my kayak he would be vastly impressed at how far I had come with such a small vessel. Maybe he would even have dinner with me at which we would consume that first-ever catch of mine?

But all he did was blurt out: '*Où est le passeport?*' Never mind seeing the kayak, he wanted my passport! I was completely taken aback, confused by this unexpected response. Now the mayor began getting peremptory – clearly he wanted answers, and fast.

'*Moi passeport* à *la chambre,*' I replied, still trying to figure out what the problem was.

'Bring to me,' he said, switching to English. And now my stubborn nature kicked in (although I hope it was more of a commitment to my principles). Since he didn't seem to appreciate my humble approach and only interpreted it as weakness, it was time to stop playing the wounded deer.

'*Pourquoi?*' I asked. In other words, why did he want to see my passport? Had I done something to create this hostile, rude, aggressive response? I did not intend to simply back down and let him think that it was OK to treat a visitor to his country like this.

'*Pourquoi?*' I repeated, with more feeling this time, and standing straight up. '*Moi* no *bandit. Pourquoi l'agression avec moi?*' Basically I was saying that it was time he explained his aggressive attitude towards me.

Well, he obviously didn't think so. He spoke a few words in Malagasy to the policeman on his right, and seconds later I had two of the soldiers trying to hold me by my elbows. I resisted in a calm but very firm manner, while keeping eye-contact with the mayor. Almost immediately a crowd started gathering, and fortunately one of its members was Natasha. Politely she suggested to the mayor that I be allowed to go and fetch my passport, even if that meant being escorted by the soldiers.

The mayor allowed himself to be persuaded, and back I went to the hotel with my armed escort. By the time I returned the mayor had lost interest in me. He had had his ego fix for the day and had shown the village that he was actually a very big shot who could tell

The crowds came out to see me off. It was very different from the 'Round Africa' cycle send-off, with an intimidating harbour for the launch and a bumpy sea to follow.

Much later I admitted that as I paddled out on the first 20 km of the journey I was nauseous with fear. Physical fear? Possibly. Fear of failure? Probably.

A man must eat ... fish, anybody? The 30 kg kingfish took me three hours to land and nearly sank my kayak.

Thomas the Rapala lure was my closest friend and confidant on the trip – we caught most species, but not even one dorado. There was nothing like a huge fish to ensure a warm welcome from my Malagasy overnight hosts.

Seamus damned well went and caught not one but two more sizable fish, while I managed to hook the reef. I reckoned I was not going to hear the last about Seamus's triumph for a while, and I was right.

The giants of Morandava's Avenue des Baobabs make you feel pretty puny ... my friend and I confirm that our arms don't even go half-way round ... but the Lover's Baobab makes up for it by promising fertility to its visitors.

My favourite place along the entire Madagascar coastline was Cap Masoala. I met a lot of other people in dugouts, dhows, pirogues and sailboats – though I didn't expect the 'pirates' in the speedboat. I needed directions now and then – but most importantly, contact with humans, pirates or not.

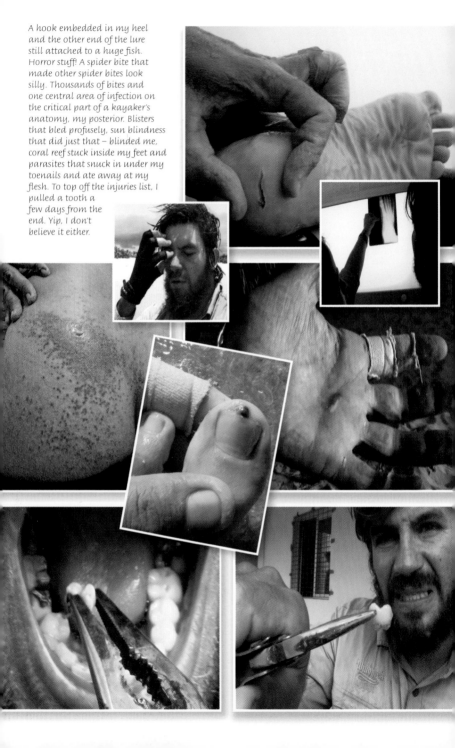

A hook embedded in my heel and the other end of the lure still attached to a huge fish. Horror stuff! A spider bite that made other spider bites look silly. Thousands of bites and one central area of infection on the critical part of a kayaker's anatomy, my posterior. Blisters that bled profusely, sun blindness that did just that – blinded me, coral reef stuck inside my feet and parasites that snuck in under my toenails and ate away at my flesh. To top off the injuries list, I pulled a tooth a few days from the end. Yip, I don't believe it either.

Eric and Fanele were the terrible twins of the year's cyclone season. When you have two of them arriving simultaneously it's like a couple of gatecrashers who roll up uninvited, eat more than anyone else, drink your best wines, break expensive glasses, cause disharmony among your real friends ... and then, to top it all, won't go away.

The Church at Belo sur Mer. Mother Mary survived and the faithful still attended mass the next weekend. Beaches change shape yearly as nature landscapes them, whether you like it or not ... nature did some serious rearranging while I was there. The bicycles are called 'pousse pousse'. I tried out everything – once.

Sometimes it was 5-star accommodation, mostly not ...

Ockie – legend of Sainte-Marie (opposite top). Being tired is the secret to a good night's rest; luxury for me was keeping the rain off. It was great to have a roof over my head and a view of the sea; mostly I pitched the tiny tent on mosquito-ridden beaches. Sometimes I was too spent to even unpack the tent, and slept with the crabs. Church hall accommodation had an awkward revival feeling about it.

I had to see more than just beaches ... and there was more than enough, from French colonial relics and ancient hand gold mining sites to the insides of way too many police stations.

The Malagasy are a very superstitious nation – bordering on fanatical. You had to know what was 'fady'! Development and traditions are in turmoil: I met people who had never laid eyes on a cell phone.

Happiness is ... selling prickly pears from your ox wagon.

Never-ending beauty ... a magazine would not print the sunset photo because they don't allow Photoshopped stuff. That picture is untouched! 'Being IN the picture' has always been a goal; rather than just taking a picture, get inside it!

The 5 000 ariary note has a historic picture on one side: my photo shows how unchanged this Fort Dauphin bay is, 300 years later. Waking up to scenes like these reminded me how fortunate I was. Imprisonment, robberies – they seemed irrelevant now.

Spaghetti bolognaise was what I craved the entire way – I was worse than a pregnant woman expecting quadruplets. Octopus is popular in the fishing villages, but people eat what is easiest to harvest – some meals would have eviscerated my wallet back home! When I didn't find food, once for four days, I survived on cappuccino sachets and energy juice.

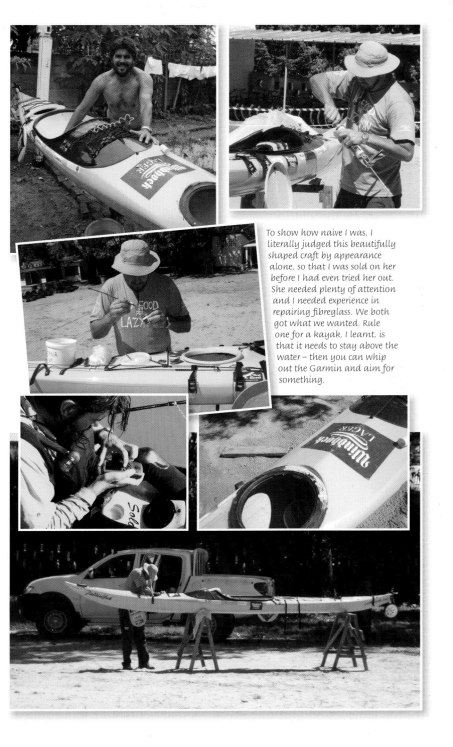

To show how naive I was, I literally judged this beautifully shaped craft by appearance alone, so that I was sold on her before I had even tried her out. She needed plenty of attention and I needed experience in repairing fibreglass. We both got what we wanted. Rule one for a kayak, I learnt, is that it needs to stay above the water – then you can whip out the Garmin and aim for something.

I feared for my life at times and spilled all my beans with God. If I'd known I'd make it through I believe I would have held back on some of the confessions. Tornadoes, 20 foot swells, 100 km/h winds accompanied me often, and there was no coastguard or back-up crew to call. I was lucky, no doubt. A five-metre kayak should never have been in some of the places I took it.

anyone, even foreigners, what to do, and so he squeezed his helmet on over his chubby face and whizzed proudly away on his spluttering scooter.

My self-appointed interrogator having left, I handed the passport to one of his associates, who turned out to be the chief of police of Soanierana-Ivongo. He opened the passport, first checked to see where I had been before and then searched for the correct visa. Since I had two Madagascar visas in my passport now because of my return to South Africa to fetch the kayak (at $100 US a go, nogal!) I was confident that he would find that I was absolutely legally in his country.

And here is where I provide the moral of the story before the story is even finished. My visa was valid only for 30 days and not for the three months it was advertised at – my plan had been to renew it in Diego Suarez, the most northerly town on the island, which the immigration staff in Antananarivo had told me could be done. Eish! Man, now I was in be-e-e-e-g trouble!

I had shown attitude (rightfully so, of course, but in the wrong place and at the wrong time), much more attitude than they were accustomed to get from lesser mortals, and now my bum visa had given them a fine excuse to get stroppy with me. I was going to be taken apart.

There was only one option I could follow: get back into wounded-deer mode and convince them that I had genuinely been under the impression that my visa was valid till the end of October. But it wasn't going to be easy. The bottom line was that I had raced down a dark alley at 100 miles an hour, and halfway down had decided, because of unforeseen circumstances, to reverse out again.

I spent the next few hours as the police chief's unwilling guest, with the two armed guards as a permanent fixture as I shuttled between the police chief's office, the holding cells and then back to the police chief's office again. I knew what I had to do – I had to get some credibility, which is always difficult if you travel alone, so

I had to get the chief to speak to Roy at the South African Embassy, and if need be with Ambassador Monaisa himself.

This was easier said than done. It took a two-hour-long battle to get an after-hours call through to Roy, and he had the interpreter explain to the police chief who I was and why my visa was expired. After a lengthy conversation the chief was persuaded that I was a genuine tourist, but he wasn't willing to budge on the question of why I hadn't got a valid visa.

It was highly suspicious, he told the embassy, for me to be travelling in this secretive manner. *'Crazy' would be a better word for me, Mr Police Chief,* I concluded, *because I was the one who sprinted over to you and the mayor so I could show you my expired visa, so that now I have to wriggle my way out of this difficult situation.*

The police office was abuzz with excitement at my arrest and the subsequent deliberations as to what to do with me. I agreed with all the obvious allegations (such as having the expired visa) but not with either of two solutions to my problem that they came up with, both of which bordered on lunacy.

One was to keep me in custody till an embassy representative bailed me out, then deport me; while the other was that I would fly to Antananarivo under police escort (at my expense, of course!) to explain my situation to the authorities and plead for leniency.

Meanwhile, as I sat helplessly in the police station Mike the cameraman was packed and about to board a flight in South Africa. As an added irritation, the policemen had now got the idea I was very rich and were openly asking me for bribes. But, furious though I was, I kept my mouth shut and told them I was awaiting a call from another friend who might be able to assist – namely Christiaan Fayd'Herbe from Tamatave.

Christiaan was very good friends with the police chief in Tamatave and also with the national police chief in Antananarivo, and could surely, by giving his personal assurance, persuade them to let me go. First prize for me would be to be allowed to go on to my next destination, Sainte-Marie Island, complete the filming there and then fly back to Antananarivo with Mike, where I would renew my visa for the full three-month period.

Then – then! – I would be able to get on with the mammoth journey that still lay ahead. Who would have thought I'd hit this kind of obstacle so early in my journey?

Christiaan got going immediately, and by 10 pm was on to the police bosses. By 11 pm he had an assurance from the national chief of police that a suitable call would be made to the police chief at Soanierano-Ivongo as soon as possible, which I hoped meant 'immediately'. By now the police chief realised that I had been unfairly treated, and his attitude softened considerably, so much so that he was willing to stay up and wait for the call from Antananarivo.

At midnight the call eventually came through. I would have a few days' grace to visit St Marie Island and then I would have to report to the main police station in the capital within the week. I was so overjoyed that I had tears in my eyes; I simply didn't have either the energy or the money to take on challenges like this for an entire year.

I was escorted to my hotel by the chief and one of his men, where they asked Natasha to serve us some celebratory beer. I wasn't in the mood for celebration, however, and I was also not in the mood for covering the tab, but I couldn't get out of doing the latter. So I paid up and did my celebrating in my head.

The funniest thing to happen on this journey thus far took place the next day. The police chief and his two assistants were so impressed with my 'business card' that they felt it only right that people of their stature should have cards as well, and at lunch-time they came to give me them at the restaurant.

The cards were made of normal flimsy notepad paper and featured very risqué designs, considering they identified the owners as officers of the law. The card of the younger assistant, for example, had a topless girl sprawled over one side, with the owner's contact details in the crucial areas. I kept a straight face, thanked him and gave a few 'knuckle ups' in recognition of the beautiful girl on his card.

Later on I laughed out loud every time I took the card out to confirm it was actually real. Africa allows more space for personality than the Western world, where, if you're a policeman or a lawyer or a plumber, there are certain things you automatically conform to if you want to be considered successful.

The home-made business cards – and, in fact, the whole ordeal– confirmed what I have encountered in many another place and country. Everyone wants to be respected and acknowledged, and perceptions and prejudice are always there to throw a spanner in the works, just to make things interesting. So when I grew excited about their interrogation of me, the mayor and police chief were seeing an attitude which in their opinion was shouting: 'I am white and therefore have no respect for a black person, irrespective of his stature.'

Everyone who has travelled across national borders in Africa will have a story about a power-tripping official. I wouldn't disagree about the power-trip description, but I believe that the innate desire of us all to be respected and acknowledged is at the root of the problem. With colonialism and its oppressive history as convenient excuses to employ these irrational power trips, we (meaning white people) cannot be surprised at the irrational behaviour of a short, uneducated, spluttering, scooter-driving, populist mayor's interpretation of our disrespectful actions toward him.

In all honesty I think I could have, should have and would have done a lot better that day. But I had little time, and cultivating trust takes time. But again, the word according to Vasti is: *Lose the battle* (which I clearly did), *so you can win that war* (which I also did, sort of).

I got some fresh insight into the Malagasy way of thinking when

Alex and I walked along the Soanierana bay's coastline towards the harbour area. I was astounded and horrified at the amount of gill-net fishing that was taking place. The catches were meagre and included just-born mackerel and other fish: and they thought this was sustainable?

I expressed my concerns about this to Alex, who explained without hesitation that the poor catch had nothing to do with this destructive ancient form of fishing but rather with the white people, who had opened factories in the town and pumped poisons into the sea. Now, as far as I could see, there was not one major factory in operation anywhere in the vicinity, and remarked that surely it was the responsibility of the elected government to protect the environment from unscrupulous activity, whether conducted by white, black, yellow or brown people?

Alex didn't agree and remained adamant that white foreigners had destroyed the sea-life and possibly the future of what had once been a successful village. He was so adamant, in fact, that he had me doubting my thought processes to the point where I decided to do some research when next I had proper access to the internet.

But that would have to wait. Right now I had to prepare for a very early start next day, because it would be my first open-water crossing, a very different (and potentially much more dangerous) enterprise than hugging the coastline.

Alex promised to be there at four o'clock next morning to help me carry the kayak back to the sea, and so he was. And to my surprise he was not the only one to see me off. One would think that this early in the day little Malagasy children would still be comfortably curled up in their beds, but all it took was a few whistles and screeches at the correct tone to have the kids start trickling out from the sprawl of old houses and tin shacks, puffy-eyed with sleep but enthusiastic.

Sainte-Marie was not visible yet as I set off, but the sharply pointed peninsula to my left acted as my reference for direction. The sea was bumpy already and I wondered how bad it would become later. I hoped that my guesstimates of the current's direction and strength were correct: I had noticed that the ferry headed south initially and later, according to the flow of the current, set a more specific course. I planned to do the same, although I had a contingency plan. If the current was too strong, I'd go northwards with it and land on the opposite end of the needle-shaped pirate island.

CHAPTER 9

PIRATE ISLAND ADVENTURES ON SAINTE-MARIE

Variables were out of my control, but on the other hand my attitude and preparation were totally in hand: a 'balanced level of danger', I told myself, quite convincingly.

Athletes who train by way of a day-in-day-out exercise programme will know exactly what I mean when I say I felt good at the start of this paddle to Sainte-Marie (Nosy Boraha) – something you *definitely* don't always feel at such a time. I knew it was going to be a hard, difficult slog, but I also knew I was ready for it. The sea conditions weren't ideal and the elements promised to be moody at best, but I just knew it was going to be a good day.

Seamus was communicating with me via SMS and wanted hourly GPS updates to track my progress. Halfway across, 19 km into the day's paddle, I was nearly two hours ahead of schedule. Seamus was surprised, but not as much as I was; that by 8.00 am I had averaged more than 10 km an hour, and this with an overloaded kayak that, I noticed, was starting to take on water again.

After 20 km I was into the open sea area, where the tide,

prevailing current, swell and wind chop met in an uncomfortable mix of powerful forces, and I was getting slapped around (I was also unhappily pondering a bit of local history that Alex had seen fit to pass on to me just before I left, namely that in this very area a ferry carrying goods and people had sunk a couple of months before, leading to hundreds drowning). But it didn't slow me down. My energy and attitude were perfect for this paddle.

And then, without any kind of warning, the sea to my right suddenly parted to reveal two bus-sized adult whales, only about 30 metres away and heading directly for me at immense speed. My heart seemed to stop at this unpleasant surprise, and in what I can best describe as a state of controlled panic I swung my feet out of my kayak and let them hang on either side for balance, then started to paddle backwards. It didn't help – the whales were still on track to plough into me. What now?

In the split-second I had left, I accepted two things: firstly, the whales were going to plough into me; secondly, the best thing to do now would be to stay balanced, and above all, to stay attached to the kayak. In the meantime I kept on reverse-paddling, and I can just imagine the anguish that must have been written all over my face as I churned the water into froth on either side with such desperate energy that several times I lost control of the awkward movement and whacked the side of the kayak.

Then, as if they were doing a synchronised swimming act, both whales ducked their massive heads down when they were only about five metres away and, still at top speed, dived under the kayak, probably only three metres or so beneath me. Most likely this was because of the unfamiliar noise made by the paddle as it hit the side of the kayak. But at that moment I didn't really care. 'Next time, just tell me so that I can announce myself in your presence,' I found myself saying ... not that they were listening, of course. But it was that sort of moment.

But I had learnt another lesson about small-boat seafaring: if you are about to be steam-rollered by speeding 40-ton whales, rap the side of your kayak with your paddle. Sounds simple, doesn't it? But there are easier ways of picking up ocean lore. My heart was beating so fast that I was dizzy – and there was a good deal of fear mixed into the adrenalin rush.

By now the entire length of the island had presented itself, and although there were no specific features such as harbours or towns visible yet, I could easily make out what seemed to be a communications tower like the one I had seen on the approach to Soanierana-Ivongo.

I made regular checks of my position on the Garmin, trying to decide which direction I should be heading in. This was easy enough, since the current wasn't too strong. I would sit in the kayak and let myself drift, and the Garmin would tell me what speed I was moving at, and where to. The subsequent calculations were almost as basic: I subtracted the speed of the current from the speed at which I was paddling, the result being my true speed. Then I could divide the remaining kilometres by this to get a fairly accurate estimated time of arrival.

Be warned, however, that this sort of calculation only works if you're paddling directly into a current. If you are at 45 degrees to the current you have to start your basic calculation by deducting three-quarters off the current's speed from your paddling speed; and remember that any such calculation only takes known constants into account and not any variables, of which there are many.

Something strange happened to me after the brush with the whales. Although my target – the little town of Ambodifotatra – was now coming into clearer view I didn't experience the boost I would have expected to get from the knowledge that my destination was close. Instead I found myself being overcome by a lame, drowsy feeling, as if much of my energy had drained away. I expect it was because my blood-sugar level had dropped too low after the hefty spurt of adrenalin that had gone through my veins – the same sort of thing that can make soldiers fall asleep in the middle of a battle.

Since I was so far ahead of schedule and still feeling reasonably strong in spite of my sudden lassitude, I slowed down slightly as I approached the harbour. But then I nearly got caught off-guard by the effect of the tide and coastal current as I chose my final angle to approach the harbour entrance. The nearer I got to land, the more I found myself being pushed northwards at a speed I couldn't match, especially since I was not as energetic as I should have been.

I adjusted my angle of approach, which was perpendicular to both the current and the land at this stage, to one that was 45 degrees further south. This worked out perfectly, and I managed to come out just a few hundred metres from where I had hoped to. Mike and local legend Ockie Snyman, about whom I had heard so much, were due to meet me at the harbour at 12.30 pm, but seeing that I was about half an hour early, I decided to reconnoitre the reef that lay just north of the harbour entrance.

What I found was shocking, to say the least – that is if, like me, you imagine Madagascar as being untouched by the ravages of the modern world. The kilometres-long reef was dead, sparse, bleached and jagged, which certainly didn't fit in with my admittedly blinkered view of Madagascar.

Awful though it was, the reef I paddled over protected pretty little beaches, with here and there a house, sometimes modern and sometimes not, nestled comfortably in the thick forest. The view made up for the shock of the dead reef, and I could understand now why Sainte-Marie had once been the home of Madagascar's pirate community. Rogues though they were, they had obviously known a beautiful place when they saw it.

When I landed at our agreed-on meeting place I discovered that Ockie and Mike's flight had been delayed and would only come in around 2.00 pm. I didn't mind too much, though, because it gave me time to experience the place as I normally do on my journeys –

alone and without benefit of a guide ... although dragging my kayak through the filthy mud of the small-craft landing site all by myself was not fun. Doing everything on your own was all very well, I reflected, but not when it meant going from feeling fresh and clean to resembling something like a human pipe-cleaner for a sewage truck.

The touts on shore knew better, of course, than to wander into the filth and lay in wait on the jetties in their crisp white cotton shirts and shiny leather sandals till I arrived on solid ground. Then a discordant chorus of 'taxi taxi taxi taxi taxi taxi taxi!' rose to the heavens, while others pushed forward to offer me a variety of souvenirs such as carved boats, umbrellas and T-shirts. The fact that I was obviously exhausted, filthy and very unsociable just then made no difference to these eager merchants. Amazing!

Across a patch of grass alongside the concrete jetty I found a coffee shop whose owners, a French couple, allowed me to lay the kayak down inside their shop – something which, in my experience, normally would not happen in a French coffee shop. I explained I was on my way north to Ockie's hotel, La Petite Traversée, and that I expected him within the hour. It was a strange name for a hotel – it means 'the small crossing' – but there was a good reason for it, as I soon discovered.

All the male half of the couple could do after hearing about Ockie was to say '*grand, grand, grand,*' while mimicking the walk and stance of a body builder. *Wow!* I thought, *what the hell type of man is this Ockie?* I had heard so many stories about him and how well he was known in the area that my original mental image of him was becoming a blur. Was he really a large bodybuilder type? *I hope he likes me,* I thought.

I spent most of the hour I had to wait evaluating my first seacrossing. There were others ahead, I knew, bigger and more dangerous ones that would make this one insignificant in hindsight. All the same, I had learnt a few things. Variables were out of my control, but on the other hand my attitude and preparation were totally in hand: a 'balanced level of danger', I told myself, quite convincingly.

In due course Mike and Ockie arrived in a rented panel van, both smirking from ear to ear as if (a) they had been naughty and (b) knew something I didn't. I wasn't worried, just relieved to find that Ockie was a normal South African guy, burly, friendly and welcoming. But he was also not like any other South African guy I'd ever met.

Sometimes you meet people who can aptly be described as 'characters', and Ockie was definitely one of them. By appearance he would have fitted neatly into the best pirate story you could imagine. A big, bushy beard hung down a hand's length under his chin, while his hair was island-style, bushy, sun-bleached and all over the place. All in all, he looked like a sort of cross between Moses and Chuck Norris. Now I knew why everyone I had chatted to so far either loved him or quite clearly feared him!

We headed south in the panel van, with the kayak firmly strapped to the roof, along the narrow but well-kept road that channelled traffic back and forth between the tiny harbour and the airport. A large hotel was being built along the beach, and I recognised another, consisting of chalets on stilts that crept out to sea nearby, that I was sure I had seen in some international travel magazine or other

It was good to see Mike, and it almost had me feeling that my journey was yet to begin (which was nearly true). I had seen the tip of this iceberg, and Mike was here to get my feelings on it thus far. It was also good to be able to repay him for his belief in and support of me in a small way by showing him that I had easily knocked off 10 per cent of the distance already and was in the right shape to conquer the final 90 per cent.

En route we passed the Sainte-Marie airport, the most unique one I'd ever come across. The amazement I had felt at seeing the Khartoum airport in Sudan – smack bang in the middle of a city – didn't come near to matching the surprise evoked by Sainte-

Marie's. This one had sea at the end of each runway. When the planes turned around to taxi into position for take-off their wings swung over the heads of herd-boys and their cattle, while cars on the road had to be careful to pick the right moment to drive past between blasts from the aircraft's propellers.

It was priceless watching the pale faces of the passengers peering through the windows, blinking in amazement as they said hello or goodbye to Sainte-Marie. The herd-boys, of course, didn't bat an eyelid because they had seen it all before, and concentrated on keeping their goats and cattle away from the shining arcs of the propellers.

When we came to the end of the road I understood why Ockie's hotel was called 'the small crossing'. Beyond the road's end was a channel about 80 metres wide that separated Sainte-Marie from a small island – a little smaller than Robben Island back at Cape Town, I estimated – on which stood the hotel. Some large dugouts were waiting for us, which I was told were the standard means of getting to the island.

Ockie and Mike crossed in the dugouts while I took the kayak, getting a bit of a wobbly ride and an occasional splash here and there, because the sea had now turned very choppy. As I paddled I could clearly see sea urchins below me and fish swimming between the rocks, a refreshing relief from the dead reef I had scouted earlier. The word 'paradise' was on the tip of my tongue, but I decided to reserve judgement, considering what might lie ahead.

Ockie's friendly staff served us our welcome drinks, after which the three of us got right down to business with a meeting out on his immaculate self-built deck reaching out over the water (as I found out from Ockie later on, most things in Madagascar have to be made by whoever wants them). It was a stunning setting: here we were, preparing our shooting schedule, which included searching for marvellous scenery, and there it was, literally on our doorstep!

Ockie had one major excursion planned for us, a visit to what he called the 'real deal' pirates' graveyard, which lay on the bank of an equally 'real deal' pirate cove. I was excited and couldn't wait to speak to the camera – I always believe that I have something more or less prepared in my head before a shoot, but when the camera starts rolling I go numb and I blurt out what my brain and my heart want to say.

It was agreed that we were going to use the first night to get to know each other, have some of Ockie's home-made Tom White Rum and, so we hoped, still end up with enough time and stability to take a walk to the other side of the island before bed-time.

It turned out that Ockie didn't just look like a pirate, he was also one in spirit who yearned for the dangers of the buccaneering life and cherished the tales of adventure that had been passed down through the centuries. One of his stories about how the Madagascar pirates became celebrities in their own right involved one Tom White, after whom he had named the rum we were drinking. Among other things, Tom White staged his own death so that he could secretly come back and marry the queen of Madagascar; their descendants, Ockie added, were still proud inhabitants of Sainte-Marie. Blackbeard? Forget about him!

It turned out that Oliver, the Frenchman who had approached me at the Bateau Ivre in Tamatave – and who, coincidentally, I had seen on the fishing DVD – had a small lodge on the west coast of the island, the opposite end to where we were now. I discovered that there was considerable (albeit friendly) rivalry between people of the two coasts, the modern version of an English–French feud that had been going on for centuries.

It was amazing to see how the French westerners still regarded Ockie (and probably me as well!) as a sort of latest generation of the crowd they historically detested most, the Englishmen who had invaded them all those years ago! Inevitably a discussion arose about which side of the island was the better one as we sat in Oliver's restaurant.

Oliver believed the west side to be better because it was sheltered from the winds and the rough seas, whereas Ockie saw the wind as a bonus to keep his clients cool while lying out on deck and – even more importantly during the summer – to blow the mozzies away. Ockie also liked the fact that because his hotel lay on the shore of a semi-lagoon his waters had a bit more 'personality' than a dam, as he put it.

We had only three days to film, and one of those would be taken up out on the deeper seas, where we hoped to get shots of me near the migrating whales. According to Ockie, the whales only left on the morning of 15 September, so we had a few days to spare. Perfect indeed (or so I thought till the time came when we actually had to do it).

The plan was for the boat crew, consisting of Mike and Ockie, to spot the whales and then for me to head off after them. Mike and Ockie would follow me, the aim being to get the 'money shot', namely the whales and myself in the same frame.

Next morning I was enthusiastic and determined, although slightly rum-tender to the point of sea-sickness! But on the first sighting of a mother and her breaching calf I got a grip on my rebellious intestines and put all I had into tailing these two monsters. It took some doing. The sea was extremely choppy, and it was very difficult to control (or even remain on) my unloaded kayak. The swell was big, too, with a strong wind-chop throwing me to left and right.

Slowly I caught up to them, however, and at one stage was only about 50 metres behind the calf as it breached. I looked back and saw that the boat was perfectly positioned to get clear shots of the whales jumping in front of my bow, and I knew that when the footage was screened on television they would look a lot closer to me than they really were. All the same, it was frightening, not to say downright awe-inspiring, to see this giant creature so close up as it leapt out of the stormy waters, completely oblivious to my presence.

We followed them for about 30 minutes, after which I was so exhausted that I had to give up the chase, and the whales gradually widened the gap between us till they were gone. But they had played their part, and now I wanted only to get into the boat and see the footage. I knew it would be brilliant.

Well, it would have been. When I got to the boat I discovered that Mike had not captured even one frame because his camera had broken down. The humidity had got to it, a common problem when one travels to tropical regions with a digital camera, and it would not switch on or do anything except flash a 'humidity' warning. Mike's only option had been to use my small Handycam, which was very efficient but just didn't have all the settings that enhanced the Professional Broadcast Sony camera with which he had shot the 'Survivor' series.

A few hours later, though, we managed to get some incredible pictures, including one of me right alongside a mother and her calf. I was able to film myself simultaneously on this occasion as well. A pod of energetic youngsters, probably males, wrestled around and beneath me for minutes on end while I just drifted around like a cork, completely at their mercy.

Fortunately it was all very playful, because sometimes this sort of jostling can become quite dangerous if the whales are pushing for places in the group hierarchy, or to get to the front of the queue to mate with a sexually ready cow. But this time the whales didn't have sex or politics on their mind, and we returned for lunch, followed by another session at sea in the afternoon.

By that time the sea had calmed down, so that the afternoon session was like an advertisement in a travel agent's brochure. It was a privilege to be out on the water then and to see and experience what I did that day, not to mention the fact that my nerve-pinched lower back could enjoy a much-needed reprieve. Then came the return to my log cabin for a hot shower (the only hot water on the island at this time) and a slow migration to the dining area for fresh fish, salads and blasts of recordings of the hard-core rock band AC/DC.

What a day!

Ockie was amazed by how small my kayak was. When he had originally heard of me he had believed that I would be in one of those huge rowing-boats that people pull across the Atlantic in, complete with toilet, shower, DSTV and on-board entertainment system. His amazement set me thinking again as well. Maybe I should have gone bigger? Well, it was too late now.

One thing which people only find out about Ockie when they stay over in his hotel is his passion for music – especially AC/DC's. AC/DC, I discovered, was usually unleashed while guests drank their freshly brewed coffee after dessert – just in time to divert your thoughts away from your soft and inviting bed. Ockie liked to share his favourite DVD, of a live AC/DC concert somewhere in Europe, and pass on numerous facts about Angus, the band's guitarist, with his famous school uniform, and the other band members. I have to admit that these post-dinner education sessions turned me into a huge AC/DC fan as well.

I certainly badly needed the four days here after my ordeal at the hands of the police in Soanierana-Ivongo. I had communicated with home via the cameras and the radio interviews, and I had seen the faith people had in me, just as I had found during the Africa trip. I was well aware I had only done about 10 per cent of the 5 000-odd kilometres so far, and I could imagine the journey starting from scratch – in theory, of course – but this time with some invaluable experience and an idea of what to expect.

The most memorable land moment I had with Mike was when we went to the pirates' cemetery under the guidance of one of Ockie's staff and walked around, inspecting the centuries-old graves and squeezing in a few more interviews. This was not as easy as it sounds, however. A cemetery with its tranquil atmosphere might sound like a good venue for this sort of thing, but thanks to the local tour guides it was anything but.

The guides were fed up because we hadn't hired them, and so

they avenged the perceived snub by harassing us. They yelled at us while we were trying to do the interviews, threatened to report us if we walked in certain areas which, they claimed, were out of bounds by regulation, and generally made deliberate nuisances of themselves. Perhaps, I thought, it was because most of them were genuine pirate descendants and were just following their ancestors' lawless example.

As a result of all these bad vibes I had a nervous moment when Mike decided to use one of the gravestones as a seat while he changed a lens on his camera. 'Ai, Mike,' I ventured hesitantly, not wishing to cast doubt on his judgement, 'do you think it's a good idea to be sitting on that grave?'

'Huh?' he frowned, a bit confused about what I was getting at. Then the penny dropped and he swivelled his upper body around so that he was now facing the vertical part of the headstone itself. 'Please, man, if ...' he paused, trying to read the pirate's name, mumbled something and then carried on '... if *he* wanted to sit on *my* grave, I really would have no objection. And anyway, these guys don't deserve respect, they were all thieves, murderers and rapists. The least of all his (indicating the pirate's headstone) worries now should be whether I sit on his grave or not.'

That eloquent statement pretty well summed up the situation, and immediately I felt more confident, because I knew that I was in the company of a man who had no difficulty in separating the (good) sheep from the (bad) goats. Case opened, case closed.

Work on the interview schedule Seamus had given us went so smoothly that we even had some spare time to put the Sony underwater camera housing through a real test. The camera housing worked well, except that no one, not even Mike, could solve the problem of the lens area misting up. Mike speculated that Sony might have targeted it for a kinder family environment rather than the over-heating and abuse it was taking at my hands. They were certainly getting their gear tested big time!

Then our time was up, and I had to leave for Antananarivo to fulfil my promise to the Malagasy police and immigration. I went to book a seat on the same plane on which Mike was leaving, and by a small miracle snagged the last available space. I felt positive again as we took off.

CHAPTER 10

A NEW VISA –
AND A LONG, LONG HAUL

*I made a bargain with myself and conjured up a tempting
offer to make it worthwhile: if I could make it around that
southerly point of the bay before the entire sun ducked behind
the horizon, I would eat as much spaghetti bolognaise as my
body could take when I got there.*

At Antananarivo Mike climbed on to a direct flight to Johannesburg, while I headed for the Country View Guest House in the suburb of Ambohidratrimo, Ockie's local branch. It was only a few kilometres from where I had stayed originally in Antananarivo, so I felt very much at home.

What made it even better for a rugby addict like myself was that I arrived at the guest house on a Saturday afternoon, just in time for Round 13 of our domestic trophy, the Currie Cup – the oldest trophy competition in world rugby, incidentally.

The cherry on top was that the team from my native province, the Natal Sharks, were playing the Golden Lions from Johannesburg. The Joburg boys might have represented South Africa's economic powerhouse, but the Sharks were not overawed and continued to display the exceptional form of their earlier games.

That gave me another little personal goal to work into my itinerary, as I had managed to do during the Africa trip, which was to make sure that in two weeks' time I would have accomplished the near-impossible and be somewhere with a TV set so that I could park myself in comfort and watch the Currie Cup final. I had managed this in the deepest and darkest parts of Angola, so could it be any more difficult in Madagascar?

Naturally I could only begin updating my visa on the Monday, which meant that with the rugby out of the way I had Sunday at my disposal. And what a special day it turned out to be, deeply personal, rejuvenating and moving. I had a late breakfast, played a few rounds of *boules* with the guest house's driver's son, Deon (*boules* is that game you see in the French movies which is very similar to 'old men's marbles', as juvenile wits like to call lawn bowls till they actually try to play it).

Afterwards I went back indoors, and while surfing the channels of the South African DSTV satellite service I came across a movie I had heard about, called 'Faith Like Potatoes', which had a somewhat unusual subject but ended up giving me a much-needed new injection of inspiration.

For those who don't know about it, 'Faith Like Potatoes' is a true story which recounts the leap of faith taken by a farmer, Angus Buchan, who relocates his family from Zambia to the KwaZulu-Natal midlands and decides to do the impossible: raise a crop of potatoes right in the middle of the worst drought in living memory.

A strange subject for an expatriate kayaker marooned in Madagascar, perhaps, but what happened was that I found myself engrossed in this extraordinary film, derived from Angus Buchan's real-life experiences, which were first published in book form. Essentially it is a story of faith in God and a spiritual renewal that took Angus from being a borderline alcoholic to a builder of rock-solid relationships with those around him in spite of – or, more accurately, because of – the trials and tribulations through which he journeyed.

And it is an epochal journey before he sees any results from his venture into the unknown. He suffers so much that he nearly loses faith in his faith. He goes through excruciating heartache and at the same time hacks his way through relationship complications with both his wife and his black labour force. But he is determined to go on, to hold on to all he finally has left; his faith.

Some of the scenes in the movie really worked magic in my spirit. One was where Angus, motivated mainly by the drought, racial tensions in the local agriculture industry and the appalling murders perpetrated on farmers, decides to get all the farmers and all the labourers together in one venue to pray.

Not in a church hall, mind you, or even a conference centre; Angus's vision is of filling an entire rugby stadium. And he does it, so that you see him in front of the grandstand of a monster stadium with thousands and thousands of people of all races waiting for him to speak.

Angus begins to pray; not the usual evangelical rant but a very everyday way of speaking, as if he were alone with God. He prays for strength and guidance and continued energy. He condemns the unseasonable weather caused by El Niño to hell (this sounds very revivalish, but it wasn't), along with other similar challenges, and ends with sincere thanks for the blessings he and his fellows have received thus far.

Hmm, I thought. *Power, passion and commitment to see something through, no matter what. Ay, I want some of that.*

The end of the movie literally had me in tears as I sat all alone in the empty lounge of the guest house. Angus is under the impression that people in his village, especially the white folk, still believe him to be naive and a bit crazy. He has no hope of assistance additional to his current and meagre work-force.

One morning he and his right-hand man, Simeon Bhengu, walk together out on to the farm's vast fields, great expanses of what looks like dry and barren wasteland. Underneath lay ... well, they didn't know. Potatoes grow about 30 cm underground, and the farmer doesn't know what sort of crop he has till he harvests it.

Angus and Simeon are beyond anxious, but also eager to see what lies below their feet. Angus kneels down with Simeon at his side, pauses to look him in the eye and says with great emotion: 'Simeon, no matter what comes out of this soil today, I want to thank you, thank you for being a brother to me and member of our family. I love you and my family loves you ... Let's pray.'

They pray, and Angus thanks God and asks Him to bless the crop, however it turns out. Angus then parts the soil, breaking open the dry dirt to reveal ... monster potatoes of a size he has never before seen in his life. Angus and Simeon laugh and roll around in the dirt like schoolboys, so overjoyed that at first they do not even notice the entire village population winding down the valley with shovels and wheelbarrows; they have come to harvest both his potatoes and his faith, which had kept theirs alive.

At first I wasn't exactly sure why I cried, although I knew I was an emotional guy and that my emotions were what made me strong and determined. But of course it was because my emotional commitment to what I was doing was being recharged. Without faith and a vision there is no life in your actions. They are hollow and very short-lived, and Angus's story had reminded me of that.

Come Monday, I went to the visa application offices prepared for wading through a very complicated process, which it would have been but for the help I received from Christiaan Fayd'Herbe and the special effort put in by Ambassador Monaisa and his staff at the embassy to fire up what the Madagascar Tourism Office believed to be a lost cause.

The result of all this effort was that just three days later I had a

60-day extension on my visa as well as paperwork in the pipeline for an 18-month one.

I took all the tension calmly, believe it or not. Was I negative or burdened by these challenges? Not an iota! Surprising, considering what I had endured to date! I was just concerned that my embassy and the Malagasy Tourism Association would not have the same staying power.

The next day I was on a direct flight back to Sainte-Marie, where I was duly reunited with the Pirate of La Petite Traversée and got ready to go. My kayak was in good shape, except for its persistent leak, I was well fed and, above all, I was now as legal as it was possible to be. All I needed was to find and fix that damned elusive leak.

I spent one more day with Ockie, packing and repacking my gear and looking for the leak. I was frankly baffled. I had plugged, sealed, replugged and resealed every possible place where water could get in that Johan the kayak-builder had suggested, and then some. But the kayak was still taking on litres of water every time I put it in the water, and it was freaking me out.

How was it possible to seal everything so thoroughly and then still find the water seeping in? It was literally a matter of life and death. If the kayak took on enough water it would sink if I encountered rough seas, and I would drown. End of story. So I simply had to have an answer. But I wasn't getting one.

In any case, there I was in front of the kayak, kneeling like an old-time supplicant at a shrine, except that I wasn't praying but running the design's finer details through my mind, to the point where I was beginning to imagine leaks where there weren't any. Ockie stood by in a supervisory role, offering moral support as required.

Then – the great revelation! It came as I was inspecting the custom rear hatch for about the tenth time. Johan's factory had fitted a larger-than-normal one for me with a neoprene cover wrapped over a circular lip. Something made me give the hatch a closer look, and suddenly I could see and feel that the lip wasn't smoothly joined to the kayak's deck, so that there were a couple of gaps. I did a simple little test, involving splashing some water over the kayak. I was right! I could see the water pouring in through the gaps.

I was flabbergasted when I realised what I had got away with, and how fortunate I had been to survive through all the rough seas I had encountered so far. I knew that any experienced kayaker would not have believed it possible that my kayak and I could have made that 40 km crossing from the mainland to Sainte-Marie with a leak like that.

I also remembered now that back in Cape Town Johan had explained to me that because of the pressure in getting the kayak to Madagascar on time he had not had time to test it himself. With his experience he would have spotted this easy-to-repair flaw in a heartbeat, and repaired it just as quickly. I had promised him that I would make checking the hatch an early priority, and I had forgotten. I felt bad about that, but all the same I was over the moon at finding the fault before it killed me, and felt even more confident than before.

Ockie took my kayak and myself back to the spot in the harbour where he and Mike had originally fetched me. There he reminded me of a honeymoon offer he had placed on the table days before (sorry, this is a little private joke between us), then said goodbye. The kayak kissed the water and I was off at last.

My plan for getting back to the mainland was to head up Sainte-Marie's west coast and overnight at a place called Lokintsy, which lay almost exactly at the island's half-way mark. From there I would paddle north-west across the channel between Sainte-Marie and the mainland to a place called Manompana, which all the locals agreed would be the best day-destination. Then I would continue up the coast to Antanambe, considered one of Madagascar's most beautiful bays.

From a little higher up the coast I would lay a course slightly east of north which would take me across the mouth of the Bay of Antongil, after which I would continue up the east coast. That would be a tough leg, I knew. It is Madagascar's largest bay and bites far into the coast, with a sizeable town called Maroantsetra at the deepest point of its inner coastline. By cutting straight across its mouth rather than following its coastline I would be doing only a third of the distance. But it was a tough third, something like 40 km of open sea.

I had a very good reason for doing this the hard way. Vasti was due to fly out and meet me at the northern tip of Madagascar before too long and there was no way I was going to miss out on that. But she had a fairly inflexible work schedule that did not allow for vague arrangements, and so I wanted to 'save up' on travelling time in case of unscheduled delays. All I hoped was that the weather would be good when I headed into the open sea.

In any case, having said goodbye to Ockie I wasted no time following the rocky coastline, and I managed to reach Lokintsy in very good time. I was now outside 'British' territory, so I had not yet received any form of hospitality from the French expats, but rather to my surprise one of them, named Rian, welcomed me into his home for the night. Among other things this involved eating his cheese. I thought it was quite appropriate: here was Riaan eating Rian's cheese! It could only be a good omen for the day ahead.

It was here that I noticed for the first time something I was to see over and over in Madagascar – the number of expatriate Frenchmen, mostly deep into their retirement years, who were married to or living with young local women. I couldn't help wondering about this phenomenon. Some seemed to be genuine love matches, but I couldn't help feeling that many of the others appeared to be unions of the sugar-daddy type.

I recalled that one of my friends in Tamatave had told me that every expat he had met who claimed to have fallen in love with a Malagasy woman also claimed that his relationship was 'different'.

Well, my friend commented, such a relationship might be 'different', but they seldom lasted, because quite often he would hear this assertion and then a month later see the same girl at his restaurant, still in a relationship ... but with another partner! Perhaps I'm wrong about this because it is admittedly a strictly subjective observation about the nature of these relationships, but there you are.

Next morning I was glad to find that the sea was fairly calm as I set off into the most stunning island sunrise I had seen in Madagascar. Gold seemed to be splashed on to everything the sun came in contact with. Magical! But I couldn't spend too much time admiring it. I planned to hit things hard for the first few hours and then, if required, take stock of my progress and crawl the rest of the way to my destination.

That was how it worked out. The morning went better than well, and by midday I was within comfortable reach of the mainland. My energy level was still high, though, and I reckoned it would be a terrible waste if I simply paddled over to the nearest bit of land. So I studied my map and made a brave call (or a foolhardy one, given my near-zero amount of experience).

I would get to Manompana in less than two hours at my present progress, but if I stopped off there I would have to double back a considerable way eastwards before getting to the open sea for the big crossing. What if I simply kept slogging on past Manompana till I reached Antanambe around sunset? It sounded good, except that it would mean I would have to cover nearly 60 km in one day.

Could I do that? What if the sea turned nasty? Where would I be able to land in an emergency? The coast showed no good spots for bailing out. It sounded a little dodgy. But I decided to risk it anyway (after all, I'm a self-proclaimed adventurer), so I turned sharp right and headed for Antanambe.

After about 40 km I began to get a very uneasy feeling that I had made the wrong decision. My lower back was in spasm and my right wrist throbbing with pain. *Ooh la la!* Big mistake, yes? I was still going well, but I could feel my body threatening to pack in. I needed smaller goals if I wanted to clear this huge hurdle, so I decided to do 15-minute slogs at a time, and only assess the distance covered every 60 minutes. This way I would get sufficient rest breaks as well as the least amount of disappointment if I had not covered as much distance as I had expected.

So that's what I did, and every half-hour I would also jump out of the kayak to stretch my back and, most importantly, cool down – the temperature was in the high thirties, so that I was dehydrated and tired even before 3.00 pm ... and a first for me on these regular cooling-down dips was answering nature's call without too much fear.

I recalled that a famous Australian adventure paddler, Andrew McAuley, had died while trying to do a solo crossing on his kayak from Tasmania to New Zealand. Rescuers found his kayak with all his gear still on board, but McAuley himself was never seen again. The theories that were floated afterwards suggest that he could have been out of his boat when something happened – a shark attack, perhaps or something that led to him drowning ... or, perhaps, doing the one thing that's impossible to ignore? The truest saying in the world is that when you gotta go, you gotta go.

That didn't give me much comfort, though. Each time I got that irresistible urge I would spend a few minutes peering down at the seemingly bottomless waters below me before I went. But the stress didn't go away altogether, and I found my body still involuntarily cramping up whenever I heard the clarion call.

The sun was going down now, and I just could not convince myself that I was moving fast enough to get into Antanambe Bay by sunset. So I made a bargain with myself and conjured up a tempting offer to make it worthwhile: if I could make it around that southerly point of the bay before the entire sun ducked behind the horizon, I would eat as much spaghetti bolognaise as my body could take when I got there.

I presented this offer to myself, decided it was one I couldn't refuse and formally accepted it. Then I bit back any whimpers and settled into a machine-like paddling rhythm (except that this particular human machine's chassis started to hurt), and eventually I was only a kilometre or two from the southerly point of Antanambe Bay.

It was beautiful, all right, but not too welcoming at first glance, with surf about six feet high rearing up and crashing over the reef. I was in no condition to quibble, however – I was so far gone that it was the surf or nothing. It was true that I hadn't negotiated too many reefs like this one to date, but I had seen fishermen on their dugouts on the other side of the foam and believed there had to be a safe passage somewhere between these crashing waves. And in any case I was fresh out of options.

I headed cautiously but fairly confidently into the danger zone, relying as much on gut feel as anything else. On impulse I headed for a spot that I felt was deeper and safer, with the big waves breaking on either side of me. It turned to be just that, and I could literally thread my way between the never-ending breakers into what I found to be a narrow, shallow lagoon which reached all the way into the bay mouth and made the final kilometre a rather comfortable warm-down.

When you are as exhausted and lame as I was then you always hope that everything will be just right when you come to your destination, and what I wanted right then was cheap accommodation just inside the bay. But that didn't happen. I still had to paddle some way into the southern part of the bay to find a cluster of A-frame bungalows.

As I finally neared the shore I noticed a man swimming about 50 metres out and surprised myself at the direction in which my conversation with him went. Having greeted him in French and asked how he was, I found myself going on to an incongruous topic that somehow seemed very important all of a sudden: 'Does this place with the bungalows serve spaghetti bolognaise?'

He took this unexpected question with equanimity, considered it while he paddled lazily around and replied that he didn't know the menu too well, but would ask on my behalf. We went ashore together, and while I prepared to carry my kayak up the beach he went ahead to (so I presume) warn the hotel's proprietors that they were about to meet up with a spaghetti-mad kayaker who had just paddled in from nowhere.

Apparently he did and they believed him, because an elderly lady with plaited hair came out to meet me. 'Hello, you are Italian, *si, si*?' she greeted me.

'No,' I replied, 'I'm from South Africa, and I would like a place to stay.'

'Ok, room is 20 000. No problem,' she smiled.

Now for the big one: 'Do you have spaghetti bolognaise?'

'Yes,' she answered, laughing loudly. 'You *are* the Italian madman on the kayak. My customer tell me about you come here! You are welcome.'

Now, 20 000 ariary was the equivalent of 13 US dollars, which was way above what I had had in mind. But right now I could not care less. I would have a bed and lashings of spaghetti bolognaise. Hell, what more could I ask for?

Chez Grondin, as the hotel was called, was exactly the resting-place I needed. Besides all the spaghetti I could eat I could relax properly in complete privacy, while the owners' daughter, Eve, spoke good English and not only charged up most of my electronics while the generator was on but also gave me good advice on what I could expect further up the coast. Among other things she told me that just north of Antanambe was a beautiful little island just 520 hectares in size that was a unique nature reserve, the sole home of a type of fruit bat called the Madagascar flying fox. However, it appeared to be in danger of being ruined by tourism developers.

There were some other tourists staying at the hotel, including a philosophical middle-aged German bicyclist called Rudolph who planned to cycle around as much of Madagascar as he could. I didn't tell him that I had already circumnavigated *Africa* on a bicycle, because it really would have brought a serious damper to our conversation. I must add, though, that I genuinely love hearing people's stories, although it's not humanly possible to maintain the same enthusiasm after you hear the twenty-fifth one on the trot. But I gave him my website address and said to him he could follow my travels there.

A lovely – and valuable – bit of travel experience and advice Rudolph shared with me was to call to children in their mother tongue when arriving in some remote village or other. As I discovered, this was a classic bit of advice. It breaks any tension and gets the kids laughing, and – most importantly – trusting you, which in turn gets the grumpy adults on board. *Zaza kely* was the magic phrase Rudolph taught me, which means 'small Malagasy' or 'children', and it definitely works when you are surrounded by what feels like hundreds of them.

It was a pleasant first-time experience to sit there and listen to the other people's adventure stories, but I swear I could feel my backside swaying from side to side, a most odd sensation. When I mentioned it, one of the other tourists laughed and said it was a common one for kayakers which was generally referred to as 'sea bum', and was the small-boat equivalent of sea legs. I had to lie down to have the world beneath me stop swaying.

Apart from ordinary fatigue, the very long paddle had left me dehydrated, and I spent most of the day after my arrival trying to sleep off a persistent headache. A strong northerly wind delayed my departure on the next leg, so I took advantage of it to have a rest. I could afford a day off – I was in credit as far as distance covered was concerned, and it was only 26 km to my next destination, a little village called Seranambe. From there it was about 20 km to

Mananara, which would be my jumping-off point for the journey across the mouth of the Bay of Antongil. So I could laze about in good conscience and, naturally, indulge in my favourite food.

CHAPTER 11

CASH CRUNCH AT SERANAMBE ...
AND A LOVE-NEST AT MANANARA

*My kayak was humming with joy (so it seemed) as we
reached speeds over 20 km/h. For a 70 kg sea kayak this was a
crazy rate of knots, and before I knew it, I had passed
four whales, covered all of 14 km and had Mananara
clearly in sight.*

I hit the water at 6.00 am next day so that I would be able to cover the maximum distance before running into the usual afternoon head-wind. Since Seranambe was only 26 km further along the rocky coastline, I calculated that I would easily be able to cover about 70 per cent of the distance before running into the head-wind, and judging by the map the village was tucked neatly into a sheltered bay.

It was an easy leg, but I felt I needed to give my body a break after my last exertions. That back-breaking lap to Isle Sainte-Marie had been my first real taste of the sort of thing I would have to do from time to time along the endless kilometres that still lay ahead, and now there was the prospect of another long paddle.

The swell was breaking big all along the northerly reef of the little bay when I left next morning. It never ceases to amaze me that the surf can look so small at a distance, but then seems to grow as you get nearer, so that when you eventually find one of those 'small' six-foot crunchers looming overhead you feel like screaming for mercy.

It was the same thing with this launch, but I got smoothly over the reef: I had timed it perfectly and shot over during a lull, and there was just enough water in some places to keep my kayak afloat – 'just enough' meaning less than about 10 cm in some places! But it was a close thing. The kayak would have been smashed if I had been caught by the breakers, and the partly healed cuts in the sole of my left foot from my encounter with the Foule Point reef were there as a reminder of how sharp and dangerous the coral was.

A few kilometres north of Antanambe I spotted the island Eve had told me about. It was stunningly beautiful in its cloak of rock and jungle, wrapped around with huge snow-white billows of foam. I gave it plenty of room as I paddled around the outside of it, partly to keep at a safe distance from the huge swell breaking on its reefs and partly to let me feast my eyes on a good panoramic view of this unique and now possibly imperilled piece of Madagascar, because according to Eve a French cartel had applied to the Madagascan government for a licence to build a hotel on it, complete with ... wait for it ... a helicopter pad!

Deep inside the Bay of Antongil, I knew, there was a much better-known island reserve called Nosy Mangabe, which was just about the last refuge of the strangely named 'aye-aye', a type of lemur that is in danger of extinction because illegal logging and similar activities have nearly wiped out its natural habitat. The aye-aye is so near permanent oblivion that some years ago a few breeding pairs were shipped out to Nosy Mangabe, where they soon settled in.

During my previous travels I had picked up some experience of the sort of maniacal tree-huggers who are opposed in principle to all and any development, but as I cruised past the islands I knew where my sympathies lay in this case. I just couldn't shake off the shocking memory of that long stretch of dead reef at Sainte-Marie.

I knew from my researches that Madagascar needed as many nature reserves as it could get to protect all the unique plants and animals it had that could be found nowhere else on the planet. To the casual eye it might look unspoilt, but it is in great danger from population spread and, more particularly, large-scale illegal logging of the rain forests, which has enriched a select few to the detriment of the common people as well as the country itself.

One international authority has even warned that unless a stop is put to illegal logging Madagascar is going to find itself in the same position as Haiti – one of the very poorest countries in the world – which also destroyed its original wealth of great forests by short-sighted logging. So, although I had no facts or figures to back up my feelings, there was no sympathy in my heart for the would-be hoteliers and their helicopters.

But I didn't have much time to spend on such depressing thoughts. I was in such good form, and the sea was so co-operative, that by 10.30 am I was worming my way through a tight spot over the reefs that protected the bay in which nestled Seranambe. It was a real Robinson Crusoe sort of place, but its appearance turned out to be deceptive – Seranambe might have looked sleepy, but I soon found out that its people were wide awake.

Although I came in quite quietly, without any noise or fuss, the beach was packed with inquisitive villagers, from the pastor to the schoolmaster, within minutes of my setting foot on dry land. Arrogant in my ignorance, I thought that my fame had preced-ed me, but it was not the case. What had pulled them in was that gaudy green-and-yellow kayak of mine, which was just about bright enough to be spotted from space, never mind a small Malagasy beach! I was strictly a secondary attraction.

After touching and pulling at everything they could reach, the lo-

cals offered to help me (for a fee!) to carry the kayak to suitable accommodation, which turned out to be pretty much what one could
expect from a village that, so I discovered, had never even heard of
spaghetti bolognaise: namely, a sagging cane-framed bed inside a
room whose walls consisted of reeds draped with cloth, topped by a
rusted, holey corrugated-iron roof, all for a bargain (I don't think)
5 000 ariary ($25 US) a night. Ouch.

I suppose I could put a positive spin on this less-than-ideal accommodation by saying that the room might have been expensive,
but the company was free. The latter consisted of hordes of children pressed up against one 'wall' of my room, making small holes
between the reeds and drapes to watch me as I lay there, trying to
fall asleep amid their heckling and giggling.

Eventually I gave up trying to sleep and decided to satisfy the
children's curiosity by going public, so to speak, so that they could
all have a good look at me. So I ventured into a section of the village
where women and younger girls were making flour in the old style,
rhythmically crushing corn with the help of heavy, round-headed
poles that they slammed into wooden bowl-shaped vessels.

It was a familiar sight for me. Everywhere in rural Africa you will
find two or three women standing around like this, pounding their
poles into the bowls at their feet with the precision of a Swiss watch.
It looks easier than it is, as I discovered when I talked my way into
a flour-making group and recruited one of the children to film me.

Much as I tried, I just could not stay as focused on the rhythm
of the thing as my fellow pounders. My conclusion was that a two-
pounder group worked better and I might as well retire, but the villagers who had gathered to watch my clumsy efforts would have
none of this – it was far too entertaining to watch. As a result, flour
production hit an all-time low that day.

Eventually I managed to shake off my admirers to take a short
late-afternoon nap, and at dinner that evening I met yet another of
the Malagasy girl/foreigner couples you see everywhere on the is-

land. Many of those I had seen so far had struck me as being sugar-daddy liaisons, but this one looked like the real thing.

The male half of the couple was a charming and highly opinionated German guy named Folker, who was on his way south towards Tamatave in a 4x4 after having spent some time with his young Malagasy wife in their newly acquired home in Maroantsetra, deep inside the Bay of Antongil.

Maroantsetra, incidentally, enjoys the same status among Madagascan tourists as got-to-see places elsewhere in the world like the pyramids in Egypt, the Taj Mahal in India or the cave-city of Petra in Jordan. But Folker's wife had become bored in their piece of paradise and longed for her family and friends back home.

Folker spoke many languages fluently, was extremely intelligent and full of facts on almost every subject, even South African history and politics. The mere fact that he knew considerably more than the canned holier-than-thou CNN and BBC stuff on apartheid that most tourists are so clued up on made him a breath of fresh air.

He had good insight into the minds of me and my fellow Africans, and knew a lot about my country that I was shamefully vague about: things like the relevance of President Paul Kruger and General Jan Smuts to our country's historic Union of 1910, as well as Smuts's involvement in creating the League of Nations, the fore-runner of the United Nations.

Folker even knew all about the long-gone Dutch East India Company, the world's first multi-national corporation, whose decision to set up a 'truck stop' at the Cape of Good Hope in 1652 to service its trading fleets had changed the history of the sub-continent.

Amazing! I had paddled up to a truly forgotten part of the world with no greater immediate ambition than to find a meal and a place to sleep, and by chance met a European who had a lot more knowledge of, and insight into, Southern Africa than a lot of Southern Africans.

As I lay down to sleep that night I mentally girded my loins for the future. Some isolated stretches of paddling lay ahead of me in which I would really be on my own. No more electricity or Coca-Cola or any other of the small comforts of civilisation, just sand, wind and survival at its most basic, right down to the point of having to find my own food. I fell asleep dreaming about the fish I was planning to catch next day.

Things are never as simple as that, though. For one thing, a traveller has to have a little money on him, even when he is heading into places no one has ever heard of, and while I was preparing for my departure next morning I found that the currency I had stashed away was, in fact, non-existent. In a nutshell, I was completely and utterly broke.

Of all the places to be cashless, this was the worst (well, so far – who knew what lay ahead?). Where was I going to get some cash? What if I couldn't catch any fish? Maybe I would visit places where there really were no banks and people didn't use money. Maybe I could barter for my daily bread. Maybe, maybe, maybe ... hope is a fine thing, but sometimes it can get a little thinly stretched.

But all was not lost. According to my map my next destination, Mananara, had an airfield, so surely it would also have a bank or financial outlet of one kind or another where I could lay in some cash. The problem was that I would arrive on a Saturday, which meant that even if it *did* have the necessary I would still have to get through the weekend without so much as a red cent to my name.

It was not a pleasant prospect, but then I decided to put it out of my mind. If I couldn't survive a minor crisis like this, considering what might yet happen to me, then I was in big trouble. Immediately I felt better.

It's truly amazing, the way a small reality check and a touch of self-honesty can turn an insurmountable problem into a molehill. Right! At best I would be able to scrounge my way through the weekend. At worst I'd be sleeping rough and going a trifle hungry for a couple of days. So what? My stomach might growl a bit, but I had water and I had vitamins. Perfect.

Seranambe had even more of a Robinson Crusoe look to it as I sat comfortably on my kayak, 50 metres out into the bay, with 300 or 400 people seeing me off, the mist steaming off the sea and the odd cloud or two hanging on to the jungle cliffs that rose from the sea around me.

Today we know so much about everything around us that sometimes I feel almost like a cheat when I tell people that I do adventure for a living. The old seafarers of five centuries ago who first clawed their way up the eastern coast of Africa had to take a leap into the unknown literally every time they set foot on land. I had Google Earth, accurate maps, a cell phone and GPS, whereas at best they would have had an ornately drawn but fairly useless chart which owed more to the cartographer's imagination than to his actual knowledge.

Admittedly my aids couldn't tell me everything I wanted – for example, they couldn't warn me of the sudden and sometimes quite drastic changes in the winds and currents when I came into a bay from the open sea – but they were certainly a vast improvement on what my predecessors had to rely on in the days when it was quite common for cartographers to fill in empty spaces on their maps with drawings of strange beasts or warnings like *hic draconis* (here be dragons).

And they certainly could not bet on the likelihood of any stopping-place having some sort of inn, no matter how rickety, where they might be able to order a plate of spaghetti bolognaise!

But then I put all such philosophical ramblings out of my mind. I had things to do and places to go, and I was full of energy; it was as if I drew strength from my awe of the beauty of my surroundings. I might have it easier than the hard men of five centuries earlier, but I was still an adventurer, and in spite of all my modern gadgets I would also have to face the perils and hardships of the adventuring game. Mananara, here I come!

In addition to being Madagascar's largest bay, the Bay of Antongil was also a famous calving area for whales, which naturally posed a certain hazard. I didn't expect to encounter many of them, though, because most would have headed for the cooler waters of the Antarctic by now, but I was holding thumbs for some encounters of the non-lethal kind with the stragglers.

I knew that rounding the southern cape to reach Mananara would be difficult. I had been warned that the northerly winds became more common at this time of year, and that the tides over these reefs could drain all your energy as you paddled till your tongue hung out, and still didn't move a metre. At the same time it was easy to make a mistake while navigating around the reef, because the swell would not only keep hitting me from the east or south-east but would also bounce off the inside of the bay and the smaller coves, making the going very wet and bumpy.

The fishermen had not gone out today, and I could see why. It was choppy and unpredictable, and in a dugout the chances of sinking in such conditions were strong. After 7–8 km I had to take a decision.

The absence of the fishermen was a warning flag for me, too, and I had earlier agreed with myself that for safety's sake I would not hesitate to take my cue from the locals. On the other hand, I reasoned, firmly ignoring my compact with myself, it was such a short paddle to Mananara – just 20 km – that turning around after covering less than half the distance would be even more stupid than taking a chance and carrying on. So I paddled on, and not for the first time Dame Fortune favoured the foolhardy.

When I reached the half-way mark the wind was squarely at my back, and so was the swell. Although I didn't get to run (surf, that is) with the swell as a more experienced paddler might have done, I was going nearly double my usual speed all the same! My kayak was humming with joy (so it seemed) as we reached speeds over 20 km/h. For a 70 kg sea kayak this was a crazy rate of knots, and before I knew it, I had passed four whales, covered all of 14 km and had Mananara clearly in sight.

The sea became calmer and calmer the further I turned left around the cape and moved into the bay proper. Mananara had a huge tidal lagoon in front of it, and I could see what looked like a cell-phone tower near which a small airplane that had circled above me earlier now had landed.

I couldn't go wrong, I thought, so I tucked my Garmin away and decided to wing it, heading straight for the comms tower ... a decision I found myself regretting an hour and a half later; I discovered that the approaches were very shallow indeed, so that I ran aground in the middle of my final lap and ended up dragging my kayak landwards. I wanted to know whether I was heading in the wrong direction or not, but my attempt to get some directions turned into a futile and distinctly bizarre exercise.

This involved a woman wearing a scuba mask who was sitting hunched over, ducking her head into the water to look for edible sea life, one breath at a time. Somehow she was unaware of me – strange, since we were the only two people in that part of the bay – and didn't respond to my calls of calls of 'azaha fady' (pardon me), even though I timed them to coincide with her emergence for air. Eventually I shouted at maximum volume, and this finally attracted her attention.

Her reaction was anything but what I expected. She looked around, spotted me to the left and behind her and gaped in horror-struck surprise. Then she began to howl like a terrified child and scrambled away on her knees in the opposite direction to get as far away from me as possible. Clearly this conversation was not going to go anywhere.

Since running through water is a tiring business, her screams soon got softer and her speed slower, and after a while she stopped dead and looked back at me, begging wordlessly – for what? 'Please don't abduct me'? Or perhaps 'please don't eat me'? From the expression on her face it was definitely something like this.

I made myself look as harmless as possible, repeated my *azaha fady* greeting and by means of sign language tried to explain that I was looking for Mananara. It didn't work; she couldn't understand me and clearly had no intention of helping me. Frustrated and disappointed, I gave up my clearly unwelcome attentions and faced the facts: I would just have to keep on dragging and trust to my Garmin to get me to Mananara, which it confirmed was in the direction of the comms tower.

So I struggled on, paddling sometimes and at others dragging my kayak through the very shallow shallows, asking directions when the opportunity presented itself. But I got nowhere fast, and at length I was so tired and desperate that when a guy in a dugout appeared out of the mangroves and offered to show me the 'back way' I took him up on it without a second thought.

We headed up a narrow, winding waterway, with my good Samaritan setting a stiff pace which forced me to paddle quite hard to keep on his tail. It was the first time I had seen any mangroves on my Madagascar journey, so in between all the paddling, chatting and hand-waving I kept my eyes busy trying to take in my new environment.

Like so many other countries I had visited before, Madagascar's reputation had preceded it. I had read over and over that the huge island's mangroves were slowly being destroyed to provide firewood. But first-hand experience and investigation is what gives a person a more balanced view than what can be derived from a reading of *Lonely Planet* or the Bradt travel guide.

The distant doomsayers faded into background noise as I feasted my eyes on my surroundings, particularly the little kingfishers with their rich colours, bright blue or purple four-inch-high balls of energy that flew over the bow of my kayak to attract my attention, then winged off for about 20 metres to sit and wait on a branch. Then they would do it again, and eventually fly straight back to where our paths had first crossed. What this harassment actually was, I reasoned, was a clever tactic to divert attention away from their nests.

In the meantime my guide was still forging ahead. By now we had covered about a kilometre through the mangrove jungle, and my tired muscles forced me to believe him when he said that the village was 'just here'. I didn't argue. If this 'back way' was a short cut, that was OK by me.

Well, it didn't turn out quite the way I had expected. In fact, what happened was positively the last thing in my mind at that particular time and place. We pulled in at a spot on the bank where several other pirogues had been parked, and he waved me nearer. As I started to get off my kayak he gave me a big grin and a request that I understood perfectly, even given our fractured English and French:

'Me want kiss,' he said, to my complete astonishment. 'Kiss, kiss, kiss. Me want kiss.'

Kiss?

I goggled at him. Had I misunderstood him after all? But the answer was 'no'. The devil-may-care paddler of the mangroves had vanished now, I noticed, and he had become quite shy and nervous, but there was no doubt about what he was saying: 'Me want kiss, kiss.'

For heaven's sake! Here I was, half-way out of my kayak and falling around in the mud, and I was being propositioned in the depths of a tangle of mangroves in a place no one had ever heard of (or, in my case, even seen). I felt frustrated beyond belief, but certainly not to the extent of buying directions to the village with a bout of kissing, even if I had had the inclination.

I huffed the universally recognised 'are you crazy?' huff, flopped back into my boat and headed back down the winding way we had followed from the bay. I had been thoroughly misled – there was no sign of life in the vicinity, and the mangrove jungle was so tangled that I doubted if even five men would be able to carry my kayak. I needed to get to the village, but I could get lost without any help from my amorous new acquaintance.

Back in the open, I consulted my Garmin, which told me that to get near the village the 'front way', so to speak, required that I rounded a point west of where I had originally entered the bay. Doggedly I prodded my worn-out self into motion and started dragging my kayak seawards across a now completely deserted bay so that I could get out over the reef and into deeper water and then turn left around the point, a needle-shaped sandbank covered in palm trees. I had wasted three hours on this bay and its mangroves, and now I badly needed to rest.

Fortunately for me this attempt worked. Before long Mananara harbour with its clump of huts came into view, and soon I was dragging my kayak up alongside a number of pirogues and small fishing boats that dotted the stretch of beach in front of the huts. In no time a crowd gathered around me, and within a few minutes three locals and myself were wobbling across the soft sand, the kayak on our shoulders, towards what I was assured was accommodation for a *vazaha* (white man). This was more like it!

The Caucasian-style accommodation turned out to be a cluster of bungalows called the Aye Aye Hotel, after Nosy Mangabe's famously rare and shy lemurs. Awaiting me was the hotel's co-owner, a Frenchwoman named Lisa, whose first words were: 'Aaah, we have been waiting for you, mister kayak man! The South African has arrived. *Bienvenue!*'

Bienvenue indeed. I couldn't have put it better myself.

It turned out that Rudolph, the cyclist I had met at Antanambe, had passed by earlier and warned Lisa of my imminent arrival. I felt very, very welcome in this village, which was different from all the others I had visited so far because Lisa and her husband, unlike most other expatriate inn-keepers, seemed to have become genuine members of the local community, rather than resident outsiders who stood out from the other inhabitants by virtue of their different nationality, skin-colour and economic resources. In a nutshell, they were part and parcel of Mananara.

The Aye Aye Hotel was situated next to my original aiming-point, the airstrip where I had seen the small aircraft land a few hours earlier, and Lisa explained that an Air Madagascar flight came in once a week with much-needed supplies as well as tourists. I was surprised – I honestly did not expect this poor island nation's national airline to service such isolated towns, although I could understand it when I reflected on the remarkable lack of even half-way decent roads. A tourist would never get to see the 'real' Madagascar if it wasn't for the airline's commitment to less profitable destinations.

It was here that I made my first face-to-face acquaintance with Madagascar's famous lemurs – although not in the way I had expected. While we were having tea and scones about half a dozen half-tame lemurs jumped around in the trusses above our heads and poo-bombed us, so that I felt like a World War II ship under attack by dive-bombers. Then, having manured us to their satisfaction, the lemurs (I could identify two different species) jumped down on to the tables and helped themselves to our scones and milk.

Lisa didn't like the fact that the lemurs had become semi-domesticated, a feeling I noticed was shared by the two Belgian girls who were also staying over. They were active conservationists back in Belgium and told me how disgusted they were about how tame the lemurs were – they were in Madagascar to see its 'wild' life, not spend their time travelling through a zoo.

I felt much the same way, but I didn't venture an opinion about the matter at this stage of my journey because I could see that Lisa was more or less helpless to prevent the lemurs from domesticating themselves, something which was pretty inevitable in the circumstances.

In any case, I had a more pressing matter to attend to, namely my serious lack of liquidity. Before actually breaking the bad news to Lisa, however, I decided to give my baggage one more solid scouring for the 50 000 ariary ($25 US) I was convinced I had hidden somewhere. And I turned out to be right; my problem was that I had hidden it much too well. Sure as eggs, I found the cash carefully stuck away inside my medicine bag between the nausea and diarrhoea medication. I decided right away that I was not going to wait for Monday but would carry on to my next stop, Antalaha.

However, when I told Lisa that evening about my no-longer-missing money and my plan to waste no time in heading for Antalaha, she refused to accept payment and said she would give me her Bank of Africa details rather, so that I could deposit the money for my stay when I arrived at Antalaha. It was a fine gesture towards a total stranger, and although I would rather have paid right away and headed off debt-free, her innate generosity wouldn't allow her to let that happen. So next morning I set off with her banking details. My bill totalled 50 000 ariary for two nights, dinner and breakfast included.

Yes, you're right – a bargain.

CHAPTER 12

DRUNKEN BEGGARS AND FRIENDLY FISHERMEN

Three or four more of these 100-stroke sets, I knew, and I'd be safe on land. I remember clearly how my weary mind struggled to accept something I would not have believed possible an hour or two earlier ... then a breaker helped by picking me up and flinging me sideways on to solid beach sand, kayak and all.

My intention was to get going early. That was the standard routine for me now – start off early in the morning so that if things went wrong or took longer there wouldn't be a serious delay to the day's stint. If you leave late, you start on the back foot and your capacity for dealing with unforeseen problems diminishes. This time, however, my good intentions were frustrated because everyone overslept, and so I left an hour or so later than I had planned. However, the weather seemed OK for the time being, although I realised that I was still in the relatively sheltered waters of the bay.

But I had other things on my mind than just the likely weather conditions I would face. The time had come for me to ask myself some serious questions; questions I had been dodging for a while. But not just yet: first I had to work out a weather strategy, because as I paddled further outwards I spotted an evil-looking dark horizon approaching on from the north-east.

I didn't let it upset me, though. It was still a long way off, right on the other side of this wide, wide bay, and it might come to nothing. Of course I might have decided differently if I had had as thorough a knowledge of weather conditions as the local fishermen, who had been dealing with it all their lives. So I didn't even worry about plotting my course too precisely at this stage because the bay between Mananara and my immediate destination, Manambolosy, was not deeply indented. I would just stay 10–15 km offshore, and that would be good enough.

I paddled on without much effort; the sea was calm and the only obstacle was a swell of five or six feet. Then I saw that the dark sky was approaching much faster than I had thought it would, and now it began to drizzle as well. *Keep at it, it won't be so bad*, I told myself. But soon the sky above me thickened, and the wind coming over my left shoulder started picking up strength. *Stick at it – focus*, I told myself again.

This was all very well, but the swell started losing its shape, while the small wind-chop grew larger with every passing minute. Now I faced an entirely new situation. Paddling can be defined as a continuous repetitive motion that creates a constant forward momentum, but that was not what I found myself doing – I had my work cut out just trying to stay on my kayak and keep it pointed in the direction of my destination. I couldn't keep to my course, and so without further ado I started steering for the shore about 7 km away.

It was a quick, simple decision because I did not have time to think too long about it. Waves were smacking in from all directions and every fourth one was knocking the kayak on to its beam ends and spilling me into the water. Thanks to my re-entering practice back home and my subsequent experience at it I wasn't worried about my ability to climb back on, although it wasn't easy with the water breaking over me as I clawed and wobbled on to the kayak after every spill. I had also never forgotten the advice to always keep the paddle attached to the kayak on a leash.

The most worrying thing, one that I couldn't do anything about, was that every time my kayak flipped over it would suck water in through the small openings in the deck. After a while it was about 70 per cent under water, and I was heading into a state of controlled panic. The bottom line was that the kayak was sinking, and the wind had begun gusting so ferociously that at times it felt as if I were going backwards. Now those 7 km between myself and the shore seemed impossibly far, and a feeling of helplessness started to take hold of me, so that I felt disorientated and lethargic.

This was truly life-or-death stuff, and after about an hour of increasingly desperate struggle I began talking loudly to myself between each splutter and plunge, trying to pump back some of my old determination. Was I willing to die for what I called an adventure? My instantaneous response was obviously 'no', and that meant I had to go into survival mode, or the adventure would be over for good. Survival – nothing less.

That was easier said than done. The fact was that my boat was sinking, I was getting very tired and I was involuntarily swallowing so much water that I was just about slowly drowning. The only way I could survive was to get ashore, or else more than just this journey would be over. For that I needed more than just a short-lived shot in the arm: I had to have a determination-spurt that would last for several hours.

If you're not willing to be determined now, you never will be! I told myself, over and over. *Nobody can help you here except yourself. Do something, starting with your attitude!*

But what sort of 'something'? Well, first of all I had to work out a way of staying on the kayak for longer intervals so that I could make some forward progress in addition to just staying alive. So the next time I had to climb back on I threw a leg out over each side. It worked – instantly I was more stable.

I still couldn't move very fast, but I found I could manage about 100 strokes between being thrown off. So that was the pace I maintained for the next three gruelling, desperate hours. Splash! Climb back on. *One ... two ... three ...* Splash! Climb back on and swallow the sea-water filling my mouth. *One ... two ... three ...*

It seemed to go on for a very long time. Then suddenly I was within reach of the shore, where a growing collection of locals of all ages was awaiting my arrival. Three or four more of these 100-stroke sets, I knew, and I'd be safe on land. I remember clearly how my weary mind struggled to accept something I would not have believed possible an hour or two earlier ... then a breaker helped by picking me up and flinging me sideways on to solid beach sand, kayak and all. I dragged the kayak about three metres up from the waterline and slumped down next to it, head between my knees. I didn't know whether that was far enough from the waterline, but I didn't care; I was still struggling to believe I was back on terra firma at last.

I could sense the crowd growing thicker around me as I sat there, head down, all of them consumed with curiosity about me and my little boat. Soon they were so close that they were actually bumping into me as they jostled for position. Not one of them greeted me: all they did was stand and stare at me in wonderment. Then they began laughing when I croaked out a whispered request for them to stand back and give me a little room.

After about 20 minutes l had recovered enough to stand up and begin communicating properly. I saw now that the crowd consisted mainly of primary-school-age kids and elderly people. Most of the oldsters seemed to be a bit tipsy, while some were very drunk indeed, and it wasn't long before the drunkards started demanding money from me, belligerently and persistently. I was very obviously in pretty poor condition, but these juice-hounds didn't care – they just wanted my money. Then the children joined in, teasing me relentlessly and enjoying my reaction.

The last straw was the arrival of an officious middle-aged character who ordered me to hand over my passport, obviously not caring a fig about how wiped out I still was. That was it. Distress and fatigue gave way to anger. I filed the idea of camping here for the night in the 'stupid idea' folder of my brain and started dragging the kayak back to the water, which had calmed down dramatically while I was being tormented. Rather the sea, even though it had been trying to kill me not long before, than these heartless drunkards and their nasty children. At least it would give me the solitude I suddenly craved.

It was still possible to reach Tanjona – according to my Garmin it was only 20 km away, and I still had four hours of daylight left. So I got the kayak out into deep enough water, climbed on board and set off.

In between paddling I pondered the day's adventures, and it was only now that I realised what a risk I had taken. What was probably more important, though, was that I also realised that I had managed to roll a huge mental boulder out of the way.

I am all for the belief, clichéd though it might be, about overcoming difficulties by means of a positive attitude, but I'll also be the first to acknowledge that positive thinking isn't enough – there has to be follow-through. I had learnt two really important lessons from this ordeal: I had to time my big bay crossings more accurately and not give in to my ever-nagging, stubborn, impatient spirit, and I had to accept that up to this point I had not really been honest with myself.

I hadn't cornered myself as decisively as I had done before my Africa circumnavigation and asked what I was willing to offer up in exchange for conquering Madagascar. Was I willing to risk my relationship with Vasti, my health, my financial welfare and, in all truthfulness, my life?

In the months leading up to my journey I had flirted briefly with my supposed willingness to do whatever it took to achieve another world first. But was I truly that willing? Till today I had glibly said 'yes' and left it at that. Now I knew that I was – fortunately or unfortunately. Suddenly I felt re-energised and ready for anything. I knew I was in the correct frame of mind to take on whatever lay ahead of me. But I needed more experience – experience that might save my life.

Landing at Tanjona was an exciting mix of dodging rocks and sliding through breaking waves around the small bay's easterly cape, and once again there was a reception committee of local inhabitants. But this time they were a bunch of super-friendly fishermen who didn't let the fact that they could not speak a word of English and not much more French stand in their way.

Through pouring rain they helped me up the beach towards a sports field of sorts, where they helped to clear an area under a large tree where I could pitch my tent. Most of them were in hysterics when they saw how small the tent was – *la petite maison*, or small house, as they called it. I marvelled at the difference between these guys and the surly drunkards I had met earlier. I decided it was because these ones were hard workers who went out to sea every day to provide for their families, while the other lot didn't appear to have the same work ethic, if they had any at all.

The fishermen presented me with two litres of locally brewed lemonade, called 'Bon Bon Anglaise' for some reason, which went down very well. Within minutes of crawling into my tent I was asleep in spite of the furious sheets of rain, only waking occasionally, but very briefly, when the thunder and lightning reminded me where I was.

I needed every minute of that sleep, not only to recover from my very hard day but to prepare my body for the 40 km slog across the Bay of Antongil. For all I knew, it would be a repeat of what I had just gone through. I didn't waste time worrying about the possibility, though. There was nothing I could do about it, and I had gained some valuable experience about dealing with rough water. So I was ready for the crossing.

Next day conditions were cool but perfect, without even a breath of wind over the calm sea as I set out in the darkness of early morning with my fishermen friends coming along to see me off. As I left them behind I made a mental note to return to Tanjona one day, and perhaps to do something for them that would repay their kindness. I had arrived there out of the blue, a total stranger, and without hesitation they had opened their hearts to me, although they had had no idea of what I'd gone through that day or how desperately I had been in need of a friendly welcome.

I set a course that would take me directly eastwards across the mouth of the Bay of Antongil. My destination would not be one or the other dwelling-place – the coastline directly opposite was part of the Tampolo Marine Park, and according to my Garmin there was only one village along that stretch. So my itinerary was quite simple: aim for the nearest piece of dry land, and decide what to do when I got there.

I set to with a will, the idea being to get the bulk of the day's distance behind me as soon as possible. Thanks to the fine conditions this worked perfectly. I fell into a steady rhythm, gliding over emerald-green water that was so clear that when I peered over the side it seemed much deeper than the 100 metres or so that it actually was. By lunch-time I had covered nearly 30 km, and in the distance I could see land.

Decision time: where was I going to land, and would it be for a rest or for the night? At this stage I was flying blind, with no information about the coastline ahead except for that village indicated by the Garmin. It didn't take me long to decide. Instead of heading for the village I'd do another 5 km down the coastline and go ashore at a rocky outcrop outside the border of the marine park.

All right, this might be slightly risky if the sea and weather conditions were to change as abruptly as they had yesterday, but on the other hand it would cut the next day's paddling by an hour or two. I might even be able to reach Cape Masoala – the eastern tip of the bay's mouth – by sunset.

Scattered clumps of jagged rocks greeted my eyes as I got nearer to my revised destination, such as it was, but then I spotted the entrance channel of a small natural harbour. It was narrow, but easily wide enough for my kayak (and, I presumed, for pirogues) to get in without being smashed apart. I wasn't taking any chances, though, and I was concentrating so fiercely on getting safely through to the harbour that at first I didn't notice that two girls were walking down from some almost invisible grass A-frame shelters to welcome me. I was both surprised and relieved. If there were people there was life. Good news for me – I could use some congenial company.

The afternoon was still young, and I had plenty of time to set up my tent on rocks instead of sand, which I had not done so far. I felt vastly content. This was the campsite I had dreamt about; it had exactly what an adventurer paddling around Madagascar should have. I would be sleeping no more than a few metres from the waves breaking on the rocks, and would also have time to use the sun, which had now broken through the clouds, to charge my various batteries with the aid of the solar panel. I felt very much the modern adventurer as I spread out the metre-wide panel over the boulders that rose out of the foaming seas. Vasco da Gama, eat your heart out!

Although friendly, the girls were very shy and formal in their welcome – probably, I calculated, because they felt a little apprehensive about this large, bearded stranger who had turned up out of nowhere in a bright green-and-yellow boat of a type they had never seen before. It wasn't till later that afternoon, when their husbands or boyfriends (I wasn't sure which) returned, that I discovered the truth of it.

When I went to greet the menfolk and explain as best I could what I was up to I found that my usual smiley-smiley approach didn't have the desired effect. The men, and especially one of the younger and more muscular ones, were very grumpy about my presence and growled instead of laughing when I tried to make a joke.

I didn't have to be a brain surgeon to realise that they, and the young guy in particular, felt threatened by my presence among their women. I felt threatened in turn because I was badly outnumbered, and so I decided to keep a very low profile – climb into my tent, knock back some energy juice and the remaining Bon Bon Anglaise, then mind my own business till I fell asleep.

As it turned out my evening wasn't as dull as that. A late arrival who didn't have a woman there and thus obviously felt less threatened invited me to share his evening meal of crayfish and rice. We got to talking over this unexpectedly exotic repast, and he told me he and his colleagues were gypsy crayfishermen (or, to use his exact words) crayfish poachers. The bags of crayfish these guys would harvest along the rocky coastline would be taken by foot to Maroantsetra for sale to hotels and the tourist trade.

When I mentioned to him that he must surely be a big fan of the Madagascan tourism organisation, though, his reaction confirmed my suspicions about the reason for my chilly welcome. He scoffed at what I thought was a reasonable assumption and asked me why I would think so. 'These tourists,' he sniffed, 'are here only for sex.' Quite the opposite, I thought, of what the average businessman would have felt about his sole source of income – after all, whatever tourists came out to Madagascar for, they still had to eat.

We were just finishing off our meal when I experienced a 'sundowner moment' that was better than a strawberry daiquiri: two young humpbacked whales passing right by us, no more than 10 metres away and heading out of the bay at a leisurely pace through the last glow of the setting sun.

I crawled into my tent without feeling the 'wow factor' rush that

I would have expected such a scene to conjure up only hours before. Then I realised why: *This is what I expected from the outset, and I'm relieved and awed that the dream is actually being delivered. I can't wait to see more.* The rocks I lay on seemed to be massaging me as I stretched out, with a small one doing duty as a pillow. Around me the night was quiet and restful, with the splashing of the waves and the sighing of a gentle breeze to lull me to sleep.

CHAPTER 13

CAPE MASOALA AND SOME FISHING ADVENTURES

*Accepting your flaws and mistakes is the beginning to finding
a solution for them, it's said, and I wasted no time in
accepting defeat when I saw the six-foot surf crashing over
rows of jagged rocks.*

All I could think about as I paddled south-eastwards next morning was catching myself a fish. Well, and also massaging some semi-negative self-rebukes about not taking a more direct route and crossing straight over the bay to Cape Masoala.

If I'd done that instead of lazing about with a bunch of grumpy crayfish poachers I would have been two days ahead of schedule. A day saved here and there would mean that I would get home a month earlier. That was the argument my ever-impatient mind was flinging at me. I resisted it, but all the same I couldn't help feeling that I had let my own side down to some extent. I decided to put the one-man dialogue aside and rather think about catching that fish I had set my heart on.

Then I must have passed some invisible cell tower because an

SMS popped up on my phone. It was from Seamus, and the news he was passing on diverted my thoughts to matters which had become remote amid all my adventures and misadventures. What the hell was going on back home? President Thabo Mbeki had resigned the evening before, and Kgalema Motlanthe would be acting president till our general election the following June, an election that was expected to be comfortably won by KwaZulu-Natal's Jacob Zuma, the very man Mbeki had fired from the deputy president's post a few months earlier.

Mbeki had, of course, been in an uncomfortable position when I had left South Africa, with the African National Congress clearly split into two camps, one backing him and the other shouting for Zuma. Mbeki had been under attack from all quarters for the way he was handling things like the Aids epidemic and the repulsive President Robert Mugabe of Zimbabwe, but no criticism had seemed as personal and vociferous as that from within his own regime. All the same, Mbeki had faced some tough times in the past and I had thought that he would survive this crisis as well, and still be in place when I got home.

Obviously I wasn't as good a political prophet as I thought, so I put all this aside and returned to my first priority, which was to get that damned fish which was paddling about somewhere near me, waiting to be hauled in so that he could make the acquaintance of my stomach. Politics and religion, I decided, were not fit subjects to be polluting a real death-or-glory adventure, never mind dinner parties and family get-togethers.

The rain came down with enthusiasm while I filmed myself at sea talking about my new ex-president, the lack of fish and the passing dugouts, overloaded with people and cargo, which were moving about in the sheltered area below the cliffs. Initially I had been surprised to see them putting out in such torrents of rain, then I was mystified when I heard the people in the dugouts shrieking their heads off, obviously sort of freaking out about something – what, I didn't know.

I decided to paddle about 300 metres out so I could trawl over the reefs. This position obviously added extra drama to the dugout theatrics. I must have looked lost and doomed amid all the rain, which was not only splashing down and into my eyes from above but was actually splashing up from below, too. All very dramatic.

Then things got even more dramatic when the reel started screaming as well. A fish had taken my bait! And from the sound of it, it wasn't a small one either, although the water seemed dark and was so full of reflections that I couldn't make out its size or shape. But one thing was sure – it wasn't fooling about getting away.

I swung my legs over the side and fought this brave fish for about 10 minutes. The line on my Shimano coffee grinder filled up as the fish's movements became more accentuated. This was really something! Then that damned impatience of mine scuppered me.

I knew the fish was a few metres under my kayak now, and I couldn't wait to hoist him up on to my lap, so I tightened the drag another quarter-turn before giving one last firm pull. *Dwang!* The line snapped, the rod flicked skywards and I nearly tumbled into the water. AAAAAAH, no, man! I wanted – I *needed* – that fish!

But he didn't need me. Broken-hearted, I examined my gear and saw what had happened. The fish had decided to make another run for it at the same time as I exerted pressure from my side, and the combined push-pull forces had been so great that they had snapped the metal leader – 20 cm or so of steel wire just above the Rapala, designed to cater for aggressive fish that would simply bite through the normal nylon line.

What the hell had I gone and hooked? Maybe it was just as well that the leader had snapped. Oh, well ... as the saying goes, there were lots of fish in the sea. Next time, all going well, I'd do better.

I got down to the job at hand and made very good time, so much so that I was within sight of my selected landing spot – a small village marked on my map in the small bay on the western edge of Cape Masoala – considerably earlier than I had expected to get there. I had thought I would have difficulty pinpointing the right place, but some photos Ockie had shown me of his fishing trip up this way seemed to bring the coastline to life, so that the islands that ringed the outer edge of this little bay were unmistakable from any angle.

I turned in – I was in deep water, about a kilometre from the shore – and got going, expecting to make short work of that last little stretch. But then my luck ran out. Without warning a gale-force north wind arose and smote me. Well, there was nothing to do but press on. I got my head down and put every ounce of grit and force I had into pushing my way through that furious wind, so busy trying to get somewhere that I didn't once look at my watch or check my GPS position.

For those who don't know, paddling directly into the wind is a kayaker's nightmare. It's almost impossible to maintain any sort of regular rhythm, and before long your wrists, lower back and elbows begin to hurt, probably from tendon strain. With prolonged exposure the tendon pain is likely to worsen to the point of being positively debilitating.

Anyway, I made it, but it took me a full hour to cover that one measly kilometre. This time there was no crowd of onlookers on the beach when I finally dragged myself on to dry land, just a couple of kids who came running up to greet me and then sprinted off, giggling, in the direction they had come from.

I couldn't see the reed-and-bamboo huts that Ockie had told me would be there for accommodation, so I decided to ask the owner of the little beach shop. It turned out she was also the huts' proprietor, and seemed chuffed to be able to offer me this basic form of accommodation. And I mean basic: no electricity, no communications, no water, but the hut she offered me was right on the beach, snuggled into a plantation of banana trees. Stunning, stunning!

The only question now was how much it would cost for the night. Her answer was 5 000 ariary, which was the equivalent of

$2.5 US – very cheap. Needless to say I took her up. Tonight I would decide if I would spend a day resting up or head on immediately; it would depend on how my body felt and also what the sea conditions were like.

My hut gave me 180-degree views of the sea and island, and for a while I relaxed and watched the fishermen rowing past on the way out to one or other of the local islands to check their nets, while children entertained themselves and each other on the beaches. Then I looked around for a bit and found that the village proper – a mellow, relaxed sort of place with 30 or 40 huts – was about a one-kilometre stroll inland. It had a good mixture of young and old inhabitants, which gave it a genuine family vibe. At first glance Masoala seemed exactly what tourist postcards advertised to the world, a little haven of perfection.

But it wasn't perfect, as I found out when I made friends with a sailor named Alain, who was temporarily on the beach because his ship had run aground on a reef about 15 km out of Cape Masoala (I remembered having seen it on my journey) – many ships ended up aground in this area, Alain explained, because their skippers misjudged the distance to land and ventured too close to the reefs.

In any case, Alain's ship was carrying fuel cargo up north to Antalaha and Sambava when it ran aground, and his duty now was to safeguard some of the fuel that had been landed and also go out to the ship by speedboat every couple of days to check that no local pirates had vandalised it or stolen anything. Just the night before, Alain added, someone had stolen a barrel of fuel while he slept – fuel, he said, that belonged to the president – and he needed to catch the thieves and, if at all possible, get the fuel back.

Well, you couldn't have the citizenry play fast and loose with the president's fuel (I didn't quite understand how the head of state featured in all of this, but I didn't ask, since I had learnt by now that Madagascans did things their own peculiar way), so I helped him to set up a trap.

The plan was to leave two truck wheels in the open and unsecured as bait, with an empty tin containing pebbles attached to act as an alarm. That done, we chose three lookout spots that would be dark when night fell. Alain reckoned that the wheels would be too tempting for the thieves to ignore, and when they came he would be ready for them. I wouldn't actually be on guard myself, but would be on call if he needed me. (As it happened, we slept soundly and undisturbed by the rattling tins – the thieves did not return that night.)

I decided that I would take a rest, laid out my solar panel and left it there for the entire day, so that most of my electronics were fully charged by evening. I spent a lot of time staring at the panel, imagining what was happening inside it with no help from anything except the sun. Solar technology still amazes me – it is very close to the classic loafer's dream of getting something for nothing.

I also conducted a long-distance interview with OFM, the favourite radio station of our landlocked Free State province, on a breakfast show expertly guided by two of South Africa's naughtiest DJs, Pieter and Christie, who are living proof that age is more in the mind than in the body. They are both middle-aged, but still full of the zany zest of youth and have the time of their lives cheerfully tormenting anyone who makes an appearance – willingly or unwillingly – on their show. Now that's what I call enjoying the dreaded mid-life crisis.

I enjoyed bantering with Pieter and Christie as I sat on the beach at Cape Masoala, because I was fond of Bloemfontein for a number of reasons. I had served there in the paratroops in 1991 and later had given many corporate talks there, among others at two legendary schools: the best rugby school in the world, Grey College, and South Africa's oldest girls' school, Eunice (pronounced, for some reason, as 'yoo-nee-see'). But what I liked most of all was the infectious humility and honesty I had found there – the real thing, not just pretence.

What I liked most about this link with OFM was that I was speaking to people who saw the ocean once a year at most, but who could now live this sea adventure through me from beginning to end – and without risking an encounter with a great white shark's teeth.

Talking of which, one thing I kept noticing as I mingled with the villagers of Masoala was the terrible state of their teeth. Most people had mouthfuls of decaying stubs, sometimes no bigger than maize pips, which were stained a strange purple colour. Others had the purple stain in one part of the mouth only, usually the four front teeth. But the most surprising thing was that no one seemed in any pain. How could this be? Sugar-free for me, I thought with a shudder. Brush twice a day and floss regularly, and I'd be OK. With a ghastly example like this I wasn't likely to slack off on my dental care routine.

Next morning early I climbed on to my kayak with mixed feelings. I knew from experience that I tended to tarry in places I liked, even if it was only for an extra day or two, and Masoala was one of the places I really liked. But those extra days have a way of mounting up, and I dared not hang around too long. All right, I was a professional adventurer by choice, which meant I got to visit places where most people didn't go, but unless I kept moving I would deny myself interaction with new worlds, ideas and cultures. I would never get around this island unless I kept my eye on the ball.

So here I was heading out of the little bay in the half-dark and a slight drizzle, not knowing what I would find around the next corner – and I mean that literally, not figuratively. The bay was still sheltering me, but within a couple of kilometres I would have left it behind and would be travelling slap bang into the face of a northerly breeze that, I could see, was already building up some energy and might easily turn into something similar to what I'd experienced two days before.

What perplexed me about this wind's direction was that along the two-thirds of the coastline to the south the winds were consistent south-easters for 360 days of the year. But now, as I left the Bay of Antongil behind, the wind was coming from the north about 60 per cent of the time.

Oh, well. I only had a few hundred kilometres to go till I reached Diego Suarez, the most northerly city on Madagascar. Vasti's visit was getting closer and I was longing to see her. After Diego Suarez I'd be heading south down Madagascar's west coast, and – touch wood – I'd have calm seas and a tail-wind. A kayaker can't ask for more than that.

I was heading north before the sun had even stuck its nose over the horizon, but even in the half-dark I could see waves on my right, breaking over a reef. What if the bay didn't have a northern channel to the open sea? If that was the case I would have to come all the way back and leave by the same channel through which I had arrived. But I wouldn't know, one way or another, till I got there. Go back or take a chance? Like any good adventurer I decided to take a chance.

This decision was based partly on the fact that up ahead I could see a lighthouse looming high up out of the jungly cliffs ahead of me. Seamus had been doing some research on my behalf because I had wanted another project to lend extra meaning to my Madagascar circumnavigation, and he had made contact with a professor from the University of North Carolina in the USA who was involved in worldwide studies relating to lighthouses and how they affected migration.

The angle was a bit extreme, the lighthouse being high above me, but I snapped a few pictures which Seamus had said the professor would like as a document of my journey – the closer the better, the prof had added. Well, I wasn't going to be able to get closer than about 300 metres, but it felt good to be doing something as significant as this.

The lagoon was typical paradise material: crystal-clear water with fish gliding past and underneath me (it still surprised me to see them so clearly). The barrier reef was dead, though, probably as a result of hundreds of years of hand-harvesting, as I noticed after leaving the lighthouse behind me. But now I had something that needed my attention far more. I was almost certain that I was not going to get into the open sea from there. The white water was just too dense, and that indicated waves, a shallow reef and danger.

Nevertheless I continued till I saw I had reached a dead end. Accepting your flaws and mistakes is the beginning to finding a solution for them, it's said, and I wasted no time in accepting defeat when I saw the six-foot surf crashing over rows of jagged rocks. I turned the kayak around and headed back, although keeping an eye open for a possible exit channel I might have missed. If I didn't find one – well, I would just have to carry on and leave the bay where I had entered it. It was a good thing that I had started so early.

The five-kilometre paddle back took a long time and at one point I was overcome by an attack of impatience that drove me to clamber up on to a protruding tongue of reef to see if I could make a dash for it. I had learnt my lesson, though, and I put on my Salomon Amphibeas shoes to protect my almost-healed feet. But I soon abandoned the idea. If I were knocked off my feet at any stage and then had one of these waves smash over me I would have had parts of my body ripped open; possibly even ripped right off! So I returned to the calmer waters below the lighthouse and carried on back.

I found a text-book perfect spot for fishing behind the reef, where the depth dropped almost straight down to about 30 metres. With the white water and the deep water right alongside one another, and distinct small-fish activity to be seen, I felt sure I would attract something big with my Rapala lure. I dropped it in. It was an exciting moment.

And sure enough, it wasn't five minutes before my reel began to scream. So far, so good. The problem, however, was that I couldn't sit and fight this fish at leisure like last time because the waves, some of them about three metres high, were breaking over a huge bus-sized boulder a few paces from me; I needed to paddle a few hundred metres into deeper water and then fight the fish in relative safety.

That's what I did, and my idea worked. Twenty minutes later I had hoisted about six or seven kilos' worth of sparkling blue-finned kingfish on to my lap. Dinner! I was both relieved and excited – in conditions like this, I told myself, it was impossible *not* to catch anything.

I put the Rapala in the water again without delay and carried on trawling as I headed north along the reef. About 20 minutes later I hooked another fish, this time a king mackerel, a long, slender fish that has been recorded at speeds of nearly 100 km/h – mostly reached while attacking its prey! Thomas (as I had now decided to call my Rapala) had better watch out, I thought.

The king mackerel – which is also known in South Africa as a cuta – was too big for me to bring on board. Well, I suppose it was not too big and I could have hauled it in, but to be honest I was just too scared of having this wild fish smacking me around or even biting me! So I let him go, pointing out to Thomas that we needed to respect the fish we caught as well as eat them. 'Take only what we need,' I preached as I unhooked the cuta and threw him back into the water.

I know it sounds crazy to have a philosophical discussion with a fishing lure while wrestling with an escape-bent fish, but travelling alone can do funny things to your mind, and I might need Thomas's full co-operation later on. I don't think Thomas quite believed me, because I could have sworn he looked a little dejected when the cuta departed at a rate of knots. Sorry, that sounds even crazier.

Apparently Thomas bore no grudges, because 20-odd minutes later I hooked *another* cuta, this one smaller and manageable, so that I decided to keep it as an ice-breaker at any village I might reach later in the day. I had been told that if I came bearing gifts it would definitely sweeten my reception, and in my circumstances, what could be better than a fish as my gift of choice?

Thomas was certainly living up to the claims that had been made for him (incidentally, I didn't simply pick 'Thomas' out of the air because it sounded cute – I named my lure after the American boxer Thomas 'The Hitman' Hearns. And I must say that so far my Thomas was beginning to build up an impressive string of victories, as you will agree).

What with all this *ad hoc* angling we were not making as much progress as expected, although we were still moving north. I left Thomas trailing behind me as I paddled, and not even half an hour after catching the cuta we had yet another strike. That one was saved by the bell, because I set it free. I seemed to detect a certain feeling of disapproval emanating from Thomas, but that was just too bad. I was the captain of this tiny ship, the 'master under God', as they used to say in the days of sail, and I would not tolerate any mutinous mutterings from the crew.

CHAPTER 14

SCORING AN 'OWN GOAL' NEAR ANAOVA

Amid all this chaos I had a very special moment of interaction with the creatures of the sea. I was paddling away with all my strength to cut through the waves, concentrating on the area two or three metres ahead of me, when suddenly a large, dark, mollusc-covered creature appeared so unexpectedly in front of me that there was no way I could avoid hitting it.

Thomas was now attracting everything that moved, and I seemed to be spending more time fighting fish than actually paddling north-wards. Fortunately the sea was glassy smooth and the coastline easy to navigate, with long reefs protecting the even longer beaches, and plenty of lagoons.

The ocean around me was populated both by fishermen's pirogues and by larger cargo-carrying boats which were passing me a bit further out to sea, probably heading, I guessed, towards the famed vanilla region of Madagascar, as Alain's much bigger steel-hulled ship had been when it came to grief.

The last two fish of the day were very noteworthy. One was a points loss for Thomas: we caught a glimpse of the fish – it looked like a giant trevally or kingfish – underneath the kayak, and then it headed steeply downwards, putting up a violent struggle. I tried to resist, but the fish seemed to get stronger and faster with each passing second, and eventually it bent the thick steel hook right open.

I was impressed and not a little intimidated by this spectacular show of strength; now there was no doubt in my mind that it had, in fact, been a giant kingfish. The encounter gave me some food for thought. I needed to respect these fish, especially since a man on a kayak was not really well-equipped to take them on. I knew that many fishermen on larger boats rarely won a fight with a giant kingfish. How was I supposed to achieve what they couldn't? The only answer was: with experience and respect.

My first lesson in respect was not long in coming. Having repaired the damage wreaked by the giant kingfish, I put Thomas back in the water, albeit with some reluctance. Not that I wasn't enjoying the action, but I wasn't on a fishing safari and wanted to cover a few more kilometres before I got another customer.

Naturally it didn't work out that way. A little further on we got another bite, and after some aggressive work with the reel I had him next to the kayak. This was a big one, a cuta which must have weighed something like seven or eight kilos, with too much grunt left in him for me to lift him on board. The struggle had taken about 25 minutes, and my impatience to get going again was beginning to take hold of me, so I decided to unhook the cuta and let him go to fight another day. Then Thomas could take a well-deserved break.

With this aim in mind I decided to be even more aggressive and bring the fish closer and closer to the kayak without tiring it out completely. To my left the fish, still tethered to my rod, was swimming in circles, showing definite signs of exhaustion now, so I thought I would bring him around one more time, then grab him as I coasted past and do the necessary.

I guided the cuta into the right glide path, so to speak, making sure that my dangling feet wouldn't get caught in the line, because any sudden moves by the fish could see one of my toes being sliced off as cleanly as if it had been stuck into a guillotine. This done, I leaned and glanced back to where the cuta was heading towards me, apparently tired to the point of docility.

Then suddenly he went into supercharge mode and made like a torpedo, screeching past at top speed just underneath my left foot. I was startled by his new-found energy, but what happened then was even more startling. My left foot shot up out of the water till it was as high as my chin, shaking furiously from left to right – and attached to it was my victim the cuta!

Gaping, I tried to grasp what had happened. It seemed to take a long time but was probably no more than a microsecond. The bottom line was that the fish and I were both firmly attached to Thomas.

The Rapala, for those who aren't familiar with it, consists of a cigar-shaped plastic fish with two treble hooks, one at its tail and the other hanging below its belly, and the dire situation in which I found myself had come about because the belly hooks had the cuta by the mouth, while the tail hooks were embedded in my left heel.

My first reaction wasn't too smart, and I paid for it right away – instinctively I grabbed at the cuta's head with my left hand to stop his frantic jerking around; my two middle fingers ended up in his mouth and then it was crunch time – literally. A cuta has gnashers like a terrier, and with a shake of his head he was tearing the flesh off my fingers. Suddenly there was blood everywhere.

I remember holding as tightly as I could to the fish's head to cut down on his movement, which was causing all the pain and damage. By now blood from my foot was pouring into the kayak's cockpit and, which was much worse, into the water around us, so that other fish began milling around underneath me. I knew it was only a matter of minutes before sharks, which can smell blood at an incredible distance, would find us as well.

More from instinct than thought I tore my Leatherman tool out of the front pouch of my lifejacket, opened its knife-blade with my teeth and began frantically stabbing away between my fingers at the cuta's head – a sort of deadly serious version of a game my friends and I had played at school, where one boy would put his splayed-out hand on a desk, and another would stab away with a pencil in between the outspread fingers. It worked. Blood began to spurt from the fish's head – over me, over the rod and reel, over the kayak.

Now I realised that while I had been dealing with this emergency the swell had pushed the kayak dangerously near to the reef. If I touched the reef and capsized now, the cuta would be back in the water and would make an energetic attempt to escape, and to escape meant ripping those hooks out of my heel. It was a nightmare almost as bad as that one about an unfriendly neighbourhood shark or two rolling up for a free lunch.

Fortunately the cuta was starting to calm down – which was hardly a surprise, seeing that by now I must have stabbed it 20 or 30 times with the maniacal strength born of sheer desperation, so that its head was a bloody pulp. How I managed to avoid cutting off my mangled fingers in the process remains a mystery.

My most immediate problem, however, was not the cuta but the reef. I was wobbling from side to side, still astride the kayak but only just, with the waves crashing on to the rocks only about three metres away – and there was nothing I could do about keeping clear of the reef till I had parted company with the cuta ... immediately, if not sooner.

Logically I should have turned the Leatherman from a knife into a pair of pliers and snipped off the shanks of the hooks in my heel, but there was no time for that, so instead I took the quickest (and most painful) way out: I leaned forward, grabbed Thomas by his plastic body and kicked my left foot forward as hard as I could to rip the hooks out by sheer brute force.

I remember bracing myself for several kicks, bearing in mind how tough the skin of one's heel is, but by great good fortune the hooks came out right away. This meant I could drop my mangled left foot back into the water and regain my balance, so that I had the time to convert the Leatherman into pliers mode and attend to the hooks in the cuta's mouth, which was a lot less painful (for me, in any case) than getting the others out of my heel.

The cuta drifted away, very much the worse for wear, and when I had put some distance between myself and the reef and started heading for a suitable landing-place I took stock of the damage ... and there was plenty to take stock of.

Thomas, the author of all this misfortune, was looking a little punch-drunk but was in fairly good shape. The handle of my rod bore its own wounds where the cuta's snapping jaws had taken chunks out of it. But my foot was the real victim of the fierce little battle. It looked awful, with flesh hanging from the wound, and as I paddled grimly towards land it let me know in no uncertain terms that whatever pain I felt (a lot of it) would just keep getting worse. A crazy thought passed through my pain-addled head as the shoreline approached: I had just played the lead role in my own budget horror movie ... with no effort spared on providing realism.

According to my map and GPS I was close to a seaside village called Anaova, and some passing fishermen pointed me a little more to the north, to a small but distinct cape, where a motorised boat of cargo-carrying size was anchored. I put aside my navigational aids and aimed at the boat, and in due course I was dragging my kayak up through some marshy sand and reeds, wracked with pain and tired almost beyond endurance.

The first person I met was one Jean-Pierre, who, so I gathered, was the main man around there. I asked him for a place to sleep and he introduced me to his daughter and her boyfriend, showed me his shed-style house and said he would be happy to charge me one fish for the night's accommodation. I was equally happy to oblige. It was a cheap price to pay for a good ending to this day of horror.

I realised that evening how isolated an area I was in. The young couple who were hosting me spoke not a work of English or French – they had been given their instructions by Jean-Pierre, and as far as I could see were following them to the letter. The girl cleaned the other fish and began to smoke it for me so that I could take it with me as nutritious dry rations. The boyfriend politely showed me where I would be sleeping, but I sensed he wasn't happy having me around: he never smiled and always made sure his girlfriend was never alone with me.

Again, as had been the case at my last stop, I got the impression that he felt threatened by my presence. I was too tired and full of pain to care, however, and after doctoring my foot I just sat around waiting for night to fall. Night meant sleep and, at least to some extent, recuperation.

The barn was divided into two main parts, with my half being a room on its own, separated from the other half by some makeshift curtains beyond which Jean-Pierre's daughter and the boyfriend slept. Well, 'slept' is perhaps not the right word, at least at first. I was completely knackered and dozed off as soon as my head hit the pillow, but later on I was aroused by a series of giggles and lay there wide awake while the two of them got down to a variety of sexual activities that were embarrassingly easy to identify by sound alone.

I lay there, stunned but powerless to do anything, as we – I say 'we' because I was now an involuntary participant in the slap-and-tickle in progress on the other side of the blanket – went through the whole gamut of mattress-wrestling, starting with ever less discreet foreplay, and then headed with ever-increasing speed towards the inevitable conclusion.

The boyfriend, I gathered, wanted to stretch things out a little, but the lady was impatient to gallop down the home stretch, as it were, and get past the winning-posts without delay. I listened willy-nilly to the entire thing, petrified of making some sound that would tip them off about their unwilling audience. It wasn't easy – I couldn't help smiling at first, mainly out of sheer embarrassment, but after a while I had to fight to stop myself from laughing out loud.

Fortunately the boyfriend wasn't endowed with much stamina, and soon enough all three of us were asleep. I don't know about the other two, but my sleep was a deep one, so much so that I was barely conscious of something hitting the headboard of my wooden-framed bed and bouncing on to my chest some time during the night. A second object followed the first, and this got me more or less awake. Dazedly I sat up. What the hell was going on? I felt about in the dark to find out what was falling on me, and after some scrabbling around I found one. It was small and round, like a bon-bon or perhaps a Lindt Ball; I could even feel the wrapper. But why should either be raining down on me in the dark in a forgotten corner of Madagascar?

I searched for my headlamp, which I usually stashed on my chest when I had a snooze, switched it on and identified the objects that had disrupted my sleep ... baby onions, neat and firm, each with its neck sprouting on top like a wrapper. This discovery only deepened my mystification.

I took a deep breath to clear my head a little and suddenly remembered what had seemed like a dream, about thuds and bangs on my bed's headboard. The thuds and bangs had been the onions, of course, hitting the headboard with considerable force and then bouncing down from there on to my head and chest. Then I remembered another part of the dream, which had Don Juan next door muttering a few sleepy words in Malagasy in a clearly disgruntled tone of voice.

Suddenly I realised what had happened. I had been talking loudly in my sleep, an old weakness of mine, and since this wasn't helping my neighbour's nocturnal tranquillity he had decided to launch a few onions over the curtains to help me end my demonic night activity. Well, he had succeeded, but I felt a bit bitter – there was no need to get ugly and start throwing onions; he could simply have asked me nicely to shut up and I would have stopped shouting in my sleep. Well, maybe not. After all, the only reason I had been talking in my sleep was because I wasn't awake to keep myself from talking in my sleep.

Anyway, I didn't let myself become upset by all this, because I hadn't yet achieved my main aim, which was to sleep as long and deeply as possible. I must have talked myself out, because no further onions came raining down on me. Next morning I didn't say a word about my sleep-talking (or, of course, about their bedtime stories), and none of us mentioned the onion bombardment. On these tactful terms we parted company and I got going, my next stop being (according to my map) the village of Amparavoana.

Although it was not even sun-up yet the sea was bumpy already, and it looked like another rough day for me, although one good thing was that the wind was easterly and sometimes south-easterly, which meant that I wouldn't have to struggle with it directly in my face. I dug in the paddle and got going – I wanted to get the first 20 km out of the way as soon as possible, or else I was going to get nowhere that day.

I had absolutely no idea of what I was heading into. All I knew was that I needed to round Pointe Est, Madagascar's most easterly point 70 km away, in the next two days – the first of the 'big four' I needed to conquer if I was to get around this huge island. My maps showed a village on the other side of the cape but didn't say anything about a suitable place for me to land. So tonight the end of my day's journey was going to be a surprise – though whether it would be a good or bad one I wouldn't know till I got there.

My fears of the early morning proved to be correct. The weather became progressively worse, and I found myself fighting through a storm which was twice as bad as the one I had experienced in the Bay of Antongil. I'd duct-taped the front hatch closed to stop any extra water from getting in, which had been the major reason for the kayak's instability in the Antongil storm.

Johan and his team had not had time to test the seals, so they were not as secure as he would have liked, and he had warned me to redo the entire hatch myself when I had the opportunity. Well, I was running the test now, and the tape was saving the day (and probably my life) because the sea was out of control.

The swell was gigantic, easily five or six metres, with the waves breaking at times as if hitting the shore, although I was kilometres away from land, and I couldn't keep going in one direction for more than 20 metres at a time. But being well out to sea didn't mean safety from reefs either, as I discovered when I looked to one side and then the other at one stage and was stunned to see rocks on my left, looking almost palpably eager to turn the kayak into matchwood, while on my right there was nothing but a boiling mess of swells and foam marching relentlessly down on me.

The nose of the kayak was much more buoyant now that it was free of water, and allowed me to punch through waves that would previously have knocked me out of my seat. I still fell off from time to time, but thanks to the menacing rocks so close by I could see that I was making some forward progress. *Keep going, keep going!* I chanted soundlessly to myself as I frantically plied my paddle.

The storms here seemed to be compact and aggressive, turning calm seas momentarily to a froth of turmoil, and while I was scared, as any normal kayaker would be, my previous real-deal storm experience made this mad second one seem less intimidating.

I couldn't help asking myself: *Would I have been able to make it through this one if it was my first?* And the answer I got from myself was short and sweet: *Not a chance!*

But it wasn't all trouble and strife. Amid all this chaos I had a very special moment of interaction with the creatures of the sea. I was paddling away with all my strength to cut through the waves, concentrating on the area two or three metres ahead of me, when suddenly a large, dark, mollusc-covered creature appeared so unexpectedly in front of me that there was no way I could avoid hitting it.

At first I thought it was a baby whale. Oh, shit! 'Baby' was a relative term – even a little whale was large enough to destroy my kayak if I rammed it. Then the kayak hit the creature, but instead of a meaty thump there was a cracking sound, and as I glanced down I saw the mysterious animal break into several smaller pieces. I realised for the first time that I had run into a group of giant turtles, probably mating away on their version of a water-bed. A second glance not only confirmed they were turtles but also gave a clear indication of how confused they were at being interrupted at this time and place: their big heads were popping up and down as they surfaced to try to figure out what had just happened.

In other circumstances I might have slowed down to give them a good once-over, and perhaps have a laugh or two about having left them in state of coitus interruptus. But just now I had no time to relish the moment. I had to keep moving forward, because if I kept moving forward my little boat would not sink. *Focus, Manser!* But I did take the time to film myself for a couple of seconds, to show the people back home that in the paradise of Madagascar it was not all sun, sea, sand and roses.

One thing was sure: Thomas was not going to see action today, because I simply couldn't risk hooking a big fish in such treacherous conditions. All I wanted now was a place to land safely, because I had spent a long, long nine-hour day battling those mountainous seas. I needed to get a good night's sleep before attempting to round Madagascar's most easterly point.

ON TO CAP EST

*I couldn't stop staring at the pictures, zooming in and out over
and over. The detail was incredible – on the first photo I could
clearly see the whale's mouth and even one of its eyes.
And to think I had been on the other side of the lens,
barely 15 metres away!*

The chief at Ampanavoana village charged me just 5 000 ariary (just under $2.50 US) for my night's rest in one of his huts, and next morning personally served me with breakfast coffee. It was a small but gracious act that brought my flagging spirits up to the necessary level to tackle the undoubtedly tough day that lay ahead, and it cheered me even more when he, his grandchildren and even his mother came to see me off as I paddled away into the early-morning mist.

I had anticipated a tough day, and I had been right to do so. The sea was huge, and time after time the 10–15 foot swell, moving at incredible speed, would lift me up, shake me and push me back towards the shore. But once again my early start proved crucial, because conditions got even worse as the morning wore on, with even the wind occasionally changing direction and coming from straight ahead.

I was not surprised. By now I had learnt that whenever I left the shelter of any solid land form that jutted into the sea the chances were that the ride would be exciting and bumpy, thanks to so many forces from so many angles refracting in every other direction and creating an uncontrollable mass of liquid energy. Cap Est, Madagascar's most easterly point, was clearly not going to be conquered easily.

During all this battering I found time to put my companion Thomas over the side again, and he delivered with ease once more, this time a 9 kilo cuta. As I was unhooking him from the cuta, I told him (yes, I was still chatting with him) that I was going to rest him for a few minutes. To my delight the underwater footage of Thomas doing his thing that I got with the Sony in its waterproof housing had turned out incredibly well. The fact was that Thomas was very photogenic, though battered by now.

But that was merely a diversion. Reaching Cap Est was not just a case of ticking off another destination on my list. The symbolism of Madagascar's eastern tip would keep me fired up to prove to myself that this journey was indeed possible. It wasn't difficult to stay motivated, now that Cap Est was within reach, but I have to admit that I felt a little heartsore and homesick, because I knew where Vasti was going this day ... namely to her good friend Renate's wedding to JG, a quiet but very pure and sociable late-nighter sort of guy. I have never been wild about attending weddings unless they involve people close to Vasti or myself, but this was one of those times.

Renate was a great girl and JG a great guy. He was the sort of fellow who would see any party through to the very end, and Renate was the poster child for a mature hippy surfer girl; beads and blonde wavy hair to match. What was more, she could easily blend a fruity chardonnay in your bath if necessary, since she was a qualified Stellenbosch winemaker! I would really have liked to see them take their wedding vows.

So I had a lot on my mind as I plugged away at getting to Cap Est. The sea became more structured than the day before, so that eventually I was only being thrown about when I encountered rocky areas, and by midday I had made good progress – with the bonus of seeing, to my surprise and delight, two large humpbacks pass right in front me without even knowing I was there. Before I knew it I had the actual easterly point in sight. Satisfaction filled me. That distant land-mass represented so much more than just another chunk of Madagascar: when I got to it I would enjoy my first genuine taste of success.

I had to work for it on that last stretch, though. A kilometre or two of giant six-metre swells had me fearing for my life at times as I approached the dramatic jut of the cape. What sort of crazy landing would I have to make this time? I consoled myself with the thought that there was a lighthouse on Cap Est, and where there was a lighthouse you had to expect some sort of safety. After all, a lighthouse was there to warn mariners of danger and provide an alternative to shipwreck 99 per cent of the time. There was something screwy about this reasoning, but I didn't have much time just then to work out what it was.

The surf was so huge as I approached that I took a very wide swing out to sea and pulled Thomas the Rapala out of the water, making very sure that I didn't capsize, because if that happened in such a wild sea my kayak and I would be separated instantly and we'd both be obliterated on the rocks. My change of course worked, and eventually I could see the entrance to the lagoon. It wasn't very wide, but it was calm, and soon I was on the beach, with a reception party of young children clustered around and giving me directions to the local hotel.

The 'hotel' consisted of a cluster of basic but surprisingly comfortable bungalows which were not quite finished, so there was no running water for showers as yet, but working flush toilets were a welcome highlight for me and all in all I was very comfortable.

Whether I would actually occupy one of the bungalows was still a moot point at this moment, because, once again I had absolutely no money to my name, and would have to find a sponsor or work out some sort of arrangement with the proprietor. I was worried that I might run into a language barrier, since any negotiations would obviously start off badly if we weren't able to understand one another.

It didn't make me feel any better to discover that the woman in charge was only the manageress, and that the owner, a Mr Leon, was a vanilla farmer who lived elsewhere. But all I could do was persevere, and after an hour or so of bargaining by way of back-and-forth telephone calls filtered through an interpreter I was allowed to strike a deal: I could sleep the night and pay up when I arrived at Antalaha. Phew! Now I could relax.

At dinner that evening I met a couple who were also staying over, a German woman and her Malagasy husband, who introduced himself as a guide from Moransetra, and I remembered now that the two Belgian girls I had met at the Aye Aye Hotel at Mananara had praised him to the skies. My dinner friends tonight remembered them just as well, and with even greater pleasure.

The evening proved to be very instructive, because this couple told me some interesting things about Madagascar's culture that were completely new to me, particularly the extent to which the average Malagasy is hamstrung by superstition – *fady*, they call it, which in translation would probably come out as 'wrong', but in this context meant something more like 'taboo'.

If something was *fady*, they said, it was considered an absolute no-no, because the consequence of ignoring the taboo would be some happening or event that would bring bad luck to your family, your village or whatever. For example, if an aye aye lemur came into a village it meant that someone in that village was going to die.

Another superstition that astounded me involved menstruating women travelling in ships. If there was a menstruating woman on a vessel that was entering the area I had just passed through in the last few days, she would have to declare her condition, the result being that she would be dropped off as soon as possible; if she wasn't left behind, the ship would sink and everyone on board would die.

I thought this was really preposterous. I had just fought my way through the wild seas of that alleged death-zone on a little five-metre kayak, and as far as I was concerned I would rather do so in a big sea-going vessel, even one crammed full of menstruating women.

I remembered now that at one of my earlier stops a chameleon had crawled all over me and I had been told that a young unmarried girl should never touch a chameleon. I had never found out why, and so I asked the guide. He replied that if she touched the chameleon she would become infertile and nobody would marry her ... all this with a perfectly straight face. Was he pulling my leg or did he believe that too? I couldn't tell. But in my world seeing is believing, so I just added it to my grab-bag of experience and reflected that it looked as if I was going to be skating on some pretty thin ice.

Next day I was on my way again, my destination Antalaha, 45 km up the coast. I was feeling some strain after the previous day, and what I would really have liked was a couple of days of crossing a lagoon with some flattish water that would allow me to paddle faster and longer instead of battling an angry sea, day in and day out.

It was more than just a desire for some peace and quiet, though. I had to get to Diego Suarez (Antsiranana) in time for Vasti's visit, and as matters stood now I would have to average more than 30 km a day, excluding any rest days or unforeseen complications, to make it in time. But currently I was doing much less than that if my rest days were included. So getting to Diego Suarez on schedule was going to take some doing.

I didn't spend too much time worrying about it, though. It wasn't the first time I'd had to change a mountain into a molehill. I would find a solution, no matter what happened.

My lagoon dream remained just that. When I discussed the matter with the locals they said it would be impossible – I would get cornered by the coastal reef, just as I had at Cap Masoala, if I tried to travel north on its landward side. The best would be to start early, get beyond the reef and cover as many kilometres as I could while the sea and wind were at their calmest.

I bowed to their expert opinion and did just that. It turned out to be very good advice, so that when the wind and sea lapsed into their bi-polar frenzy at midday nearly 60 per cent of the 45 km to Antalaha was behind me. But then things got a lot worse, and very quickly.

At times the swell was hurling me forward at huge speeds – my GPS registered one run at over 29 km an hour. Can you imagine my combined weight of 170 kg hurtling forwards at that speed? Crazy! The boat whistled as it whizzed over the water and air was sucked out of the cockpit from the foot-holes.

All very exciting, but the down side was that at such a speed it was almost impossible to steer the kayak, because when the nose started to choose a path of its own the rudder became useless. As a result I got tossed violently off the kayak every second or third run, the longest run going only a little way beyond 100 metres!

My aiming-point throughout had been a large mountain, which in the absence of anything else I had assumed marked my destination, but after a couple more hours of fighting the swell I got a more accurate fix when the big satellite dishes and communication towers of Antalaha became visible. What a lovely surprise! It couldn't be more than about 15 km now, and at my current speed I would be there in another hour at most. I pinned my ears back and concentrated on my paddling, already tasting the spaghetti bolognaise.

Thomas the hitman went over the side as usual, but wasn't at all successful. By now he was definitely the worse for wear, chewed to pieces by all the fish that had attacked him over the past two weeks, and was actually taking in water, which added plenty of weight and had a bad effect on his performance – the equivalent, I suppose, of what too many head-punches did to a boxer.

The fact of the matter was that Thomas had had his chips, and I was 90 per cent sure that I wasn't going to put him in the water ever again. On the other hand, there was that remaining 10 per cent that was urging me to give him one last stab at getting a big one … a sort of golden handshake, so to speak, before he hung up his hooks for good.

In my eagerness to get to the finish-line I had my head down most of the time as I paddled instead of looking ahead as I would normally have done, and so it came as a distinct surprise when I glanced up and saw a whale launching itself right up out of the rough seas like a submarine missile right in front of me. Wow! Talk about good timing!

This near-encounter made me pay a little more attention to what lay ahead, though, and I had another stroke of luck when this same whale breached completely out of the water, no more than 400 metres away. What unbelievable luck! I was excited beyond words and decided I wanted to get even closer for the third act in this little drama.

My good sense (which is never very strong at times like this) pointed out that it would be crazy to do any such thing, but as usual it didn't take much effort for me to convince myself that it would be worth the risk. If I could paddle in line with the first two breaches, I calculated, I might get right next to where the next one would be.

OK, there was the possibility that the whale, all 30 tons or so of it, might land right on top of me and cause a serious case of death, but imagine if I could actually get that picture of it bursting out of the water right in front of my kayak and only 10 or 15 metres away! Right! I altered course landwards and paddled hard for a few minutes till I got to where I estimated the whale would reappear, then put down my paddle, swung my legs over the side for extra stability and got my camera in the ready position on my lap.

Whatever happens next doesn't matter, Riaan, I told myself, *just press the shutter button, hold it down to get a few shots and continue to point calmly. Even if it's about to land on you.* My sense of self-preservation was screaming like a car alarm now, but I was committed. I had a chance to get a super shot and a super memory, one that I would be thrilled with (and surely Sony, too).

But nothing happened. I felt very disappointed: maybe I had been expecting too much. But I hadn't! Suddenly, just 15 metres or so away on my right front, the water exploded as the bus-sized whale burst into thin air. I gasped with excitement, fear and joy all combined, but I remembered to press down on the button. I recall that moment very well. I had stopped breathing, frozen with awe as the great body soared into the air.

Could it really be happening, or was I hallucinating? If it wasn't a hallucination and was really happening, had I got the shot? Surely not – it was all happening so fast that I didn't think my reflexes would be able to keep up.

Next moment the whale slammed into the water again. A ball of furiously disturbed foam and water towered up 10 metres above me, then fell in on itself and created waves and splash that had me fighting for all I was worth to keep from being thrown off the kayak. But I was so full of adrenalin now that I was past caring: what I really wanted to do was jump up and down and shout in exultation.

Now I noticed that my jumping whale wasn't doing a solo act but was one of a pod of four, probably boisterous young males, who were all caught up a bout of robust jostling and activity; it looked as though one was leading the jumping, with the other three excitedly following ... all of them completely oblivious to my presence.

I knew then and there as I set off on the last few kilometres that this moment was going to be the one that set the bar for my entire trip – not that anyone was going to believe my story. I had just experienced the sort of ultimate adventure I had been aiming for on this journey. I might as well go home now, because surely it couldn't get any better than this!

Now I was close inshore and heading into what I assumed was the harbour entrance, my long-anticipated portal to civilisation where, all going well, I would be able to get to grips with that bowl of spaghetti bolognaise I craved (why? I don't know, but that was what my heart and stomach were crying out for).

Anyway, I wormed my way in between the surf and the reef to where I presumed the harbour was – there were plenty of wooden pirate-style boats anchored behind the protection of the reef. But somehow it didn't feel quite right, and it wasn't: a crowd of young children who came to greet me pointed further north, shouting: '*Un kilometre ... deux kilometres.*' OK! They must know what they were talking about, and I could handle another couple of kilometres.

And they did, because I found myself in a real, genuine harbour, jetty and all. But a harbour should be littered with boats, and there wasn't so much as one anywhere. It just seemed all wrong, like an airport with no aeroplanes. I headed for the jetty, feeling unhappy about the emptiness all around me. Just *one* boat wouldn't have been too much to ask for, surely? Oh, well, maybe I was just feeling grumpy.

I got myself and the kayak ashore and headed for the Nanie Hotel, which was literally 10 metres away over a tarred road, a very welcome sight, and went into the reception area to ask if there was a room available. '*Oui, oui,*' came the reply. Right! Now for the crucial question: 'Spaghetti bolognaise?' I said, with just enough of an inflection to show that this was not some weird greeting but a question.

I got it right, and once again – happy days! – the answer was '*oui, oui*'.

Okay! Now I just couldn't wait a moment longer (what the hell was wrong with me?). '*S'il vous plaît, possible spaghetti maintenant?*' In other words, I would like my spaghetti right away, if not sooner.

It would most definitely be possible, I was told. The hotel staff helped me to carry the kayak to the front door of my room, where I quickly packed away my video camera and other valuables and then, without even taking a couple of minutes to change, I went straight down to the restaurant for my long-anticipated meeting with the spaghetti.

While I waited for it to be served I stifled my impatience by checking my stills camera to see how the whale pictures had come out. Hairbreadth-Harry shots, where it is more point and shoot and hope for the best than anything else, have a habit of being disappointing, because a fraction of a second can make all the difference in the world. All I wanted was for just one of the whale pictures to have turned out well.

Apprehensively I scrolled through the memory. And there it was! Or perhaps I should say 'there they were'. No fewer than two pictures captured the moment perfectly. One showed the whale's head breaking the surface, and the second caught it landing in a gigantic ball of foam, with the kayak neatly framed at the bottom left of the picture.

I couldn't stop staring at the pictures, zooming in and out over and over. The detail was incredible – on the first photo I could clearly see the whale's mouth and even one of its eyes. And to think I had been on the other side of the lens, barely 15 metres away! At this stage the spaghetti bolognaise arrived, and it was the best I had had in a long time, plenty of meat and not too much sauce. I went at it like a Trojan, then used up the last dregs of my energy to stagger back to my room, where I hit the sack and didn't move for the next 15 hours.

Next morning I reviewed what I had to do. It would be a rest day or two to get my body in shape for the big onslaught up the coast that would take me up to Diego Suarez for my rendezvous with

Vasti, and I had other unfinished business to take care of, namely to pay Lisa from Mananara the 50 000 ariary I owed her, and Mr Leon 27 000 ariary for my night at Cap Est. The kayak had to dry out, and the front hatch needed some serious repair work, because it was sucking in plenty of water.

The hotel's owner was a Mr Momo, a Frenchman married to a local, and a real character. He spoke very little English, and although he wasn't very friendly at first he soon warmed up, my love for his spaghetti amusing him no end. I gave him copies of the whale pics, which astounded him, and he said he was going to put them up in the hotel restaurant.

Mr Momo introduced me to the expatriate NGO/volunteer community of Antalaha, consisting of some American and French youngsters. Evin and Ronda were American Peace Corps volunteers who were there to teach English to the locals, while Eduard was a Frenchman doing his compulsory military service – the French government, he explained, gives conscripts the opportunity to volunteer for civilian work in the Francophone countries that had once been part of the French empire.

Awesome, I thought. I am an ardent supporter of national service – not military but *national* service, something that I think my own government hasn't got right yet. The excuse that we are a developing country can't be used for ever. I mean, national service is a form of repayment for what our world-class constitution offers us: free education, health care and, in some cases, government grants. In my opinion South Africa should do the same thing with school-leavers as the French government.

I wish I had spent my time in military service helping others rather than enforcing ideologies I had no understanding of. How can a country not see the overall benefits of this sort of volunteer system? Eduard's assignment was to assist the local tourism department in getting structure, destinations and activities in place so they could begin to attract tourists, as was happening with the more obvious places like Nosy Bé and Sainte-Marie. He thought that my influence and knowledge could help his work.

I liked the American couple, too. Evin and Ronda were what you would expect from Americans, and they knew a lot about a lot. Their generation had the misfortune of inheriting an unfair reputation as far as mine was concerned, thanks to having George Bush as their nauseating praise-singer. But – as I have discovered over and over again – most Americans are not like George Bush.

Evin and Ronda were genuine and willing to hear others' opinions, but in all other respects they were vastly different. Ronda was black, large in stature, flamboyant and bubbly in personality, while Evin was a slightly built, shy-looking white guy who, I discovered, came from North Carolina and probably even knew the university professor Seamus had communicated with regarding my tracking of the lighthouses of Madagascar.

The US elections were looming at that time, and the world was in the throes of 'first black President of the USA' mania, with Barack Obama making huge inroads into Hillary Clinton's perceived white strongholds. This gave us plenty to talk about.

A cynical reader might ask what that had to do with anything. Well, quite a bit, actually. It didn't take a genius to understand that Obama's 'change' slogan was not just based on change away from the clown figure of Bush but more a change from white to black. Personally, even though I had seen little of Obama, I was very impressed with him. A talented speaker always has the advantage over someone who is a policy maker and nothing else. And anyway, by African standards Obama wasn't black, since he was as much white as black.

Now here is my point. Can't the lobbying be on purely the issues? Which shows how politically naive I am! Politics is exactly *not* about the real issues. Ronda and Evin and the other American volunteers were planning a big party for the night of the primaries, apparently a big thing in the States. I wished I could be there when they celebrated Obama actually winning the presidency. But in spite of this pleasant encounter the best advice is still to never ever talk religion or politics. Most of the time the end isn't pretty!

Madagascar had its own problems, I was hearing through the grapevine. The mayor of Antananarivo had publicly criticised the President and had now been relieved of his duties, and one of the President's allies was taking control of the capital city. Maybe it was a good thing to be at sea. Things were changing at home and in America as well, and now the paradise of Madagascar seemed to be catching the virus. The sea was surely the safer place to be.

CHAPTER 16

DISASTER AT ANTALAHA

*My welcoming committee had now grown from five to about
20 in a matter of seconds, all of them laughing at me. The only
thing I could do was pull myself together and film everything –
the damage, my disappointment and the pleasure the locals
were getting out of my bad luck.*

The two days I spent at Antalaha were more than just a physical
break. They gave me time to finish the mental debate I had started
a little earlier and get my thoughts in order. This journey was not
a sort of water-borne version of the Africa one. Nothing from the
Africa circumnavigation, apart from my unwavering (unavoidable!)
perseverance, was applicable here. In fact, as I noted in my diary, it
was beginning to seem real powder-puff stuff!

My ripped heel from the fight with the cuta was festering slightly,
probably because I was on land, which I calculated had more germs
than the sea, so I took a three-day course of antibiotics. I wasn't
too keen to do this, because I wanted to save the antibiotics for
really serious situations. My philosophy is that if at all possible,
your body should be allowed to learn about a germ and conquer it

on its own, but with Vasti virtually on her way I wasn't taking any chances – I knew that one of my predecessors on this stunt had given up because of repeated infections that had made him fear for his life in some of the isolated spots.

Seamus, too, was in contact with me. He was planning to visit Nosy Bé on the west coast and wanted a guarantee that I would make it on the dates he had set – we had been offered a week's accommodation on a South African-owned yacht called *The Gecko* which would give me time to get properly back in shape and allow Seamus to shoot footage for our planned documentary piece.

It was truly awesome to have him assisting me like this. He didn't know how much it meant to have his involvement, which went far beyond merely logistical support. In every chat with him his constantly reiterated message of confidence and steely will to succeed reminded me of how determined I was.

I always tell people that I am a lucky guy, which I am, but usually this luck relates to a scary story of near-death or destruction. But having Seamus as the manager for this trip was one of the most extraordinary strokes of luck I've had in my life. And every day I realised more and more that this journey was going to need all the luck it could get.

I set off out of Antalaha harbour with all my new-made friends waving goodbye and a schedule that required an average 25 km a day, which I intended to stick to come hell or high water. There was no way I was going to miss first Vasti in a few days' time and then Seamus a few weeks later. But I didn't feel pressured – 25 km a day I could handle easily.

Naturally it turned out not to be as simple as that. The sea was choppy as I set off, and gradually it grew beyond my ability to control, with the swell created by the wind causing some chaos of its own. At about the 20 km mark I began to wonder how much more I could take. The kayak was being flung around, sometimes almost 180 degrees, at such regular intervals that I was sure I had paddled double the distance I had reached so far.

I am not one for cursing, but I know that day had me hurling expletives at the sea with liberal abandon from sheer frustration as well as a re-awakening fear for my life. The kayak was sucking in water faster than I could drain it manually, and the logic was simple: sooner or later I was going to lose this battle.

Eventually I had had enough of being the Indian Ocean's punching bag and was pretty sure that I had done 30 km, so I turned and headed straight for some dugouts I had spotted near the shore; surely there must be a place to land near where they were.

And sure enough, there was; as I got closer I could see that the dugouts – much larger than those I'd grown used to, I noticed – were bobbing around in a relatively sheltered area. But there was no easy way in, and I could see that the guys in the dugouts were nervous.

Still, in for a penny, in for a pound. I aimed for a spot where a few dugouts had been pulled up on the beach, being careful to time my landing in between waves. The water swept me forcefully up the bank, and I jumped out to grab a handle in the bow and drag the kayak on to dry land. I'd done this many times before, but this time I slipped, missed the handle and then had to watch my kayak being sucked at speed back down the bank, lifted by the next wave, about a five-footer, and smashed on to the hard sand.

Normally the kayak would have managed that much abuse without suffering any ill-effects, but not this time. As it made contact with the ground it flipped over on to the side on which the fishing rod was sticking out at an angle. I expected the rod to snap into pieces – the force of the impact was just too great. *No, man!* I thought. I needed the rod to survive. I couldn't afford to have it damaged! I didn't realise then that this was actually the lesser of two evils.

I lunged forward to meet the kayak as it came in again, and that was when I saw what had actually happened. Shimano make their rods strong – too strong in this case, because it had withstood the impact and had ripped out the entire chunk of the deck behind my seat.

I was so down. I had been hoping the rod wouldn't snap, and it hadn't, but now something infinitely worse had happened. I slumped down in disbelief next to my kayak. Why did this have to happen to me now? Come on!

My welcoming committee had now grown from five to about 20 in a matter of seconds, all of them laughing at me. The only thing I could do was pull myself together and film everything – the damage, my disappointment and the pleasure the locals were getting out of my bad luck.

That done, I considered my options. Vasti was due to arrive at Diego Suarez in three days' time, and I would never make it if I had to spend time repairing the kayak first. I sat there for about an hour, pondering my misfortune under the eyes of the giggling crowd and feeling sorry for myself. Then I gave myself a mental shake and began working on a plan of action.

I considered various possibilities, but there was only one that made sense if I wanted to have my time with Vasti, and that was non-negotiable. I would only have five days with her, and I didn't intend to waste one minute of it. So I would have to find a village where I could store the kayak safely, go back to Antalaha via Sambava and get to Diego Suarez by public transport in time to meet Vasti. Then I would return, take the kayak to Antalaha, repair it properly and get going again.

Almost immediately I felt better – it's incredible how poring over your bad luck only makes you feel more suicidal; the thing to do was plan an escape route before it was too late. It was good to be reminded once more about how actually doing something can change both your mood and your situation. In a moment I was up and about and after negotiating a fee with some kayak-carriers headed for the nearest village. There I would go into phase two, which was to find transport big enough to take the kayak to Antalaha after my return from Diego Suarez. After that the rest should be straightforward.

The chatter among my helpers was that I needed to be presented to the 'president' of the village (or the region, I didn't know which), who apparently had to vet me and approve my movement through their town. Now, normally I am opposed to someone regulating my freedom of movement, but this time I would just have to put up with it, because if anyone was in a position to help, it would be the president.

The president lived in a hut alongside the famed tarmacked road to Antalaha. He was younger than I had expected, and was evidently a popular guy. I explained to him where I had come from and what had happened. He understood I needed to get back to Antalaha. I refrained from going into elaborate detail about my rendezvous with Vasti in Diego Suarez in three days' time – it would simply complicate things, and I didn't need more complications than I already had.

I was also careful not to let him see how desperate I was to get to Diego Suarez. I was, of course, but to judge by my experiences elsewhere in Madagascar this would involve handing over a large wad of cash.

I made an arrangement to leave my kayak with him, although I would take all my baggage with me to Antalaha, where I would attend to some 'business' (no details) and return after five or six days. Needless to say I was actually going to be away for eight or nine days, but I was afraid this would scare him into turning me down, since he was obviously not all that keen on my leaving the kayak with him.

I finally managed to catch a taxi to Antalaha and sheepishly returned to the Nanie Hotel to plan my journey to Diego Suarez via public transport. I had heard this would take a day or two, which meant that I would have to leave next day or the day after at the very latest, otherwise I wouldn't get there in time to meet Vasti. Geez! This timing was as tight as a guitar-string.

Mr Momo introduced me to his brother-in-law, one Donald. Donald was Malagasy, fluent in English and a few other languages, clued up on Madagascar travel and a super guy all round. Best of all (and this was the most freakishly lucky thing) he was leaving for Diego Suarez the very next day. He knew what time the bus was leaving and went with me the next day to book our seats.

This was Thursday, so I'd travel tomorrow and, all going well, would be on time to welcome Vasti at the airport on Saturday morning. Two days to go and just 24 hours available for travel! The drivers at the station claimed the trip would only take 12 hours. I didn't believe them. Donald said it would take a bit more, and I believed *him*.

I spent the rest of the day having my clothes and a torn bag repaired by a friendly roadside tailoring stall. The amazing thing about my shirt was that actually I only had to have it taken in. The First Ascent adventure shirts have generous waistline space, which I hadn't needed in the first place, but now that extra cloth had become positively cumbersome because I had lost so much weight. I marvelled as the tailor took in the waistline. Only three months into my journey, and I had already metamorphosed into another shape!

Donald and I were up at 4.00 am and 45 minutes later were waiting outside the alleged bus, which looked more like an oversized horse-box. The fact that Donald had reserved seats for us made me relatively confident about our comfort over the next day, though – except that as it turned out this applied to somebody who was slightly built and not taller than about 5 feet 10 inches, which is about the maximum for the average Malagasy. Since I stood six feet tall in my stockinged feet and was heavily built, I knew the journey would not be without pain.

On the other hand, the road to Sambava turned out to be

From mangroves to rocky areas and desert isles, the terrain wasn't all cocktail bar to cocktail bar. The surf can look so small at a distance, but then seems to grow as you get nearer, so that when you eventually find one of those 'small' six-foot crunchers looming overhead you feel like screaming for mercy. I spent a lot of time bailing out.

Giant leatherback turtles, dolphins, sharks, whales, seahorses and plenty of jellyfish. The world underneath the sea is unknown to us. Every human is a temporary visitor.

When on land it always took a while to switch over from 'sea legs'. I swear I could feel my backside swaying from side to side, a most odd sensation but apparently a common one for kayakers, generally referred to as 'sea bum'.

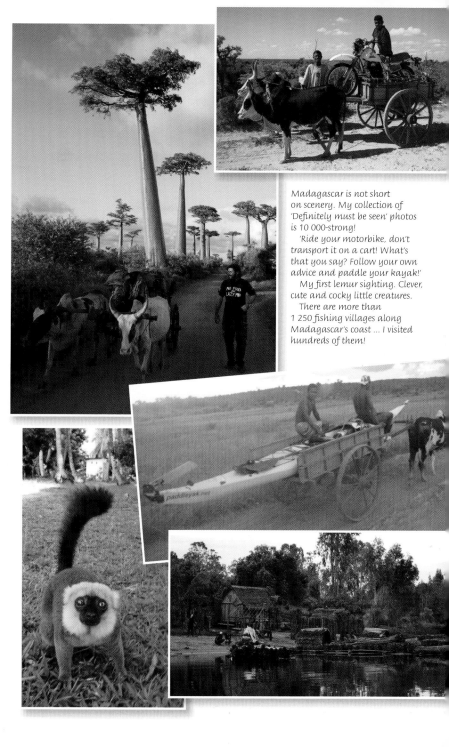

Madagascar is not short on scenery. My collection of 'Definitely must be seen' photos is 10 000-strong!

'Ride your motorbike, don't transport it on a cart! What's that you say? Follow your own advice and paddle your kayak!'

My first lemur sighting. Clever, cute and cocky little creatures.

There are more than 1 250 fishing villages along Madagascar's coast ... I visited hundreds of them!

I'd try to cool down by splashing myself, though sometimes the water was warmer than me. East, North, West, South ... my biggest geographical goals. Cap d'Ambre, the northernmost point of the huge island, signified success and progress. The dancing children had me doing what I never do – dance!

The south was rocky and dangerous. Caught in between a 100-metre high cliff and 20-foot surf, I risked everything to carry my kayak up the cliff and a few kilometres along the ridge to a safer launch site.

The Pangalan Canal was designed by the French to navigate the mid-east coast. The best decision I made was to spend 10 days of my journey on it, experiencing another world and history of Madagascar and her people.

The last day was not easy, with 15-foot swell and choppy seas reminding me I was not done. A fight with the sea is one that you will always lose. Don't even attempt it. I risked too much at times (easy to admit with hindsight!).

smooth sailing compared to what your average African road offers, although the driver seemed to have a sadistic streak. He delighted in passing as close as possible to pedestrians and cyclists using the road's shoulder, and once actually clipped off a piece of sugar cane hanging from the back of a teenager's bicycle.

But he was not content with these near-misses, as I discovered when we saw a chameleon on a snail's-pace dash across the road. When the driver spotted the chameleon his eyes lit up and he aimed right for it, and while I accept that even on the best of days the chameleon probably would not have made it, the driver made sure by swerving over on to a collision course, then showed obvious satisfaction when the truck's right front wheels flattened it with an audible crunch.

I was revolted; you can tell a lot about a person's character from the way they treat animals, or any other living thing, for that matter. I said something about this to Donald, who explained that the driver had wanted to eliminate the risk of the chameleon causing any *fady* in someone's life. Pathetic!

We passed through Sambava and several other inconsequential dots on the map, and late that afternoon reached Vohémar, otherwise known as Iharana, the first and only big town so far, going down a dramatic drop from the high mountain road into the beautiful harbour valley area. I found the view a refreshing change: every time I saw Madagascar it was from sea-level.

We had now covered more than half the distance to Diego Suarez, and I reckoned the rest would be easy – just follow the road northwards. But the bad news was that, according to Donald, 'now we have the difficult part. Maybe we cannot even get through because of the rains.'

That was the last thing I wanted to hear, and Donald turned out to be right. The road was almost impassable in some parts, and many times the trailer threatened to break loose from the truck and tip over. That wasn't my only concern: after something like

14 hours of being bent out of shape my body just couldn't handle my 'comfortable' seat any more. I asked Donald if he could negotiate for a bigger one, which he managed, but it was too late. After a few more hours I was hurting just as badly as before in spite of a few pee and poo stops which allowed me to unscramble my skeleton a little. So much for the promised 12-hour journey!

In the middle of the night we reached the village of Ambilobe, clambered out of the horse-box and had midnight coffee and dinner. By this stage I needed the food, but I needed the stretching even more. Then it was back to the horse-box again. By this stage, I knew, Vasti had already ended her first day in Antananarivo and was staying over at Ockie's guest-house branch there before catching the early flight to Diego Suarez (later I heard that Ockie's staff had pampered her to the utmost, making sure she felt safe and then taking pains to get her on to the correct flight).

Before leaving Antalaha I'd given Vasti the bad news that I would be arriving late, and that she would have to get a taxi from the Diego airport and find a hotel for us, the idea being to surprise her by being there in person when she arrived. She had been slightly worried, and now, too, so was I, although for a different reason. Was my stupid joke going to backfire on me, or would I actually make it in time to meet her at the airport?

To my relief things started to look more promising after we had left Ambilobe. There was a drastic improvement in the road, and along with most of the passengers we transferred to a minibus taxi. We were 'very close now', according to the driver, and would probably make Diego (as everybody called it, I noticed) by 9.00 am. That was about the time Vasti's flight landed, but I would be cutting it fine.

The road was now very reasonable indeed, though, and having got out of the clutches of the horse-box and its murderer of chameleons we were flying along at a good clip as the sun began to rise. But not fast enough for my liking, and every two minutes or so I would pester Donald with: 'Are we there yet?'

I was still pestering away when the taxi suddenly began to slow down and then stopped, after which everyone else just sat and stared at me. Puzzled, I stared back. Then they started calling: '*Allez, vazaha, allez,*' which I translated as 'go, white man, go'. In other words, move your arse. The message was perfectly clear and I got out. Then I saw why: we were parked opposite the airport.

Donald, who was just as surprised, helped me to retrieve my bags and pointed me safely over the road. I said goodbye with genuine gratitude, and made plans to meet up with him later in the week so I could introduce him to Vasti.

Inside the airport building I felt like jumping for joy – even after 28 sleepless hours – when the staff told me that the flight from Tananarive was not expected for another 40 minutes. Unbelievable! How much more perfectly could I have timed it?

I couldn't help following through on my joke; Vasti knew that with me around the likelihood of one was always present, although she had a tipping point at which she began to panic about a situation – such as, for example, being thrown into a very exotic foreign country all on her own and knowing no French or Malagasy. I reckoned she must be near the tipping-point now and ready to give a piece of her mind, on the lines of: 'How dare you leave me all on my own? A girl can't be expected to sort herself out – this is dangerous!'

Nevertheless I decided to go through with the joke to the bitter end. Well-camouflaged by the pillars of the airport building and the other people standing around, I watched her disembark and then sent her another SMS to say sorry, I was going to be a few hours late, but that the good news was that I would definitely be there, and we should both simply be grateful for that.

She went to stand next to the old-style conveyer belt as the baggage began to appear, glancing back and forth between the belt and the exit door, and I guessed at her thoughts: 'He can't be for real, of course he's here somewhere.' It was too much for me, and my resolve to carry on melted away. Pretty weak of me, maybe, but this was Vasti, for whom I had longed so much. So I sent her another SMS to say it was OK, I was waiting for her on the other side of the door.

A few minutes later she came out, looking so pretty and fresh and enthusiastic. That's the way I know her, and sometimes with the humdrum stress of life she didn't always reflect that wonderful glow. I wanted her to have it permanently.

Then she came out through the sliding doors and we headed forward to hug – only, of all things, to be pushed away from one another by a cloud of over-eager taxi and hotel touts – Madagascar's tourism had gone down in the past few months and business was scarce. But eventually we managed to get together for that hug, and then we went out and found a taxi that was only reasonably overpriced to get us to the town, 15 km away. Although I knew we were paying the '*vazaha*' price, I didn't care.

With only five days at our disposal, I planned to pack each one with as varied a round of sightseeing and relaxing as possible. Vasti enjoys beaches and warm sea-water, so after spending one night at an over-priced shit-hole, we caught a taxi at a bearable exorbitant fee to take us to Ramena beach, Diego's tourist hotspot. From there, we decided, we'd play it by ear.

All I wanted was for Vasti to enjoy herself and then leave with a piece of Malagasy culture, an idea of what they were about and some understanding of what I was trying to accomplish. And that's what she did in great style.

CHAPTER 17

BACK TO THE SEA

'The customer,' she replied immediately, 'is not always right.'
She broke eye-contact and turned firmly away ... I couldn't
help thinking that it must have been a very peculiar customer
services manual she had been studying.

Ramena beach had hotels scattered all along the waterfront – all, of course, owned by pompous Frenchmen who were a far cry from Mr Momo at Antalaha. The taxi-driver, who was filled with good cheer by the fact that we were paying him about 50 times the normal rate, was very willing to take us to test the waters, so to speak, and the water wasn't exactly friendly.

One encounter stands out vividly. We went down one very sandy road and stopped at a small group of beachfront bungalows, and with Vasti close behind I got out to investigate. The place seemed to be as dead as a doornail, and it took a while before my hallooing aroused some signs of life in the shape of a thin, scraggly man with long hair and all the signs of a deadly hangover who appeared out of nowhere.

In accordance with my policy of politeness at first meetings I

said: '*Bonjour, monsieur, excusez-moi, monsieur, parlez Anglais peut'être?*'
In other words: Good morning, sir, do you perhaps speak English?

To my surprise the man lifted his left arm, extended his index
finger to the sky and started waving it vigorously from left to right,
emphatically replying: '*NO, NO, NO, NO, allez!*'

Now 'no, no, go away' is not what I would consider polite in
anyone's culture. The French like to defend their culture as being
abrupt and to the point, but commonsense, not to mention a
little courtesy, should be the watchword of any intelligent person,
regardless of the culture concerned or the language being spoken.
'Do unto others as you would have them do unto you' is a good
starting-point for any new encounter.

This conversation was obviously going nowhere, and I went
back to the taxi. Vasti was amazed and asked me what I had said
to make the scraggly man so angry. I explained to her as we drove
on to the next hotel that it wasn't what I had said but the fact that
he had thought I was an Englishman. I wasn't too upset. Not that
I was used to such a rebuff – this was the first Frenchman to treat
me so rudely – but in a way I expected it, given what I knew about
Madagascar's history.

Vasti loved one hotel called the Casa El Falafy, which was built
around a swimming pool on the bushy hills of Ramena and over-
looked the sea. At 40 000 ariary (about $20 US) a night it wasn't
cheap, but my budget from Windhoek Lager made provision for
these expenses, so I had no qualms about booking us in there.

Being the ever-hungry adventurer that I am, though, the thing I
liked best about the Casa El Falafy was the seafood platter for two.
It was more like a meal for six: two large linefish, two crayfish, crab
salad (the best part, in my opinion), calamari and a dozen prawns –
all for 25 000 ariary, about $13 US.

The weather was horrendous, though. The wind pumped hard,
and when we eventually got to hike over the desert-dry mountain
to view the grand harbour entrance we saw what a really danger-

ous sea looks like. The first thought that came to my mind as we gazed down on this maniacally violent commotion of water, waves and wind was that I was never ever going to be able to paddle into this harbour, never mind get around Madagascar's most northerly point, where it was reportedly about ten times tougher than what we were seeing below us.

Diego's harbour is protected by the really huge cannon that are built into a bunker in the cliffside, and it was a strange, surreal feeling to stand behind the massive breech of one of the guns, peering through the loopholes and imagining the thunderous sound they made and the death, wounds and damage they caused when their long-departed gunners fired them at the brave ships venturing into Diego Suarez's bay in times past.

Further up on the mountainside, overlooking the entrance to the bay, a lighthouse sat perched on the cliffs, which was also surrounded by smaller – but still awesomely sized – cannon. Diego Suarez had obviously been one party you wouldn't want to gatecrash without an invitation in the old days.

Vasti and I enjoyed watching the sunsets on Ramena's main beach and met a few other travelling couples in the process. One couple approached us and asked if I was the kayak guy – it turned out Ockie had told them about my trip while they were staying with him on Sainte-Marie, and they had recognised me from a video Ockie had played them. They also confirmed that my video was played *after* the DVD with Ockie's beloved AC/DC on it. Of course! What else?

The other couple we met were very kind, too, and when we heard that they were heading for Sainte-Marie we warmly recommended that they stay with Ockie. We also introduced both couples to Casa El Falafy's seafood platter deal!

Vasti and I decided to spend another night back in the town and explore there till the sea had calmed down – that way we could do a trip we had planned before any of the others, namely visiting

Emerald Bay just to the north of the bay's entrance, the greenest area of water you will ever see in your life.

Transport now became significantly cheaper because we were willing to negotiate our fares. The law of supply versus demand applies everywhere in the world, so we acted as if we were low on demand, knowing that the local taxis were high on supply.

Our eventual trip back was funny, actually. A driver who was parked at the main boat-launching area, and obviously looking for business like all the others, came over to negotiate. He said he had seen that another driver had approached us and understood we didn't need a taxi right now, but would we at least keep him in mind when we did decide?

I decided it might as well be his taxi we took, so I tried a bit of quick negotiation, but he wouldn't budge and we couldn't reach agreement on the price. So I tried a little mind-smuggling, as South Africans call it.

Turning to Vasti, I said (in English, and loudly enough for him to hear): 'You know what, I actually don't want to go back to that dirty town right now; this is far too beautiful, and by the way, we've paid for another hotel night, so my suggestion is this: let's watch the sunset with our toes in the sand and our cold beer in our hands.'

The driver absorbed the subliminal message I was projecting, and less than a minute after our waitress placed our tall glasses of Three Horses in front of us, he appeared again. 'Zis problem,' he said. 'Come, we go.' No problem! Somehow the original fee I had offered (which was probably still far too much for the 18 km trip) had suddenly become quite acceptable.

One thing that Vasti couldn't help noticing (although I had got used to it by this time) was the number of old, grey and wrinkled white men with girls no older than about 18 at their sides – not 10 or 20 per cent but more like 80 to 90 per cent. Now, I do not believe in any way that an old man cannot get jiggy with a young hottie (I'll be old myself one day!) but in Madagascar it was just too obviously a well-organised system.

In Diego Suarez the sex trade was a real deal, as Ockie would have said, and Vasti hit the nail on the head when she remarked that the whole resort survived because of what the young girls could offer these old men – our little drop of tourism didn't even make a dent.

We dined out on Malagasy foods and now and then the odd spaghetti bolognaise, and I must say that the local cuisine is not very exotic. I had been sharing the meals of the poorest people most of the time, so I had got a decent idea of what the staple foods and meals were by then, and it was clear, for example, that rice was eaten with just about everything.

Another staple was zebu meat boiled with ramazava leaves, and the sauce created during the boiling process is hard to describe. It's not like ginger or garlic, or ultra-spicy like chilli – it has a sharpish taste and seems to numb your mouth with each slurp. The leaves look like spinach and add a unique taste to the usually tough meat, but since I'm not a big rice fan back home I wasn't always excited about this dish.

The villagers who had fed me to date couldn't afford to slaughter zebus too often, and usually served a spicy fish and rice dish instead. In towns with a larger population the dominant treat was brochettes of meat – skewers of well-done zebu steak and fat. I liked the meat part of this, and it was usually cheap, tasty and available on every corner.

Malagasy crafts, too, are just like other crafts anywhere else, and we decided on a few for Vasti to take home. I bought a hand-carved cane for my Rotary Club president, Peter Davies, who doesn't need a walking-stick but collects them. My present wouldn't be the most exotic in his collection but at least it would be from a distant and exotic (more or less) destination. Vasti bought smaller bead art and purses to take home. But we couldn't find anything featuring her favourite – the 'pampoenskulpie', a lovely type of little seashell.

We wrapped up our time together in Ramena village with a few good laughs and a deeper insight into Malagasy culture, but not at Casa El Falafy – we had moved to another hotel, not to save money but because we had been at the receiving end of an unpleasant combination of French 'hospitality' and Malagasy logic.

Vasti and I had decided to have early pre-dinner appetisers in the bar overlooking the pool. We were the only people in the restaurant area at the time, and one of maybe three couples actually staying at the hotel. We ordered our beers and then asked the bar lady if she could change the news channel to English for our benefit, since we needed an update on Madagascar's fraught political situation but couldn't understand a word of what was being said.

The bar lady did what we asked, but one beer and 30 minutes later she went in behind the bar and changed the channel to a French one. Vasti and I gazed at each other in amazement, and then I said, knowing she could speak English quite well: 'Didn't you see that we're watching?'

'Oh, I see,' she said. 'The other people want to hear French rather. We cannot just play one station. We must think of the other guests,' and she launched into a lecture about how to please one's customers.

'But we're the only people here!' I protested. 'We'd like to watch the English news channel, please.'

'I must go ask the owner,' she said huffily and marched out; obviously her client services manual didn't have a good response for situations like this. A few minutes later she returned and told me, very emphatically: 'The owner says we will not change the channel. The picture is in his room too, and Madagascar is French, so we watch what is in Madagascar.'

'You must be joking!' I said. 'Madagascar isn't French, you're Malagasy yourself. How can you accept that?'

'My husband is the owner,' she retorted. 'We are French.' Which explained a few things.

I should have let go of the subject, since I was clearly not destined to get any sort of sense out of her, but I decided to have another go, derived from pure business logic rather than psychoanalytic arguments based on colonisation and its brainwashing.

'But obviously we, as the customers, the people paying the bills, have a right to have a big role in deciding what channel "our" TV is on? Especially if we're the *only* customers?'

But she had an answer. 'The customer,' she replied immediately, 'is not always right.' She broke eye-contact and turned firmly away.

The customer is *not* always right? How was that for Lesson No 1 in customer care secrets? I couldn't help thinking that it must have been a very peculiar customer services manual she had been studying. 'The customer is *not* always right?'

I hoped she would explain herself – and she did, but not in the way I expected: 'Yes, the customer is not always right. Yesterday the customers want to swim in the pool with the beer glass. But we tell them they cannot. The customer does not always know what is the right thing.'

I was flabbergasted that she actually believed this drivel and then the subsequent supporting sewage she was spewing out. Without getting personal, though, I could understand why she was blind to this illogical approach. In exchange for sex, her French husband had given her an elevated status in her society, and since she was very much the junior partner financially she obviously was in no position to argue with him – a very nice situation for him.

Secondly, she had inherited, so to speak, part of a business she had no experience in, and so she didn't understand that great businesses are built on great service and not just on supply and demand. Normal businesses are designed around ordinary supply and demand, while great businesses are built through supplying extraordinary service once they have satisfied the demand.

Vasti was laughing in horror now, spluttering in her beer. We tried to provoke the bar lady by asking how she could equate our desire for one of the hotel's services with doing something danger-ous and stupid like taking a beer-glass into the pool. That was it. She broke off the dialogue, such as it was, packed her belongings, switched off the lights in the bar and walked away. It was a classic illustration of how to lose a customer so successfully that you never ever see him again.

Having said that, let me add that we met a gem of a guy named Serge, the owner of some newly built brick bungalows that formed one corner of the main road leading to where all the boats are parked, whom we never would have got to know if we had not left the Casa El Falafy after our clash with the bar lady.

Serge was super-friendly and we got along like a house on fire, even though he couldn't speak a word of English – he was as good at sign-language as anyone I've ever encountered in my travels. We regretted not finding him first, but when I take Vasti back to Diego Suarez one day we'll stay with him.

He helped us to negotiate a price with the Mafia-like clique of dhow owners who pressure all tourists to go on a day-trip to the Emerald Sea, setting out just after sunrise and returning at sunset. The final price was 40 000 ariary, and although I wasn't too keen at first, I changed my opinion 100 per cent.

Great snorkelling, beautiful seas, turtles, an awesome lunch and uncrowded, unspoilt beaches – all very special and romantic, and I got some great pictures to mark the occasion. One thing I remem-ber thinking as we sailed back through the afternoon wind chop was that I was probably going to have to paddle along exactly this route when I got there in a few days' time. The sea looked more manageable now than a few days earlier, but it would still not be something suitable for sissies!

Vasti and I flew together back to Antananarivo, from where she would go home and I would catch another flight to Sambava and then go by road to Antalaha for a reunion with my patient kayak. On the way to the airport Vasti got a last look at Malagasy culture when we passed a group of villagers ritually slaughtering a zebu.

This ritual is gory but interesting. The men of the village lead the animal out to the fields, usually to a spot near a tree which has some significance to them. There they say a few prayers of respect and then slaughter the animal by hand – it's considered an honour to be the one who does the throat-slitting.

The origin of the ritual is now lost in time, but probably has something to do with the Asian influence of the ancient traders who visited Madagascar. Or it might have derived from a remnant of Islamic culture. Whatever the case, things were beginning to make a lot more sense to me now as I delved ever deeper into Malagasy culture.

I couldn't help being sad as we flew back to Antananarivo, quite the opposite of how I had thought I would feel after five days of rejuvenation. Should Vasti actually come and visit me again further along? I would realise once again what I was missing and giving up to be here. Perhaps it would be counter-productive ...

Vasti got her flight out early next morning. There were tears in my eyes as I stood waving as she walked ever deeper into the international departures hall. When she was out of sight I dropped my arm and turned away.

OK, back to the sea, away from the reality of life, I told myself. *It's not that bad. Before I know it I'll be seeing her again.*

CHAPTER 18

A FIGHT WITH A FISH –
AND A FIGHT FOR LIFE

*A golden rule is to always retrieve more line than you have
lost; even if it's only a centimetre. That way the fish will
always get closer to you. I tried this and just kept that dazed
rocking motion in place as I was reeling in ...*

I was lucky enough to be able to see some rugby before I left Diego, this time the Currie Cup semi-finals – once again I had managed the timing perfectly. My home team's victory over the Lions got me more fired up than ever to put some big kilometres behind my kayak. I wanted to be going down the west coast and stopping off to see them win the finals in 14 days' time ... LIVE!

Getting back via Sambava to the Nanie Hotel was easy enough. My confidence in communicating with Malagasy people had gone up a notch as a result of the Diego interlude, and helped me to cut through the usual discrimination against whites. The big break-through resulted from being able now to speak some of the language, and also from having learnt what locals actually paid for things. I'm sure the new me was still paying too much for everything, but nowhere near as much as much as I had in those first few months!

What I could not bargain down, however, no matter what dodge I tried, was the $40 it cost me to have my kayak brought to the hotel from where it had been lying at the house of the 'president' of Tsara village. The only vehicle I could find that could accommodate the kayak was a Bedford construction truck. The Bedford was much bigger than necessary, but it was that or nothing – no favours here.

Next day I started working early and had soon repaired my Sony portable charger and bought some extra repair goodies for fixing the kayak, so it looked as if I could expect to be at sea within a day or two. Naturally it turned out not to be as simple and easy as that, because although I had picked up quite a lot of what was needed to find my way about I still had many more lessons to learn.

For example, business people on this side of the island were apparently totally locked in to the lunch-time siesta ritual: Open up shop at 9.00 am, close at noon, re-open only at 2.30 pm and then close again at 5.00 pm sharp.

I could see the reasoning behind people resting out of the blistering midday sun; for all I knew it might actually have added to their productivity, but it didn't suit my needs, since fibreglass and silicone don't set according to the ancient Malagasy siesta routine ... unless there was something else about it that I didn't know.

On the other hand, I had just about the entire expat community and then some helping me to get back in the water. One of them was Bernd, the town dentist, who was considered by the *Lonely Planet* guidebook to be the best dentist in the Indian Ocean. Ronda had had dealings with him, and Bernd's companion, Marie Hélène, who ran the region's tourism department, had worked extensively with Matthew, the local French national service guy.

Bernd and Marie were wonderful. They assisted with the repair equipment, gave me references for people and places in Sambava and even loaned me their personal bakkie and driver to take me to the exact spot where my kayak had been damaged. Bernd had often travelled up the north coast for the angling, and waxed lyrical about the huge kingfish he had caught there in his younger days, so now I was keen to land a monster of my own.

One negative thing about my stay in Antalaha was that my Leatherman multi-tool was stolen by one of a group of guides who were walking with their tourist clients around parts of Madagascar. They were camping on the concrete outside my bungalow, and when I found them scratching around in my kayak and confronted them, they responded by saying that they had just been inquisitive about my amazing sea vessel and had wanted to learn something about it.

They had learnt something, all right, opening hatches and storage spaces I sometimes didn't look into for days and seeing bits of pocket-sized portable property like the Leatherman. I didn't pursue the matter, because I couldn't waste time on what was clearly a lost cause, and knew that the Leatherman wouldn't make its first public appearance till I was well out of the way.

Bernd helped me find a Leatherman copy at one of the stores in town that I knew would last at least till I reached Nosy Bé on the west coast, and that was good enough for me. I've managed to do some amazing things with a multi-tool, and there is no doubt about the fact that it would be the first item I would reach for in a tight spot.

When I clambered back on to my kayak and left the land behind for the first time in two weeks it didn't really matter that the weather was not ideal and the sea so choppy that it was difficult to keep the kayak's nose pointing in the right direction. I had been in worse situations on this trip, and I needed to put foot down – the Currie Cup final was nearly upon us, and Seamus's arrival date in Nosy Bé was now non-negotiable.

I had a successor to poor Thomas permanently trailing behind me as I battled with the waves. This Rapala was a popular model, extra large, called a Red Head, that my Number One fishing buddy from Somerset West, Mark Stuart, had sent to me with Vasti, and I wasted no time in employing 'Red' to find a big one. And he did!

I was paddling pleasantly along when suddenly my fishing rod was yanked back with brute force instead of the usual powerful tugs I had experienced before. The reel, a small Shimano 10 000 coffee-grinder, had a maximum-strength line of a new braided type that I had put on just the night before in place of the nylon line – it was stronger and thinner than nylon, so it allowed you to catch bigger fish and also keep more of it on your reel in the same space.

This last was just as well, because the fish was screaming away from me at a million miles an hour – not down, just away, and the line was flying off the reel much too quickly. I put my legs over the sides for stability and began to tighten the drag gear to create more resistance for the fish to fight against.

But the fish took no notice. I tightened the line even more. Still no reaction, and the line continued to feed out too quickly. Soon, I worried, all of it would be off the reel and it would snap. I tightened a bit more, nearly to the maximum, while the waves bashed me about with increasing violence, or so it felt.

Now I noticed that the line was down to its last 30 or 40 metres – I could actually see the metal part of the reel's base – and it was still running out. It would be finished any time now. But I had run out of options, so I locked the drag gear and tried to win line and reel in, win line and reel in, win line and reel in, in the tried and true fashion. The line didn't snap, so I kept on forcing my pulling action and then reeling in the few metres of line I gained each time.

Soon I had the fish perceptibly closer to me and 40 metres of line back on the reel. Time to loosen the drag now, just in case, although this might mean that the fish would get its second wind … which it did, so that in no time the line was run out nearly to the end again, and I was applying the tradition win-line-and-reel-in technique once more. Get the fish tired enough, and soon he'll just about jump into your lap! That was the way to go, but to make it work you have to keep at it without tiring yourself out.

The problem with this scenario was that the Shimano rig was too light for this fish, which by the strength of him was obviously a large one. After 30 minutes of struggle, during which time I still had very little line on the reel, I concluded that there was no 'maybe' about it. There was a big boy on the other end of the line, and I was getting freaked out by the power with which he was running. I wondered if the fish even knew I was connected at the other end.

But I was determined to land him, so the name of the game was to concentrate on getting through the middle bit and deal with the landing when it happened. I knew that most fish were lost either after the original strike or during a failed landing – that's why fisherman have so many fishing stories that they can't prove because they can't produce the guest of honour, so to speak.

After a few more minutes of disjointed struggle I began to search for better rhythm – obviously my enthusiasm and determination just weren't going to be enough; my lower back was beginning to hurt and my left bicep was going lame. The bottom line was that physically I was no match for this energetic sea-beast.

In addition the waves were becoming more and more choppy, filling the kayak's cockpit to the brim, so that at times I had to stop fighting the fish and try to scoop out as much water as I could before the line ran out once more and wiped out my paltry gains.

One good thing was that the additional waterproofing I had done around the foot area of the kayak was definitely adequate, but what I couldn't prevent was the water seeping in through the rubber guides that threaded the steering-wires to the rudder. This meant that after about an hour of fighting the fish, the kayak had become very unstable because of all the water sloshing to and fro inside.

But I didn't care: I was going to bring this fish to the surface, no matter what. Part of my crazy determination stemmed from sheer inquisitiveness about what the hell I had hooked, part of it was the simple cave-man instinct to bring home the bacon (or the seafood, in this case).

The hour mark was something of a watershed. I had never had a fish on the line this long, and crossing it was a first for me. Can you believe that a fish would fight that long? But that's what it was doing, and in between being soaked I kept the tension on the line – lines usually snap when there is a drastic increase in force on them, rather than a heavy constant drag.

So the line was still holding, but after 15 minutes into the second hour I was beginning to wonder whether I would be able to last the course. I was feeling distinctly the worse for wear, and I couldn't help wondering whether my equipment, which had stood up so well, was going to hold up much longer.

The small Shimano reel was not meant for catching huge fish, and the line's breaking strain was only 16 kg. That meant there should really have been more than 250 metres of line – more like 400. And then, of course, there was the question of how I was going to land a monster fish in my current situation. I had deferred the problem till the time came, of course, but, all going well, that time would arrive fairly soon.

The hour-and-a-half notch came and went, and by now I was gauging my progress solely by how much line I was able to keep on the reel. And lately I had been making some progress. In the last few minutes I had got more than half my line back on the reel, as opposed to a mere 20 metres or so earlier.

It was as if the fish knew this, because just before we reached the two-hour mark it set off on another run in the opposite direction. At this stage there was no way that I could use any arm strength in retrieving the fish, so I had to rely on digging the butt of the rod into my left groin area and exerting leverage with the power of my entire body. To be honest, I was finished. Not that I stopped fighting the fish, but my fighting was more ceremonial than anything else. I couldn't stop this train.

A golden rule is to always retrieve more line than you have lost; even if it's only a centimetre. That way the fish will always get closer to you. I tried this and just kept that dazed rocking motion in place as I was reeling in; and then would let the fish run again. When was it going to get tired?

After two hours and 15 minutes I had zero left in my tank, and I knew that I needed to go for broke now; I was just too exhausted for anything less than drastic action. So I tightened the drag to what it had been at the beginning and set a personal target: I would give myself 15 tries at bringing it in, and if I couldn't do it, that would be it. I could see that I was gaining significantly on the fish now, but the waves had become uncontrollable and the kayak's cockpit stayed full of water, no matter how hard I bailed.

At about the ninth attempt I saw a flash of bright silver in the green depths from the direction in which the line was pointing. I was closing in at last! Now my systems were on 'go'. I was pretty sure now that what I had hooked was a kingfish, and that it was circling more than running. That was a good sign – it meant that the fish was tired.

The problem was that the fish recovered twice as fast as I did, so that whenever I took a one-minute breather he got two minutes' worth of rest out of it, and then he was off again. *I've got to go for the kill and finish the fight!* I told myself, so I kept on reeling him in, hoping the line wouldn't snap, and above all that I could hold out.

Two hours and 25 minutes later the fish was no more than five metres below the kayak. Then, when it made a turn alongside me to my left and I started hauling it in, I got a shock, because now for the first time I could see what I had been battling. The fish was well over a metre long, with a mouth the size of a dinner plate which had swallowed the Rapala lure whole. Incredible!

Well, now it was third-phase time. I started trying to haul the fish on to my lap. It was a struggle because it was so heavy, but fortunately the slippery slime on its skin helped to ease it inboard. Well, perhaps 'inboard' is not the right word, since the kayak was now almost totally submerged. This was distinctly not good!

I stabbed the fish in the head to make sure it was dead, took some pictures with great difficulty and then tried to work out what to do next. At this stage I was about 7km from land and didn't know where I was, the kayak was turning into a submarine, the fish was too big and heavy to haul completely on to the kayak even if it had not been mainly under water (as I discovered after a 20-minute struggle involving several involuntary dunkings) and the waves were still beating me, while the wind had now picked up dramatically as well. What now, Manser?

To make matters just that little worse, all the blood and commotion had now begun attracting not only small fish but also bad characters like barracuda. Sooner or later the strong-arm boys – sharks, in other words – would also start paying a call. When that happened I was finished for good and all. This is not to mention that if the half-submerged kayak sank it wouldn't matter about the sharks.

Yet I was desperately keen not to lose the fish. It was magnificent – more than 30 kg, I was sure, enough to feed a village. And it would be a sin to waste it by letting it slide back into the water. I wasn't in this fish-hunting just for the sake of killing a majestic animal. There had to be a purpose to it all.

On the other hand, loading an extra 30 kg or so on to my kayak would simply make it sink more quickly, so I decided to tie the line around my left ankle, then tow it behind me as I tackled the immediate task of finding solid ground before we – myself, the kayak and the kingfish – all ended up in Davey Jones's locker.

This I did by the simple expedient of paddling in the same direction as the swell that was moving over and past me. It worked, sort of. I was moving – slowly, but surely – or at least I thought I was. I couldn't actually see any progress amid the foam and splash and general watery chaos, but kept on going with the swells and hoped for the best.

The problem was that although the kayak stayed afloat it was im-possible to paddle, and I kept falling off and swallowing water with every wave that came over my head. Eventually I was numb, both mentally and physically, but I just kept going with the small reserve of flagging strength I had left, because that was all that stood be-tween me and death.

On and on and on ... it was only when I felt a wave actually break over me that I realised I was getting nearer to land. At this stage I should have begin worrying about how to actually get ashore with-out suffering damage from the coastal reefs, but I didn't give it a thought; I was so far gone that when I saw a whale breaching near-by while I was mounting my kayak for the umpteenth time I just kept on paddling. I just didn't have the time or the energy left to enjoy the sight.

My throat was burning now as the salt ate away at my oesophagus, and my stomach was swollen with the water I involuntarily swallowed each time I was pitched into the sea. The world had turned into a blur of colours as I huddled on the kayak, clinging to my paddle with all my remaining strength, smashed by wave after relentless wave and expecting to hit solid rock at any moment. I felt strangely unmoved by it all – I was simply past either fear or caring.

Then the beach seemed to be almost within reach. But it wasn't, and to get ashore I needed to be washed closer to the shallows by one or two waves so that I could push myself to safety. I let go of the paddle, which was something I had never done before, though it was attached to the kayak as always. But right now neither the kayak nor the paddle was important: they could make it to land on their own.

But I was not free of all my encumbrances. The fish was still anchored to me by the line around my left ankle. The loop was loosish to begin with, but I felt it tighten after the next wave tossed me into the sea, leaving me on one side of the kayak and the fish on the other. I tried feebly to free myself, but my fumbling attempts only made the constriction worse.

The foaming seas had pushed me away from the kayak, so I tried to swim nearer – to either the fish or the kayak, it didn't matter, as long as I could free myself and get to land. My efforts were as feeble as my attempts to free myself; starved of oxygen, I lost my sense of timing and more often than not sucked in foam and water instead of air.

My mind stayed clear, though, and I remember thinking wildly: *It can't be the end now, I'm nearly on shore, and for God's sake, I've been in worse seas than this!*

Then I found myself on my hands and knees in the shallows, vomiting so violently it felt as though the deepest parts of my bowels were coming out with the frothy vomit pouring from my nose, gasping for air in between each fit of dreadful nausea.

At one point I fell on to my elbows as some bigger waves washed me off balance, but I was so far gone that I didn't even try to raise myself again and just lay where I'd gone down, vomiting with my face half sunk into the grainy sand. I don't know how long I stayed like that – later it seemed to have been never-ending – but eventually the vomiting ended, and my senses started coming back.

'My kayak!' I blurted, my voice hoarse with salt, and rolled over into a sitting position to look for it. At first it seemed to have vanished, but then I saw the bright green banana was being rolled around in some breakers about 100 metres away. I got up and managed to stumble over to it, dragged it a few metres up the beach and then flopped down next to it.

My mind was pretty much a blank just then, but when I lifted my head after a while to cast my eyes over the kayak I was alert enough to notice something was wrong – not that anything was obviously damaged, but something was missing. I tried to remember what that something was, but my brain was turning over as slowly as a car-engine with an almost flat battery. Then a shaft of intelligence finally broke through the fog. *My video camera! Where was my video camera?*

Suddenly I summoned up enough energy to sit up and scan the surf. And there it was, not 20 metres away, bobbing happily up and down in its waterproof housing in a patch of still water. I summoned up another few watts of energy and waded into the breakers to rescue it and its precious digital memory. Crazy! Here the sea had almost killed me, and I was heading right into it again!

I retrieved the camera and went back to the kayak, where I propped myself up on my life-jacket so I could watch for any dangerous waves, and there I stayed for about a hour, still vomiting from time to time. I was lucky to be alive, my kayak still to be floating.

What was I thinking about as I huddled there, you might ask. The answer is: nothing. I didn't indulge in any philosophical debates that might seem appropriate at a time like this. I knew I was lucky to be alive and still to have my kayak. But this was not the place and time to contemplate my navel. An intellectual debate was not going to make my situation or my future achievements any easier. This I understood very clearly.

Having got my mind functioning again, I remembered the fish and began to track it by following the line that stretched out seawards from the rod, which was still attached to the kayak. Then I staggered to the water's edge and started pulling in the line hand over hand. It was very light, and when the last bit came out of the water I realised why: the kingfish was gone and the steel trace had been bitten right through by something ... and that something could only have been a shark, and not a little one either.

I began to feel better in a battered sort of way. I wasn't sorry for myself. After all, I had much to be thankful for. I had survived not only a drowning but a hungry shark as well; I was still in one piece and so was the kayak, my baggage was intact and my video camera was alive and well, and full of great pictures. And my spirit was unbroken, even though it was bent a little out of shape along with my body just then.

So I dragged the kayak further up the beach, found myself a safe, dry place to sleep and got ready for bed. I could see some movement on a little peninsula south of where I'd been washed ashore, but I didn't make a fire because I didn't want any company just then; I didn't even want anything to eat. Instead I drank some energy juice for dinner to give my abused innards time to recover from all the salt water, and fell asleep just after sunset. What a day it had been!

CHAPTER 19

MY RETURN FROM THE DEAD –
AND MY FIRST CYCLONE

*What followed was some vicious bloodletting that would
probably have shocked and disgusted the average European,
not to mention myself four or five years earlier, but experience
had taught me to see it for what it really was ...*

As usual I woke at sunrise and was soon was packed and ready to
take to the water again. At this stage three people came wandering
towards me along the shoreline from where I had seen movement
the previous evening. When they got nearer I saw they were obviously a family group – husband, wife and teenaged son – and were
looking me up and down with a mixture of caution and eagerness.
I could just about hear what they were thinking: 'What is this white
man doing here?'

When they came up to me I greeted them but didn't spend any
time socialising, because I was focused on heading into the new
day, with whatever challenges it might bring. But this didn't put
them off, and the son and his mother helped me to drag the kayak down to the water, with the father – who couldn't help because

he had a crippled leg – giving instructions and vocal support.

I had been learning more Malagasy every day, and by now I had enough of a grip on it to ask for detailed advice about the best way to a safe launching or landing place: '*Aiza tsara lanana?*' which if directly translated means 'what is the best route?' The father seemed to get the idea very clearly and pointed to a fairly calm-looking gully with incoming waves breaking all around but never inside it.

That seemed a reasonable enough option, but I decided to follow my own inclination and, to his horror, picked another spot about 200 metres to the north of it which seemed to be much calmer. But he didn't take offence, and the family helped me to drag the kayak 200 metres up the beach so that I was opposite my chosen spot.

On reflection it was probably rash to ignore the advice of a local who knew the area, but the place the father had pointed out just didn't feel quite right, and as it happened I got out into the open sea without trouble. That done, I got down to some serious pad-dling, because I knew by now what I could probably expect.

The sea around that part of the coast has a gentle morning time where she is probably still curling her toes in for a few more min-utes' snoozing. Then, when she wakes up, she gets grumpy and agi-tated. So I tried to do as many kilometres as I could while she was still curling her toes in, because paddling becomes very unpleasant when she is agitated: you feel as if you're hardly moving, you get thrown off by waves that sneak up on you and take you by surprise, and on top of all that I knew the kayak would begin to fill with wa-ter coming in through those cable-guide holes.

In between the paddling I took out my battered friend Thomas the Rapala lure, then put him away again and trailed out a smaller version of the ill-fated Red Head I had lost, because I was scared of hooking something as big and strong as the kingfish that had nearly done me in. But I had no luck, and that settled it: today's destination would be Sambava, come hell or high water (well, the 'high water' part was there already) because I desperately needed to get a large meal inside me.

But about 7 km this side of Sambava I made a judgement call and decided I had no option except to go ashore immediately, although I was feeling fit and strong. Thanks to the stormy sea and constant waves breaking over me the kayak was filling with water faster than I could bail it out, and if I wanted to avoid a repeat of the previous day's troubles I had get out of the water.

I kept the kayak facing in the direction in which the swell was moving, straddling it at times for stability. Where and how I was actually going to land was something I would have to decide when the moment came, and I was distinctly nervous, because the swell had now picked up to eight feet-plus, and I could hear and see it smashing its way up the beach over rocks jutting out above the water.

But as I say, I really had no choice except to go straight for the shore. I would have to try and ride in on the first big wave I could catch, and then it was a case of going for broke in more than one sense of the word, because surfing such big waves with a kayak is next to impossible, you just get flung around and sooner or later tipped off.

What I wanted to do was something similar to yesterday, to be washed ashore like any other piece of oceanic jetsam, with my kayak following me in the same way. This time I was in better shape to prepare for this sort of rough landing, so I cinched my life jacket firmly around my waist to make sure that my head stayed above water most of the time, and let go of the kayak earlier.

To my relief it worked. The sea spewed me out, I managed after some effort to stop myself from being sucked out again by the vicious rip and prevent the kayak from being damaged on the rocks, and in due course we were both above the waterline.

Coming in, I had the feeling that the sea had not been as rough as the previous day, but as I stood there, soaked and spluttering, looking back at what I had got through, I realised there was no way I was going to be able to get back out into the open sea from that spot after I had baled out and dried the kayak.

True, there were lulls when the sea went flat, and it was tempting to decide that it would be easy to make it out at such moments. The problem, though, was that the risk would be too great. The kayak was irreplaceable, and I simply could not guarantee that such a lull would last long enough for my purposes. What it amounted to was that I didn't have any choices: I would have one chance only, and I would have to use it wisely.

I did some creative thinking and realised that the first priority was to get away from the rocks that lay between this landing place and the sea. This meant setting off northwards, dragging the kayak in the shore-break till (I hoped) I came across a place near a reasonably safe gap to the open sea.

Dragging the kayak was a long, slow, laborious business because in reality it was too heavy for one man, and almost impossible to control while dragging it in the firm shore break. It just wasn't working. After a while I gave up. I would have to try something else.

I pulled the kayak up to the highest stretch of beach, planted the paddle in the sand next to it as a beacon and then set off on foot further north to find help. Before long I found some signs of human life, in the shape of four tattered women who seemed to be scouring the beach for mussels and crabs. Three of them were totally petrified at the sight of me, while the fourth was made of sterner stuff and tried hard to communicate. But somehow we just couldn't manage it, so they went on their way and I went on mine.

About two kilometres farther I came on a small bay that looked as if it might give me the access I was looking for. I was pretty sure that some sort of village or camp had to be close by, so I wandered inland and within a few metres started seeing footprints in the sand.

I followed the footprints, and sure enough, a little deeper inland I found a few huts, one with three men sleeping inside it. I made my presence known as gently as possible. They were pretty startled to see me, but once they got over it tried their best to help me, their first good deed being to climb a coconut tree to get me some liquid replenishment.

It was now that I noticed how thick this coastline was with coconut trees, almost like a plantation – something I quite likely wouldn't have noticed from sea-level. Judging by the piles of coconuts inside the huts I concluded that these guys were coconut harvesters by profession.

I explained to them that I needed help to get my 'boat' (I knew that trying to explain what a kayak was would not be worth the effort) a kilometre or two down the beach to this safe launch area in their cove. They agreed to lend a hand and soon we were on our way back with my kayak.

Next morning we duly launched the kayak, and although it wasn't easy it worked quite well. Once in the water I wasted absolutely no time in getting going. It was clear that the sea was gearing up for something big, worse than what I had experienced in the last couple of days, and that meant I had to get to Sambava as soon as possible.

I got to Sambava Bay without encountering any problems, although I was tired from the pace I had set myself. The bay is tucked in behind a blunt point of land and runs a few kilometres along a beach of brownish sand till it curls around to a more northerly direction. I hugged the coastline, dodging the small two-foot surf; I wasn't looking for any adventure – all I wanted now was rest and, yes, some spaghetti bolognaise if that was possible.

A little crowd of children saw me and started following me, growing larger all the time, so that when I eventually landed I had no trouble in arranging a posse of kayak-carriers from among the older kids. They took me to the nearest hotel, the Hotel Cocotier, about a kilometre inland from where I'd landed. To my regret the hotel didn't have spaghetti bolognaise on the menu, but I satisfied my burning hunger quite adequately with meaty brochettes and another Malagasy favourite, noodle soup.

Well-fed and looking forward to a rest, I was feeling pretty good. If I could retain my dogged determination I would round Madagascar's most northerly point in just over 10 days. The big question was whether I would be able to maintain the pace. I didn't have much doubt about my strength and determination, but the weather was turning bad, very bad indeed.

The cyclone season was approaching, and the first of the year's crop, a sizeable one nicknamed 'Asma', was hovering off the coast of eastern Madagascar. Just my luck that Asma was jumping the gun, since cyclones in that part of the world are usually expected between late December and late February. Oh, well ...

On the other hand, I was safely snuggled down in a reasonable-sized town with all the mod cons. The rain that had started falling was only a sort of aperitif to warn that Asma would hit the coast in a day or two, so I was told by Octave, the hotel's owner, who added: 'You cannot be in the sea at this time, there is little people up this coast, no one can help you.'

I bowed to his superior local knowledge and decided to stay put and use the down-time wisely by resting, doing some sightseeing and carrying out more repairs on my kayak.

My first sightseeing foray fell on a Sunday and wasn't exactly exciting. In Sambava almost nothing moved because the Malagasy regard Sunday as one long siesta. But then, when I was looking for a place to brunch, I heard about the latest open-air bare-knuckle fighting contest in the suburb of Maringi.

I decided that this was something I had to see and went off to buy a ticket, which for some reason had the word 'participant' emblazoned on it. I rolled up at the appointed time for what turned out to be a pure testosterone-driven gladiatorial spectacle.

When I arrived at the ring – an open patch of dirt with a foot-high wooden fence around it, a few metres off the main road – I discovered what that word 'participant' entailed: I was expected to whip off my shirt and start circling the ring together with a whirlpool of similarly dressed (undressed?) other bodies, tensing my muscles and either glaring around like a lunatic or smiling confidently *à la* Prince Naseem Hamed.

The aim of these laps, I found, was either to challenge someone else to a fight or be challenged myself. Any intimidatory tactic was permitted, the most common one being an extended arm with a tightly clenched fist with the middle knuckle sticking out and a general air (so I gathered) of 'I'm going to smack you with this, buddy, so come try me out.'

Each of these guys, I noticed, had a unique part-walk-part-dance that took them either clockwise or anti-clockwise, glancing around to see who was in the mix, so to speak. It was a weird business, but I gathered Marangi fighting was a long-established Malagasy institution – supposedly derived from the Malagasy people's long-distant Polynesian origins.

The good news is that nobody actually challenged me – whether out of courtesy to a lone stranger or the fact that I was very considerably taller and heftier than the average Malagasy – but I actually featured on the evening TV news that night, since the event was covered by both the national and local channels.

What followed was some vicious bloodletting that would probably have shocked and disgusted the average European, not to mention myself four or five years earlier, but experience had taught me to see it for what it really was: an opportunity for young men, and sometimes older men struggling with a mid-life crisis, to dampen their egos and rivalries fairly and, all things considered, reasonably humanely. I reflected that Western countries had their own ways of settling their issues, mostly not physically but sometimes surely far more brutally.

The Maringi fights were not the only things that set Antalaha and Sambava apart from the rest of western Madagascar. I was now in the middle of the vanilla-growing area, which had brought prosperity, for a few people anyway, to judge by the large mansions along the coast. The economic importance of the industry had also provided government-built infrastructure like roads and electricity that I hadn't seen much evidence of in Madagascar so far.

Cyclone Asma arrived in no uncertain terms. For the next four days winds shook my hotel bungalow while the rain pelted down incessantly and flooded the streets. I got plenty of rest, as I had planned, but finishing the repairs to the kayak was simply impossible. This was frustrating, because I wanted them to be the last important ones before I hit the dreaded Cap d'Ambre, the actual northerly point of Madagascar.

There was also the matter of the Currie Cup rugby championship finals, which were due the following Saturday, and although no satellite channel advertised a screening I still hoped that somehow I would be able to satisfy my craving, as I had done many times before.

Sambava had a most unexpected surprise in store for me, as I discovered when I was walking back to the hotel after an early dinner on the Friday evening and a large man burst out of a street-side eating and drinking place, shouting in heavily French-accented English: 'Ryan, Ryan. Oh, my God, you are not a dead, you are not a dead!'

For a second I stood there, stunned and then I remembered him. He was a good man named François, a close friend of Mr Momo's, whom I had met at the Hotel Nanie.

'My God, we have all been very sad these last three days!' François cried. 'I must pinch you. Is it you? Is it real?'

'What do you mean, François?' I asked when I had overcome my astonishment at this emotional greeting. 'Of course I'm fine.'

'The radio station in Antalaha and Sambava reported that some locals had spotted a yellow kayak on a deserted beach, but minus the paddler,' François explained, whipping out his cell phone. 'We knew it was your kayak, for sure! I tell Momo that I come to look for help in Sambava. Maybe my friend has a boat.'

He dialled away at the cell phone. 'I must call Momo and the others in Antalaha,' he said happily, 'they are very sad. This news will make them happy. The sea at the moment is taking many boats and lives. It is dangerous for you.'

When François got through he gave Momo chapter and verse on the good state of my health, although he himself was still so amazed that he had to break off and pinch me again, which he then told Momo he had done as proof that he was telling the truth.

It was a good illustration of the workings of the 'bush telegraph', the rural African's equivalent of the BBC and CNN. The bush telegraph is often quick off the mark, but the message sometimes gets a little distorted, as in this case. On the other hand, in all fairness the more sophisticated news media also get their facts wrong at times.

We celebrated my continuing residence in the land of the living with a few rums and agreed to meet for breakfast in the morning, and François said he would check out the larger hotels to see what rugby offerings would be on their satellite channels next day – rugby, of course, having a large following in France.

Breakfast was good next morning, but what was even better was our discovery that the French satellite service would be screening a delayed telecast. As far as I was concerned, that made all the other news, even the items confirming that I was still alive, pale into insignificance.

At the appointed time I sat with an equally enthusiastic hotel manager peering over my shoulder and watched the Sharks win the final; what a magical way to wrap up an eventful week ... which might have been even more eventful, since Asma was followed by another cyclone – but fortunately for me this one had done its worst well out of range. So I was ready to go.

CHAPTER 20

ALIVE AND KICKING

*She asked me for my pocket knife, which I handed
unsuspectingly to her, and without telling me what she was
going to do, she sliced open the swelling. I was so surprised that
I just sat there and let her hack into my toe, half horrified at
this assault on my body – and with my own knife! – and half
relieved, because it was clear that she had done something like
this many times before.*

I headed northwards through very dirty water, so different from
the crystal-clear stuff I'd paddled in thus far. The kilometres were
flying by, and I had time to mull over something that was both-
ering me: the consequences and implications of really going missing. What could I expect from those who looked forward to hearing
from me every week or so? What did I expect of two people who
were very close to me, Vasti and Seamus?

This sort of cogitation can only take place in the sort of solitude
and silence I had now, free from my earlier distractions, and I found
myself constantly conjuring up disturbing images of what would
happen if I were separated from my kayak and drowned.

For the next few nights I battled to get to sleep in spite of being tired from each day's paddling because of one picture that refused to leave my mind: of my lifeless body washed over the rocks and cast torn and swollen onto a beach, people standing in the background, afraid to come nearer. Normally I'm good at forcing a particular line of thought into or out of my head, but this time I was powerless. Night after night the same image came to haunt my dreams and shatter my rest.

Because the coast was very thinly populated and 'unguidebooked' along this stretch, I had to land wherever I thought I'd found a likely place ... and definitely before the sun set. My recurring thoughts of a lonely death had made me reluctant to undertake any tricky landings: let me rather go in while there was enough light for me to see what mistakes I was making!

One surprise sleepover was inside a calm lagoon I had got a glimpse of from way out at sea. Each time a swell lifted me I could see a rough, narrow channel joining it to the sea; it seemed worth the risk, and as before I followed my paddling friend Daantjie's advice: 'Be patient, but when you go, you GO!'

It worked fine, and a few minutes later I was in the lagoon; I was certainly getting better at following this advice and executing it with more precision. The lagoon was stunning, exactly like one of the idyllic scenes I had imagined myself in – isolated, unspoilt and, above all, wonderfully tranquil. Truly the calm after the storm, I thought as I feasted my eyes on my surroundings.

The only other people there were a small family of crab fishermen, and I shared their dinner of fresh fish and fresh crab – the sort of meal that would have disembowelled my wallet back home! Later that night I enjoyed a rough-and-ready cabaret as well. I found I had pitched my tent smack in the middle of the hunting ground, so that crabs the size of saucers were crawling almost over it with the torch-wielding fishermen in hot pursuit. Talk about having the action literally on your doorstep!

I was almost in sight now of the harbour town of Vohémar (Iharana), at which I had paused so briefly on my horse-box journey to Diego, and the temporary sanctuary its harbour promised. When I said goodbye to my hospitable crab fishermen next morning I knew I was in for a long paddle, but a do-able one.

And so it was. Lots of kilometres passed under my bow during the morning calm, followed by a struggle through an afternoon of washing-machine action, so that I was pleased when I was able to make a 90-degree turn into the harbour and approach the first set of bungalows I could find. As always, my quest had two main goals: a cheap room and a large plate of spaghetti bolognaise, and I got both.

Vohémar was full of characters. One was a French expat called Pierre who had lived in retirement in Madagascar for the past 10 years and insisted I join him on a gold-mining adventure, nineteenth-century style.

We drove for two hours into the mountains north of the town and eventually ended up on top of one range – I wouldn't have been surprised to discover that ours was the first 4x4 ever to get to that spot, which gives you an idea of the type of terrain we'd covered. After that we hiked along a ridge for another hour to reach a truly archaic mining community.

People were digging out chunks of rock which others then crushed; yet others were panning for smaller nuggets. Gold dust was being gathered and melted in small pans over open fires. I panned a bit myself without making a strike, but Pierre got two tiny specks of gold which, he said, would weigh about a gram combined.

I came away from that remote village with a great feeling of warmth towards those hard-working miners, very special people who reminded me of my own ancestors who had given up everything to come and find gold of some kind in South Africa's backveld. They returned the feeling, and clearly loved being my hosts in their little mountain world. I couldn't help wondering how long it would be before the government came along and took it all away from them ...

The day before I left Vohémar I found myself involved in applying some first aid to one of the locals, the owner of a small hotel, who came adrift from his scrambler motorbike while he was churning down the main drag at some speed. Part of the way along he slowed slightly and started to turn right, at which moment a dim-witted cyclist cut over in front of him. The hotel man swerved and fell hard with the scrambler on top of him.

I ran over to get the big scrambler off him and make sure he wasn't badly hurt. With some effort I managed to lift the bike, but that was the good news – with it out of the way, I saw with horror that his right ankle was tucked in under his calf because the bones had snapped like twigs, so that when I had wrestled him into a sitting position the ankle just wobbled loosely back and forth.

I could tell he was badly shocked, so I tried to calm him down by saying that it wasn't all that serious, although I knew it was. As it turned out, this wasn't the smartest thing I could have said, because in his shocked state he insisted on trying to stand up so that he could ride home.

Fortunately friends of his drove past at that moment and stopped to help. Now it was my turn to be insistent. He had to be taken to a doctor right away, I said over and over. First aid is just that – immediate elementary measures before expert help is given, because action early on in any trauma can prevent many later complications. After some hesitation they agreed and took him away.

I went on my way, happy at the thought that I had been able to help a fellow human being in his hour of need, not realising that before I left the very next day I would be the recipient of some first aid myself, but of an entirely more gory type.

Just before my departure I found that I had unwittingly picked up some passengers. Overloading the kayak was always a matter of such concern with me that I would convene an internal tribunal to consider the weighty matter (pardon the pun) of whether I could add even one mango to the load. But these passengers were very small, although in the sheer nastiness stakes they beat a lot of competitors hollow.

I had discovered their presence for the first time when a little pinhead-size scratch on the tip of my left big toe that I had laughed off as a minor irritation way back on the island of St Marie ripened into what looked like a boil that was almost ready to pop. I decided to let it ripen a bit more before doing anything.

Then, as I was dragging my kayak towards the water, I stopped and scratched away at the toe. The hotel receptionist, who had just come on duty, happened to see this, immediately diagnosed my 'boil' as the symptom of a familiar Malagasy ailment and wasted no time getting down to the beach.

There she promptly applied a simple but drastic treatment. She asked me for my pocket knife, which I handed unsuspectingly to her, and without telling me what she was going to do, she sliced open the swelling. I was so surprised that I just sat there and let her hack into my toe, half horrified at this assault on my body – and with my own knife! – and half relieved, because it was clear that she had done something like this many times before.

Which she had, and when she had done with the cutting she reached into the wound and deftly hauled out a little sac full of yellow snot-looking matter and a multitude of insect eggs. I must say I was impressed – not only at her expertise (where else in the world would a hotel receptionist also be an experienced bush doctor?) but also because her hotel, unlike many others I had encountered, had obviously successfully instilled the 'going the extra mile' mentality in its staff.

Some further research and the inevitable gory stories revealed that what I had unwittingly acquired was an infestation of the *tumby*, or mango fly, which lays its eggs in fine dry sand. There the larvae hatch and then lie in wait for a suitable host they can live on and feed off. Two weeks later they pop out to pupate and lay eggs of their own, which in due course hatch and find new victims for themselves.

How I had become a combined residence and meal-ticket for mango flies I have no idea, since the usual unknowing participants in the mango fly's career are dogs and other small animals, not innocent seafarers like myself. But I decided I had come off lightly after hearing some gruesome tales about people developing gangrene in limbs that had been overrun by the fly's unpleasant offspring. My before and after pics of the toe are stomach-turning enough!

Besides, I had other things to occupy my mind, one of which was how to get out to sea again. To the north Vohémar was shielded by a long, treacherous reef which was not to be trifled with, to judge by a large wrecked ship near its southern end. So I decided to stay in the lagoon inside the reef, which was very shallow in places, for as far as possible ... and learnt another new lesson – don't believe all the advice you're offered; the corollary being: be clear about the advice offered!

I picked up these new lessons while asking fishermen about the best way to go in the lagoon. Finding out exactly what they meant wasn't easy, because the Malagasy have a special but infuriating way of pointing things out.

Where I come from, your hand-gestures usually mirror the shape of the land or roads you're directing someone to. But ask a Malagasy fishermen for directions and you just about need a sign-language interpreter to get his drift.

He'll wave his hand in front of him as if backhanding a fly on the inside of his car's windscreen, at the same time casually turning his head in the direction of whatever he is directing you to. This is all very well in normal circumstances, when a mistake is irritating but no more, but when you are dealing with life-and-death matters, as I assuredly was, it is something else altogether.

I got a good display of this malign Malagasy habit when I consulted two fishermen. The younger of the two responded right away by saying that yes, the bit ahead was dangerous, and I must go back a bit and circle the dangerous area before striking on. His older companion interrupted at this stage to say no, it wasn't a dangerous area, it was actually a *tsara lalana* (good way).

Understandably confused, I tried to make sense of this widely divergent advice, at which the younger guy changed his tune and assured me that I must go ahead, it would be just what I needed. By this stage I was in no state to argue, and chose to believe him. I paddled on, and when I reached the end of the reef I realised that I was caught inside by the waves. Some expert advice!

All I could do was turn around and spend an hour paddling back till I found a risky-looking gap, which I successfully negotiated and got down to paddling. I remembered the warmth I had felt towards the miners a few days earlier, but I wasn't angry with the fishermen, as I might well have been, just very disappointed as I tried to work out why they would do something like that to me.

But all that was behind me now. I had things to do and places to go. There were still 150-odd kilometres separating me from Diego Suarez, for which I budgeted four days but was confident of doing in three. But then I needed to do over 50 km on this first day. No strategy, mine or anyone else's, dares to leave too much to do at the end, because you can never be sure about what might go wrong or affect your progress.

As I stroked my way northwards I had time to think back over what had happened so far, and to notice how the e-mails and SMSs I had been receiving from well-wishers had changed. I knew that when I had set off for Madagascar many must have thought that the circumnavigation would be considerably easier than my Africa trip. After all, it was only 5 000 km this time. I wouldn't have to cross any disputed borders or confront whacked-out teenage soldiers, or travel through countries recovering from war. All I had to do was knock off the prescribed distance each day by getting out there and paddling.

Personally I had not been under any illusions of this kind. I had realised that the Madagascar coastline was very unsafe, which was why it was not the first-choice destination for kayakers. But that was part of the reason why I had tackled it. I wanted to do a world first, something no one had ever done before.

I had not realised just how tough it would be, though. At times so far it had been much more physically demanding than Africa. Think about it: when you're on a bike and you're confronted with a downhill, you can just rest your feet on the pedals and let gravity do its thing; and if the sun gets too hot and you're sapped of energy, pull up to the side of the road and sleep under a shady tree till your body has recharged itself.

But you don't have those options with a kayak. The sea is always in motion, and not always moving in the direction you want to go – stop paddling for a while and you can quickly end up a kilometre or more in the opposite direction. If the weather starts to change drastically, the sensible (in fact only) thing to do is always to point the kayak towards the shore, paddle hard and get out of danger. But of course this isn't always possible. There might not be a suitable landing point, reefs might be churning up the waters, rips might be running considerably faster than you can paddle, or, hidden under the surface of the mighty tide, there might be savage rocks lying in wait just below the surface.

That had been my experience so far, and I hoped fervently that this north-eastern section of the coast would be toughest section I was likely to encounter ... although I had no doubt that many more surprises lay waiting for me.

CHAPTER 21

ON THE WAY TO CAP D'AMBRE

*My hands were torn up and bleeding because of the blisters
that had formed on earlier blisters that had also formed on
blisters. I was down to flesh in places, taped up in some spots
and swollen thick with fresh blisters elsewhere.*

I got in my 50-plus kilometres and ended up in a beautiful half-moon bay called Androvina, at the top end of which was a jutting finger of land called Pointe d'Andronona. My landing was like something out of an old-time comedy. I desperately needed some water and kept a sharp eye open for local signs of life so that I would know where to come ashore, and so when I eventually spotted some activity I headed straight for it.

The activity turned out to be a small gang of Malagasy children playing on the beach, and my arrival scared the hell out of them because they were so busy doing whatever they were doing that they didn't notice my arrival till I was right up close and getting out of the kayak.

At the sight of me they set up an ear-splitting collective scream– I couldn't blame them, considering my unexpected arrival in their peaceful bay, not to mention my wild hair and bushy beard – and they set off towards their village at a rate of knots with me close on their heels, making such a noise that I could follow them even when they were out of sight.

When I arrived at their village, which consisted of a grand total of three huts, I found that the men of the village were all still away at work, so I negotiated with the women for water and a safe place to pitch my tent, and I was settled in by the time the menfolk got back. For one reason or another they weren't all that comfortable with my presence either, but I got my night's rest and next morning carried on to my next destination, Irodo Island.

It was a tough slog. For most of the morning I paddled into the teeth of a north-easterly wind that eventually turned to a firm easterly and caused an uncomfortable side-on swell. It gave me some insight into what a sail would have done for me, however.

Many paddlers engaged on a long-distance trip like this one rig a kite or small sail that can almost triple their speed without using up an ounce of energy. But I had decided right at the beginning that I would do the whole trip under my own steam, although at times like this I couldn't help thinking about how nice a little sail would have been.

Just how much assistance the wind can be became clear to me now. It was at my back as I turned into Irodo Bay, and when I rested for a moment with the paddle on my lap I was amazed to find that it exerted so much force on the blades that I could literally just sit there and be pushed forward, although slowly, which was pretty incredible when I considered how much the kayak and myself weighed, and the tiny area of the paddle-blades.

Irodo Island with its fringe of mangroves had a total community of two or three families, who welcomed me, and an infinitely larger population of mosquitoes, which also welcomed me, but for a different reason. I was putting up my tent when swarms of them attacked me as soon as the sun dipped behind the mainland, so fiercely that I had 20 or 30 furiously sucking away at me simultaneously, mainly on my hands and feet.

I got my tent up and jumped inside as quickly as I could – but not quickly enough, because I found I had 20 or so of my unwanted new acquaintances sharing my personal space. I went into serious hunter-killer mode, but I couldn't get them all, and the result was the worst night I've ever had. I slept hardly a wink and by morning had scratched myself raw.

I greeted the rising sun with relief in spite of my mosquito-induced fatigue. All I wanted now was a drink and a loo, and I'd be off to Diego. The drink was no problem, but the loo situation was more difficult: the sole woman in the community explained in Malagasy that there was a 'peepee and poepoe *fady*', and pointed to the water around the mangroves, into which everyone else was wandering.

Oh, well, as an old soldier I knew all about what the military calls the 'bush crap', but even then you need a little privacy, so I didn't follow the others but went around a dense little mangrove tangle near my tent. Then I discovered why no one else was making use of this particular patch as I slipped and slid around in the thick poo- and pee-infested mud, close to vomiting.

Was this really what they did every morning? Assuming they were regular in their habits, the answer was presumably 'yes'. Crazy! Why didn't they get together, tell one another that it couldn't go on like this and make a plan? You don't have to shit on your ancestors, as one *fady* goes. A simple solution is to bury your future ancestors in formal graves and then refrain from shitting near them. Problem solved. Or otherwise call PortaLoo – these days they deliver just about everywhere.

Getting going that morning was a little painful, as it had been for some time. My hands were torn up and bleeding because of the blisters that had formed on earlier blisters that had also formed on blisters. I was down to flesh in places, taped up in some spots and swollen thick with fresh blisters elsewhere.

But I knew that it would just hurt for the first half hour or so: initially a burning sting as the salt rubbed into the wounds and then pain as the nerves were squeezed and pinched, and then the pain would die away, so that more aggressive paddling would be possible. All the same, I wrote a mental note to myself to ask Seamus to bring me some gloves; something I should have thought of before setting out.

The scenery I passed as I toiled up the coast was dry, desert-like and rocky, but still very impressive. Some of the rock formations looked just like animals of one kind or another, and one I named 'Croc Rock', for obvious reasons. It was probably a damned cheek to give a new name to something that probably had an indigenous name already, but, hey, that's what explorers do, and after all I wasn't planning to put it down on any map except the one in my head.

I didn't cover as much distance as I might have, because this was another 'interview day', and now and then I stopped off in very exotic places so that I could dig out the satphone from one of the dry bags and speak to people far away. I was keen to brag about where I had got to, but most interviewers wanted to hear about things like my near-drowning and the mango flies laying eggs in my big toe. I was happy to oblige, because people at home were loving the regular updates. If that was what grabbed them, then so be it.

And then suddenly I was just 7 km from Diego Suarez. With the wind at my back I made good time, and before long I was approaching the entrance to the harbour. I did so with some trepidation – well, let me be honest and say I was near to crapping myself as I remembered what it had looked like the day Vasti and I had gone up the mountainside. I formulated a worst-case scenario: if that was what I encountered I'd land elsewhere.

But it wasn't and I didn't. I landed on the very beach at Ramena where Vasti and I had been sunning ourselves only weeks before. As a veteran of Ramena's land-bound sharks I wasn't taken for a ride this time. I checked into a small and dilapidated bungalow which provided me with enough shelter, was situated right on the beach and was cheap into the bargain.

Next step: have a bit of a rest, wander around and generally charge up the batteries of both my body and my equipment, because next on the itinerary was rounding the notoriously dangerous Cap d'Ambre (Tanjona Bobaomby), Madagascar's northernmost point, which might well turn out to be the most hazardous sea-day I was likely to encounter.

Experienced sailors who had done this in 50-foot yachts had given me graphic descriptions of the violence that the elements produce around Cap d'Ambre, where powerful winds and currents have been clashing ever since Madagascar separated from Gondwanaland millions of years ago ... and I was going to take all this on with a kayak which was less than two-thirds the size!

The beer I had with dinner that evening didn't taste the same as it had when Vasti had been with me at Ramena. Sometimes alone is alone, even when there are many people around you.

I wasn't totally lonely, though, because I met all sorts of interesting people, among them a couple who saw me land the day I arrived and introduced themselves to me next day. When they had seen me appearing out of the sea, they said, they had joked about the fact that I looked like Robinson Crusoe. Which was fair enough, I thought, remembering how I had scared those kids.

They were heading south down the east coast, so I referred them to Ockie. If I could I would send everyone to Ockie on Ile aux Nattes. It's a Madagascar must for more than just the beauty, as I knew from personal experience.

Even better, I was able to indulge in my passion for rugby because my day off happened to coincide with the Springboks playing Wales on the Saturday evening after my arrival. I hunted down the only place at Ramena that was screening it – a seedy bar where I sat huddled on a sofa with four Frenchmen, our knees up around our ears, drinking beer from small tumblers.

A strange guy I met on the Sunday was an Italian postal worker, a near look-alike of Rowan Atkinson's Mr Bean character, who was on his annual leave – alone. He didn't think it was at all odd to go off on holiday by himself every year; after seeing so many people every day, he explained, he enjoyed getting away to quiet exotic places.

He would come and sit at the table where I was writing in my diary and do just that – sit, not saying a word till I said something. One topic on which we did not agree was my theory about malaria. My belief is that malaria is not such a bad disease, the important thing being where you have it, by which I meant that malaria was treatable, but if you were not near a hospital you could die. I also believe that it is preventable by cheap and simple methods, like taking drugs and using nets.

My Italian friend made no secret of his disapproval, although, considering that I was the only person he had to talk to, he could have given my reasoning some thought. But all he did was scoff, saying he knew someone who had nearly died of it. Big deal, I thought. I knew a man who had had malaria 40 times! Beat that, Kingsley Holgate would have told Signor Bean. Malaria is preventable and treatable, bottom line.

But he was good for a laugh as well. In a local beach bar that night Signor Bean had me smiling as he watched a Malagasy girl give a French guy a loud, fierce talking-to. Standing no more than a metre from her, my acquaintance cocked his head to one side so as to pick up every last high-decibel word, frowning with an all-knowing, understanding expression on his face. Perhaps it reminded him of one of his customers waxing wroth about the price of postage stamps ... Mr Bean goes to Madagascar!

My plan for rounding Cap d'Ambre was simple. First of all, forget about a long paddle, just concentrate on getting around it. Second, make sure the weather was decent enough, but be prepared for the worst. My Garmin showed that there were some enclaves en route, and Seamus had Google Earthed a few possible bale-out spots in case they were needed. To him they didn't look ideal, but they might save my life if worst came to worst.

I made it across the bay's mouth, passed Emerald Sea Island and turned north when I was clear of the land. Then I had second thoughts. I still had over 20 km to go before I actually reached Cap d'Ambre and less than four hours of daylight left in which to do it. So for once I decided on 'safety first' and paddled back about 10 km to spend the night on the famed island.

My only companions on this stop were the resident rats, and it was a scary evening. If the tourists who flock here in their thousands every year just knew what they would meet no more than 10 metres inland of the dazzling white beach they would be horrified. The rats scurried around me while I sat next to my fire and ran underneath my legs while I was talking to Vasti; they were everywhere, and not at all shy.

I hung up from my call to Vasti, feeling sad. Not because of the rats, but because I knew that tomorrow it might be tickets for me. Would it really end like this? Only time would tell, and I wouldn't have to wait long either.

CHAPTER 22

NORTH CONQUERED –
GOING SOUTH

*From the sheer violence of that line where wind and
water energy met it was quite clear – if I had needed any
persuading – why even the most seaworthy ship could come
to grief here if weather conditions were bad ...*

I was grateful when that long and ratty night was over, but when I woke up I realised that my unwanted companions of the dark hours had actually done me a favour. I had needed something to keep my mind off the genuine fear I felt about paddling around this fearsome northern point of Madagascar, and my silly agitation about spending a cold and lonely night with rats running over me had done the trick.

When I launched the kayak the sea was its usual morning self for that part of the world: calm, with a slight northerly breeze blowing into my face. I set off determined to pump away at maximum speed till I had rounded that dreaded point; at any time the sea could change and the pleasant breeze could turn into something brutal.

So I got really stuck in, and I was more than excited when I had made so much progress that I got a glimpse of the lighthouse at the very tip of Cap d'Ambre. Once I got around that, it was all south. So strong was my anticipation that every metre of that last bit seemed to have stretched out to three times its length.

I don't know if I started suffering from hallucinations, but the lighthouse looked as if it was playing hide-and-seek with me. I'd paddle away furiously, and the lighthouse would come perceptibly nearer. Wow! Then I'd paddle some more, and somehow it would seem to recede again. No 'wows' when this happened.

This went on for what seemed a very long time. But I was making progress in spite of what my eyes were telling me, and eventually I was at the foot of the cliff of dark rock on which the lighthouse stood, at the very spot where the Indian Ocean and the Mozambique Channel – two immensely powerful forces of current and wind – meet, tussle a little with one another and then agree to move on, each in its own direction, like two giants who have entered into a give-and-take relationship.

I could not have asked for a better day to negotiate this notorious arena, a strange sight indeed. The eastern side of the point where I found myself was slightly choppy, with a clear four-foot swell lifting me up and down. The western side, however, was as smooth as a mirror, and they met in such a precise manner that it seemed to have been engineered that way; it felt as if I could have taken a ruler and drawn a straight line along the splashing and frothing line that marked their meeting.

From the sheer violence of that line where wind and water energy met it was quite clear – if I had needed any persuading – why even the most seaworthy ship could come to grief here if weather conditions were bad ... and I had to punch through the foaming two-foot-high line of waves with my little kayak!

Well, there was nothing for it. Mentally I girded my loins, summoned up my courage and went at it, heart in mouth. I went from the smooth swells on the eastern side into the two-foot waves, which smacked me about as I had expected – and then 20 metres further on I found myself in what was almost a new world: quiet and calm, the water dark and deep. I was through! Now, for the first time in 1 000 kilometres, I would be paddling *south* instead of north. Yay!

But, I reminded myself, I didn't have time to celebrate. In five days' time Seamus was going to be in Nosy Bé, and getting there was going to be a tough slog – 170 km, with maybe a day's rest in between. That would mean more than 249 km covered in seven days of paddling.

The stories I had heard about the west coast and its calm waters proved to be true as soon as I headed into the Mozambique Channel. I actually found it hard to believe as I glided along that I had struggled through such awful conditions just a few days ago. The pictures I had seen advertising Madagascar and its idyllic island beach getaways were definitely taken on this side of the mainland. All going well, I hoped I would be able to make up the kilometres and the time I had lost on the north-eastern side.

As I paddled along I enjoyed watching the sea-animals, particularly the giant turtles when they came to visit from their mysterious world about which we still know and understand so little. Sometimes it was a humbling experience; seeing a leatherback which was almost the size of a 1963 VW Beetle and surely weighed more than 400 kg gliding past below me reminded me of my insignificance in her world.

One leatherback that popped up in front of me and took a huge gasp of air had a head the size of a soccer ball. Can you imagine that? Another turtle seemed for a moment to be nothing more than my shadow, because its body was so large that I couldn't make out its exact shape till clearer water and a sharp change in direction gave its enormous size away.

Where I come from on South Africa's east coast we see these giant turtles as part of our heritage, with a mandatory responsibility to protect them. But I couldn't hang around and hope for more interaction; perhaps the milder conditions would open the door to more intimate encounters with the world below my kayak's hull as I went along the 'Blue Continent', as one scuba diver of the 1950s so aptly called it.

The fish were abundant, and thanks to Thomas 'the hitman' Rapala, who was taken out of his early retirement, suitably sweet-talked and dropped over the side to go and fetch dinner, I had a hefty king mackerel to present to the headman of a little village huddled in the coastal mangroves, the name of which I can't remember, if it even had one.

At first the villagers were not very welcoming, but they soon warmed to me, and it wasn't long before one of them actually vacated his own hut to let me sleep in it. I had pitched my tent and made it clear (or so I thought) that that was where I would spend the night, but evidently my gift from the sea had put me in such good standing that the tent simply wouldn't do.

I protested, but only feebly, and there I was in the hut. The nocturnal scurrying of rats inside it during the night didn't bother me – been there, done that! – and I felt even less bothered when it began to rain. It beat down with meaning on the traditional leaf-thatched roof, but not a drop came through. Very good – I was pretty sure my tent would have leaked somewhere.

Before dropping off I did a few sums and concluded that I would have to average about 40 km a day if I wanted to see Seamus on time. That meant that the option I had been toying with, namely of sticking to the coastline all the way to Nosy Bé, just wouldn't work, because then I would have to average more than 70 km a day. Once again this showed how dramatically I could cut distance and time by taking the risk of open-sea crossings.

That was that, then. Tomorrow I would set off through the long Bay of Amamba, heading straight for Cap Saint Sébastien. Somewhere around there I would find food and shelter, because there were a number of islands around the cape that looked large enough to be inhabited. And I might need both food and shelter, because open-sea crossings are at the mercy of the wind, and after two days of gentle breezes I couldn't help suspecting that the odds were stacking up, and inevitably the wind would bare its teeth again.

CHAPTER 23

THE WORLD WILDLIFE FUND
PIRATES OF AMAMABA BAY

Hell! People all over my continent of Africa are starving. I've seen it at first hand. I've lived with them, and they, the real poorest of the poor, never asked me for a cent. The guys with satellite telly and BBC radio always do. It infuriates me.

My hands were now deteriorating to the extent where I had actually begun thinking of creative ways to paddle without using them. Both palms were blistered and bleeding from every blister, and since there was no such thing as handless paddling, the best I could hope for was that my few days with Seamus at Nosy Bé would provide the healing time I needed so desperately.

On top of that, my lower back was issuing warning signals as well, so that every morning started with painful cramps. On the other hand, something that had changed dramatically for the better was that I no longer suffered from sea-sickness. Being a sea-sick kayaker was something I had not anticipated in my wildest dreams. Now it was gone. Awesome!

I needed plain sailing, so to speak, as I set off across the Baie

Amamba in the direction of Cap Saint Sébastien – no bad weather, no pirates wanting my money and my boat, nothing – and the day certainly started off well as I dodged in between the reefs that from a distance I had seen sticking out of the crystal-clear blue water.

I planned to do about 50 km, with a short rest or even a nap on Nosy Hara, the largest of the islands, which was a convenient halfway mark, so I decided on a straight course from an island called Nosy Hao. The area was quiet, with not many fishermen or fish, and I gradually started to see why as time passed and I worked myself into the heart of this archipelago of volcanic islands.

My map and GPS had shown shallow areas dominating the sea between the two islands. That meant, I thought, that I would be down to a metre or so, as in other lagoon-bays I had encountered, but in some places it was so dry that I had to drag my kayak over anything from sharp reefs to soft sandbanks.

The rocks left terrible scratches on the kayak, but the sandy patches seemed to actually suck it in. The going was agonisingly slow for something like six kilometres, and it took me the better part of the morning before I struck deeper water again. When I finally got to Nosy Hara at about 1 pm all I wanted was to get to terra firma and – most importantly – find some shade.

Each of the dozen or so islands I had passed had many caves, which I knew from experience were usually the best and coolest spots in which to seek refuge, and so I kept a sharp eye open as I approached Nosy Hara. On the southern side a gigantic boulder had broken off, presumably in prehistoric times, and bits were strewn around, leaving rocky beaches where it would be difficult to land, so I continued around the westerly side.

The wind was a firm westerly and this side of the island gave me some reprieve – I had been expecting it, since the westerlies that blow over from the east side can only funnel their way in one direction here, through a huge gap in the mountains.

I was drifting along, sipping water and admiring the beauty of the scenery, when I heard a motorboat accelerating towards me. I swivelled around to see an eight-metre ski-boat coming up behind me from the north – strangely, I hadn't noticed it earlier.

In the boat were about seven people, including the helmsman, mostly men but also a couple of women, all with their gazes fixed firmly on me. They approached to within a few metres, then, without so much as a 'hello, how are you?' one of the men started hurling questions at me:

'You are alone?' Then: 'Where your friend?'

'I'm alone, why?' I replied. They looked at one another and started chattering excitedly among themselves in Malagasy.

'Come here!' another of the men shouted, leaning half-way out of the boat to take hold of the kayak's front handle. 'Bring boat here!'

I felt distinctly uneasy but convinced myself that I was over-reacting. *This is Madagascar! These guys are peaceful Malagasy people who live by the island's laid- back rules,* I told myself. *They're probably scared of you, Riaan.*

'I'm just visiting Madagascar on my kayak,' I explained, squeezing out a nervous smile.

'You cannot be here,' I was told by one man who I presumed was their leader. 'You must give us money.'

'Why?' I asked, distinctly nervous now. Had I understood him correctly? He bumps into me on the open sea and demands that I give him money? Surely not!

'You visit our country and you must pay to come here,' he explained. His colleagues, who were now laughing and showing signs of excitement, made it plain that they agreed.

A toll road out at sea? That was something new. And an *ad hoc* one at that. I decided to keep the tone of the conversation jovial but firm: 'I can't give you money, I'm poor,' I said.

'You give money now!' the guy who was hanging out of the boat and holding my kayak firmly started shouting. 'You give money now! You give money now!'

Behind him the others began shouting at me, their faces angry now, even the women: 'Money! Money! Money!' I was stunned by this sudden aggression and for a moment felt intimidated beyond belief. Here I was, literally in the middle of nowhere, with no Plan B to deal with strangers harassing me at sea.

The man holding my boat started trying to bring me right along-side so that the others could also get hold of me. That was it. Flight was out of the question, so I would have to fight. My paddle was balanced across my lap, and it didn't take me a second to slide it forward till I was holding it by one end. Now I had some serious reach, and I swung the blade straight at the guy's head, so hard that I would probably have killed him if I'd connected.

Fortunately for him the blade hissed through the air about an inch above his head, and without hesitation he ducked and let go of the kayak, his face the picture of stunned amazement.

Now the others started screaming at me. I started screaming back – real war-talk, full of blood-curdling threats. I can't remember everything I said, but the general thrust of it was that I didn't care what they wanted to do to me, but there was no way they were going to get either my kayak or my money, and if they tried to take either a lot of them were going to get hurt. I didn't give in to a bunch of bloody pirates.

As soon as I mentioned pirates they began to change their tune – to my amazement the helmsman even came forward to show me the World Wildlife Fund sticker on the bow of his boat, and then took out his camera to photograph me. I pulled out my own camera and returned the compliment, then told the helmsman, whose English was better than everyone else's combined, to go and get the police.

They were all distinctly edgy by now, and I began to worry that they might turn around (I had let myself fall back a few metres astern) and run me down, so I kept paddling to maintain my position. I calculated it would be difficult for them to manoeuvre around to me without my countering it, because they would have to circle a fair distance ahead.

If they did do that, all I could do in my turn was to stay facing them for as long as possible. It wasn't much of a defence. Fortunately, I think that by now the helmsman was worried that I had some sort of plan to sabotage them – I suppose it helped that I was a very large (by Malagasy standards) and fearsomely hairy bearded man.

All he did was throw a wide turn and do a drive-by at speed, turning sharply three or four metres away and knocking me into the water, with his pals still shouting (why, I don't know): 'Police! Police! Police!' I scrambled back on as fast as I could and sat awaiting their next move, breathing heavily from the jolt of adrenalin rushing through me and feeling pretty helpless and panicked.

But the helmsman now peeled away and sped off in the direction of a majestic cove with a white beach and giant cave. He seemed anxious and determined, and I wondered whether they were going to fetch something, maybe weapons of some kind. I needed to act, and fast.

I started paddling south with every ounce of energy in me, to put as much distance between myself and them as I could and perhaps get out of sight altogether if they stayed away long enough. I didn't look back once; every metre counted. I was now in a state of controlled panic, desperately turning over ideas of what to do.

I didn't have many options. The fact was that I had a 25 km stretch of open water with few hiding places ahead. What was I to do? Well, there was just one way out. I turned landwards and then hugged the south-western shoreline, still digging into the water as if there were no tomorrow, the idea being to get around the corner from the wildlife-loving 'pirates' and find somewhere to hide. All going well, they would be confused by my disappearance and go on to more profitable prospects.

After a few minutes more of effort I found a small pebbled beach about two metres wide that I knew would not be there at high tide. I jumped out, dragged the kayak up behind a rock, then began immediately to erect some camouflage in the form of a low berm of sand about 70 cm high and five metres long, and irregular in shape – in nature a regular outline or profile is a dead giveaway. Then I hedged my bets by strewing a layer of dry sand over the darker and damper layer to help with providing some extra sun-glare.

This done, I took out my telecoms bag and found a spot behind a white boulder, where I made myself comfortable in about 10 cm of water and some welcome shade. This done, I got on to the satellite phone without delay, because although I had won the first round I still needed help – fast.

I got through to Seamus, but just as I started speaking to him I heard the boat's engine near by, and I had to turn the adjustable aerial away for fear that that it could be seen above my head. Naturally this didn't help when I tried to explain what was going on, and my state of desperation didn't help either.

I gabbled out the story of how I had been harassed and that I was still being chased. Could he call the ambassador? But all that Seamus could hear was something about a boat and snatches about pirates and money.

Eventually he shouted: 'Riaan ... RIAAAAN ... RIAAAAAAAAAN! Shuddup, shuddup. Calm down and call me back in one minute – I can't hear you and I don't understand you. Call back when you've calmed down.'

Shit! That was the last sort of advice I needed in this predicament. Here I was being chased by a bunch of Malagasy crooks, and all the advice I got from my only source of help was to take a chill pill and call him back!

But that was what I did – well, I didn't have any alternative, did I? – and it turned out to be good advice, because it gave me time to check up on what the boat was doing. I raised my head for one quick peek, which was probably what I should *not* have done. Whether they saw me or not I don't know, but then I heard the boat's engines screaming at full power … away from me.

Highly relieved, I called Seamus back, and now that I had calmed down and got the aerial facing in the right direction again, we managed to have a proper conversation. I said I knew the ambassador was not going to be able to help in the circumstances, but at least if the police got to know about me …

Seamus cut in: 'What do you think you should do? You're there, in the situation. Tell me and then I'll plan for some contingencies.'

I decided that I was going to stick to my original itinerary and make a run for Cap Saint Sébastien, heading across the bay with the wind in my face, hoping to lose myself in the glare of the setting sun; the boat had headed eastward towards the mainland, so this could work. I agreed to call Seamus on the sat phone when I stopped for the day, and in any case I had a scheduled radio interview that evening. Either way, if they heard nothing from me they would know I had been captured.

I paddled on for an hour, the adrenalin still coursing through me. Then I calmed down as my system started reverting to normal, but I kept slugging it out, and eventually I made landfall on the northern side of Cap Saint Sébastien, just before sunset, and just in time for the radio interview. And guess what? The interview had been cancelled! Aargh!

I spent the night in a village of four huts and about 10 people. One of them was a woman with two children who allowed me to lay out my sleeping bag on her porch. She serenaded me into slumber with endless questions about whether I would give her a gift in dollars, euros or ariary.

That whining voice is going to stick in my head forever, I think; I really didn't need that tireless harassment for money as the grand finale of a day when the legacy of piracy had become a reality for me. I mentally renewed my membership of the 'give to the less fortunate without a gun at your head' club. I like giving when I'm not expected to, and especially when I have an understanding of how my contribution will make a difference with the people I'm donating to.

Anyway, doesn't kindness also feel so much better to the giver when he or she isn't pressured and/or threatened into giving? Kindness does not have a monetary value – if anything, it's negated by financial gain. Full stop.

So to the hippies out there, this is going to hurt you. I hate it when someone does something 'kind' and then harasses me for money. Offer a service and clearly state the cost involved, and we'll be friends forever. Don't trick me because you have seen on TV that white people have lots of money to throw around, even if you pretend you did something useful.

Hell! People all over my continent of Africa are starving. I've seen it at first hand. I've lived with them, and they, the real poorest of the poor, never asked me for a cent. The guys with satellite telly and BBC radio *always* do. It infuriates me. The propaganda that the West feeds into the minds of people cripples them mentally, so that they only have one skill: begging. Exactly what I saw in Ethiopia during my bicycle trip.

Needless to say, I wasted no time getting going next morning. Not just to get away from that unpleasant woman but because this was going to be a crunch day: I knew that if I didn't make it to a chunk of rock called Nosy Lava by sunset I could laugh off any chance of meeting Seamus on time.

It wasn't going to be easy. I had done 50 km the day before and now expected my body to manage another 45 km journey, once more out at sea and into a strong wind. That meant leaving as early as possible to cover the maximum distance before the wind started making my life difficult.

My beggar-hosts left at the same time as I did, going in the same direction – as far as I could gather they were off to visit relatives living on an island just off the actual cape of Saint Sébastien. But they moved slowly, and I soon lost sight of them. Good riddance!

The first stage of my day's journey was 10 km, heading directly west with the sun at my back, and then turning south towards an island just around the cape which would be my launching pad for Nosy Lava. It was quite beautiful, although it offered nothing more than a rocky shore where I could take a slug of energy drink and stretch my legs before tackling the day's long haul.

But my mind was not on its beauty. A sudden increase in wind from the south made me afraid of the open-sea crossing to Nosy Lava – so afraid that I thought again about my original plan of following the mainland coastline. Being near the coast meant that rescuers might be available in the event of disaster, whereas heading out into the open sea, as far as 30 km at times, would have only one ending if things went wrong: death.

But my calculations told the same story as the earlier ones. The close-in coastal route would increase my journey by four days, which I could not afford. I simply had to take the open sea route. But I didn't feel good as I set off at 11 am into the steady head-on breeze. I knew that I might well be taking the wrong step, and that things could go badly wrong.

The distance to the northerly point of Nosy Lava was 34 km, and I had about six hours to get there, which would require an average speed of about 6 km an hour. But as I paddled along I constantly consulted my Garmin to keep a check on my actual progress, and what it told me was that I was lucky to make a top speed of 5 km an hour. After an hour and a half I was worried.

As before, I had a chat with myself – the well-worn one in which I criticised myself for under-committing and aiming for an easier exit. I knew I had risked a lot, but that risk was premised on my willingness to give everything I had. Once again I was beginning to doubt myself and question my ability to see this big task through to the end. Everything was against me – and now my attitude wanted to join the chorus. Geez, get a life!

The chat ended in the usual way, with a silent debate about what the right action would be to remedy my indiscretion. That remedy turned out to be a reasonable one. I would give it absolutely everything for the next two hours: if I could average 7 km an hour for these two hours, I should have only 15 km left to do in three hours. Possible? Sure. I just about killed myself for those two hours, averaged 7.34 km per hour and ended up in that 'the task is possible' category, which was where I wanted to be.

But it left me lame in body, my wrists hurting and my hands even worse than before – and the afternoon wind was still blowing steadily in my face. What I needed now was a rhythm that would make it possible for me to average 5 km an hour towards that island I knew nothing about, except that my Garmin described it as 'non-urban' – meaning, I supposed, non-developed.

When the first hour had passed Nosy Lava came into view, clearly an island of cliffs and not many beaches. As I finished the second hour I realised two things: the cliffs comprised the entire coastline, and I probably wouldn't make land before sunset. A rocky landing in the dark! Please, man, I didn't need this. Right now I needed some light and a piece of that Madagascan paradise the advertisements promised.

The island drew slowly nearer as the sun set rapidly into the Mozambique Channel – beautiful, red and dramatic. I didn't pay it much attention because I was too focused on maintaining my average speed. The relevance of a chunk of earth you have never seen before is exactly that; irrelevant, because you don't know how far it really is because you don't know how high it is, and my GPS offered no height info in this case. I found that strange, because the island was not small by any means.

The 8 km-long island drew slowly nearer as darkness began to fall, and I knew that I would not reach it before night fell, but there was nothing I could do about that. I decided to stay with my plan to keep heading down the western side, which even in the dark would provide more visibility and opportunity. Then I would make a landing at the first likely-looking place.

The sun dipped below the horizon and a feeling of eeriness hung over the dark waters as I paddled nearer to Nosy Lava, peering into the darkness to see if I could spot a possible place to land. For a while there was nothing remotely suitable, and then I saw a patch of white up ahead. How big it was, and what it consisted of, I had no idea. But I was too desperate to find some suitable dry land and too tired to debate with myself about the pros and cons, so I headed straight for it.

As I neared I could hear the small one-foot waves breaking on chunks of rock. It looked dangerous and the white patch was very small. But I was past caring. If I could land here alive I would be just two days' paddling away from Nosy Bé. Good enough!

When I got closer I saw that the white patch was a length of coral bed, about five metres long, that had been washed up against the foot of one of the jagged cliffs. Briefly I considered my options. I could see now that the cliffs reached all the way down the island and what looked like more than 100 metres into the sky. I tried not to think about what would have happened if the surf had been higher and the sea more dangerous. Even though it wasn't, this was where I had to land. If I didn't get onto the coral bank I would definitely die.

The coral was rough and it was difficult to drag my kayak up onto it, but a positive point was that to judge from the distinct changes of colour in the rock it was above the high-water mark. I sincerely hoped so, anyway, as I started a fire to warm up my cooling body.

The wind was suddenly getting colder, and I could sense imminent showers, so I climbed some way up the cliff and dug around for dry wood. With this I built a huge bonfire, something I had avoided doing when camped in isolated places on my cycle trip, because it would give away my position and advertise my presence to potential enemies. In the old days an unannounced traveller would be considered a threat, and nearby communities would not wait to be attacked. But nobody was going to attack me here.

There was no activity in the cliffs above me, at least, not till the rain began to fall, which it did so fiercely that I dragged all the gear I'd packed out of the kayak in under a small ledge. The ledge offered me shelter not just from the rain but also from a huge boulder, the size of a car engine, which fell down the cliff and landed with an earth-shattering crash not four metres from where I'd laid out my sleeping bag.

At first, being still a little paranoid after my encounter with the 'pirates', I thought that someone had rolled it down on me, but after a closer look I realised that it was too heavy for any human to move. The rain must have washed away some of the earth around it and freed it to slide down onto the coral bank. Not that it mattered how it had reached its resting-place: if I had been in the way I would have been just as dead.

The highlight of this island 'getaway', as the tourism magazines would have called it, came as I collected the last few pieces of wood for the fire. One of them felt too ... well, *manufactured* ... to be natural, and when I laid the wood down in the firelight I saw why. It was a worn, sun-bleached traditional Malagsy dugout paddle. Obviously it had been lost at sea, then drifted about and over time been washed up here, high enough to stay put and wait for me to find it.

I sat fingering this forlorn artefact in the flickering light of the fire and found I was talking to myself: *This is why you do what you do. This piece of Madagascar is history – not a souvenir, but a real part of Madagascar. This is going home with you no matter what you encounter from here on, no matter what! It represents a day of what this journey is really about. The risk and the guts and the determination.*

The rain fell for only about an hour and a bit. I didn't care. I found a comfortable spot in among the coral outcrops and crawled into my sleeping-bag. Tonight I was going to sleep well. I had no food and not much water, but I was tired with the righteous fatigue of a man who has put in a good day's work and survived various perils.

CHAPTER 24

SANCTUARY AT TSARA BAJINA

I was far gone by now. My eyelids kept closing of their own accord and my body started drooping as I sat on my kayak, the odd paddle-stroke keeping me creeping forward at a snail's pace. I should have been worried about this almost imperceptible progress, but I just didn't care what happened to me now. All I wanted to do was sleep – anyhow, wherever.

Yesterday's heat had been transformed into a cool morning when I woke up on my little coral perch, and I felt good as I packed my gear after enjoying a delicious watery cappuccino. The ultimate coffee-bar mainstay on a deserted island off Madagascar? Veritably– Vasti had given me a bunch of Nescafé cappuccino sachets, and right now their caffeine and 'false' calories were a life-saver. I hadn't eaten for two days, and I needed a good large meal as much as I needed rest.

Finding food and rest: that was my main priority as I paddled away. In the meantime my body's engine was tanked up on Vasti's sachets.

Travelling down Nosy Lava's flank for the next 6 km showed me that the island had a lot more to it than I had gathered the previous evening. Far from being just a precipitous lump of ancient volcanic rock, it had some of the most picture-postcard perfect beaches anyone could ever expect to find. Blindingly white stretches of sand and palm-trees leaning over at exactly the right picturesque angle: it was all anyone could want – an exotic, secluded and safe destination. If this wasn't a tourist stop yet, I couldn't help thinking, then it would surely become one. Pity I hadn't known about this the previous night, hey? I would have carried on past those cliffs.

My immediate destination today was Nosy Mitsio, 10 or 12 km due south and one step from Nosy Bé, and I got off to a dramatic start. The sun was rising in a red haze, huge turtles were breaching to take massive gasps of breath around me, and I was where I always wanted to be: 'inside the picture'. It was the most ideal paddling I had had so far.

Soon I was within sight of Nosy Mitsio's northern point, and now it was decision time. Should I go east and find a safe landing area, or head west and into the sanctuary of the island's bay? It would save me time if I went east, it seemed to me, because next morning the early off-shore winds from the mainland would give me a push to Nosy Bé.

In the end I headed for the bay. Although I had paddled only a short distance my initial good feeling had worn off. I was exhausted and full of pain, and the heat was suffocating, even this early in the day. I needed to find a village where I could eat and rest, and if there was a village on the island, that was where it would be.

An almost immediate indication that I had guessed right was the sight of a small powerboat emerging from the bay and whizzing past, apparently trailing a few Rapalas. Right! There had to be some civilisation here. Painfully slowly I paddled into the bay, scanning the shore.

Now I could see a few huts in the distance, and as I got closer to shore I could see large, long nets draped over some small trees. I made it to shore. I stumbled out of my kayak and headed towards a group of fishermen who were working on the nets.

Shark fins as well as the odd kingfish lay scattered everywhere around them, drying out in the sun. I eyed the fins with interest: I had heard about the shark-fin fishing on Madagascar's coast, but not about where and how it was carried out. Now the unusual thickness of the nets suddenly made sense. They were not intended to catch small fish.

The fishermen were friendly and gave me a few coconuts to drink and eat, plus directions to the *'vazaha'* village. It amazed me once again that any reference to foreigner or white man automatically meant things like electricity, doctors and creature comforts. I mean, all I had asked these guys was where I could find medication, a doctor and some good food, not to mention rest – *'mila maturi, rerake bée!'* (I want to sleep, I am finished).

Unfortunately for me I would have to paddle out of the bay again and around the south-westerly point, about 13 km away according to my GPS, to get to the *'vazaha* village' – 'just around the corner,' as the fishermen put it. It wasn't far, compared to some of my previous days' travels, but in my present physical shape it seemed an endless distance. Still, there was no alternative.

I was so worn out that it took me two whole hours to reach my destination. On the way I passed a yacht full of tourists, and normally I would have made some use of the opportunity. But I just didn't have it in me right now. I was just too exhausted and enfeebled by my lack of energy – all I had had for three days now was water and Game energy drink, and, of course, Vasti's Nestlé cappuccino sachets. I needed solid food – a lot of it – and some peace and quiet to let it do its work.

The scenery on the south-westerly point was beautiful, with volcanic 'organ-pipe' rocks reaching into the skies, while below me the water was full of activity. Huge schools of shimmering bait fish swam under the kayak, and every few minutes there would be splashes and scurryings as predator fish or maybe even a shark or two would come to help themselves.

Should I use up some of my scanty remaining reserve of energy to hunt for food, or use it for finding the as-yet-invisible *vazaha* village to which the fishermen had directed me? So far there was no hotel or big village in sight, only a sprinkling of smaller islands like Nosy Lava, huge sugar-loaf rock formation that reared up out of the sea.

These rock islands didn't seem to be what I was looking for, because as far as I could see none of them had bays or landing sites. To my left and just south of Mitsio, though, was an island that seemed to be more welcoming, but the bad news was that it was about 15 km away.

Still, what choice did I have? I was in bad shape in every way. I wrestled my fading commitment back into shape and got going once more: that island was going to be my overnight stop, regardless of what it offered in the way of hospitality.

Wearily I started digging the paddle-blades into the sea again, a total wreck and yet strangely happy that I was nearing the end of this short but tough day. If all went well I would have two days for that intimidating 40-odd kilometres across the open sea that would bring me to Nosy Bé. Easy!

Fifteen kilometres later I reached the island. I insinuated my kayak into a gully of volcanic detritus and headed towards some shiny wet rocks I had spotted higher up on the cliff, slipping and sliding on the slippery surface. What I was after was water: I had run out, and needed to find some more soon, and it seemed a good place to look.

I clambered carefully from left to right up the cliff– if I fell here and broke an arm or cracked my head open I would probably die. *But if I don't climb up here I'll probably die, too,* I thought, and I found myself laughing. I had had close calls before which I had survived and then afterwards told myself: *Geez, you nearly died, but if you don't nearly die then you definitely will die!*

Maybe I was a little dehydrated and hallucinatory by now, because everything seemed to be funny, even the idea of pitching a tent on these jagged rocks.

Once again I'd guessed right and found a pool of fresh water where I drank all I could hold and filled both my water bottles. The pool was small, but inviting: enough for a return visit if I polished off both bottles that night, I thought. Less thirsty but just as weak, I clambered down to my kayak once more and literally fell into it. But it wasn't a good place to stay over – I knew that. *Nice effort, Riaan,* I told myself, *but this isn't the sanctuary you'd hoped for. You have to prepare yourself for the last big crossing, and you're going to need everything you can get.*

Much as I didn't want to get back to that endless paddling, I decided to try the eastern side of the island as a last resort. Maybe it would at least have a sandy patch where I could sleep more comfortably, even if that was all. I thought there was a reasonable possibility of that, because I had noticed that all the other islands in the vicinity seemed to have white patches on their eastern shores.

So off I went, although I was far gone by now. My eyelids kept closing of their own accord and my body started drooping as I sat on my kayak, the odd paddle-stroke keeping me creeping forward at a snail's pace. I should have been worried about this almost imperceptible progress, but I just didn't care what happened to me now. All I wanted to do was sleep – anyhow, wherever.

Then – at last! – I discovered that Lady Luck had been smiling on me all along without my knowing it. As I rounded Mitsio's northern point I saw another little island ahead of me ... not just any little island, but one with a long white beach, which had two big boats moored just off it.

The only question was whether I had enough energy left to get to this unexpected but much hoped-for heaven on earth. I had reached the point where paddling another five kilometres or so seemed an impossible task. My hands were torn open and my body paralysed with gross fatigue.

I summoned up the last few sparks left in my fading battery and forced myself to think it through. The island (I later discovered it was called Tsara Bajina) was about five kilometres away; even if I couldn't get up to more than 2 km/h I could still make it by sunset. So I would just have to keep plugging.

I settled down to a rhythm which was positively pathetic compared to my personal best. Ten strokes, rest, then another ten strokes, rest again ... It worked, and I found that a friendly tidal current was helping me, so that I was actually making 4 km/h.

Eventually I was close enough to make out human figures on the beach, although I was so flogged out I couldn't even get excited. *Keep moving.* That thought dominated everything in my shrunken little world of misery.

The last kilometre or so seemed to take so long that my crazed mind actually contemplated turning back, which just shows the state I was in. Then I was on the beach. I wobbled on to the sand and tried to pull the kayak up above the water's edge. I just couldn't do it; my body seemed to be made of rubber.

I left the kayak where it was – fortunately the tide was low – and somehow negotiated a staircase going up a dune where I now spotted some bungalows and deck-chairs. Having got to the top, which felt like a climb up Everest, I arrived at a medium-sized brick structure.

I was still recovering from this last supreme effort when a man with blonde wavy hair came out of the building. At first he didn't notice me, so I dragged myself over and accosted him.

'Hello,' I croaked. 'My name's Riaan Manser and I'd like to speak to the owner, please.'

'Yes, no problem,' he promptly replied. 'How can I help you?' He sounded like a South African. Could it be, or was my delirious state making me imagine things?

'Are you South African?' I asked.

'Yip, my name's Hilton. Where are you from?'

'Hilton, I'm a South African adventurer who is currently trying to circumnavigate Madagascar alone and unaided. I've just landed here and I need your help.' It wasn't much of an introduction, but that was all I had left in me.

Hilton didn't beat about the bush. 'What do you need?' he asked.

'I don't want much,' I said. 'If you can feed me, I'll be grateful; I haven't eaten for three days ... and then if you can help me with a place to pitch my tent for a night or two, I'd be grateful like you wouldn't believe.'

There was something else I should have said, but I couldn't remember what. Then I felt a stab of pain in my mangled hands and remembered. I held them out, palms up, and added: 'Another thing, if you've got a medical kit I could use some methiolate and plasters for my hands.'

'Bloody hell!' Hilton blurted, stepping forward to take a closer look at my hands – a gory sight, because it looked as if all the skin was peeling away from the flesh. 'You need help here, bud. Let's get you some food and I'll see what I can do.'

Hilton (his surname was Hasting) steered me to his bar-restaurant area and instructed his staff to take care of me. The care included cold beer – heaven! – and some very tasty left-overs from lunch – more heaven.

While I gobbled them down I discovered the reason for Hilton's lack of surprise when I came staggering up to him: he explained that he had heard about me from his family back home, and that his wife, who was on Nosy Bé at the moment, had read my Africa trip book. He wanted to speak to her and tell her about me. So off he went while I continued to punish the food and drink.

A little later Hilton came back with the best possible news: 'My wife said I'd better sort you out quickly, so I'm under orders now,' he told me. 'Usually we don't have people landing here and getting assistance. The clientèle are sometimes very fussy, so it's against policy to offer assistance. But we're going to let you stay in a bungalow and get you back into better shape ... for free. Maybe you can tell people about Tsara Bajina and how magical she is, as a trade-off of sorts?'

'Are you kidding me?' I replied. 'Of course that's fair.' It was more than fair, and in any case I would have accepted any offer just then, including one involving the purchase of my soul. If ever there was a classic beggars-can't-be-choosers situation it was this one.

The bungalows at Tsara Bajina, I discovered, were not of the usual type, but designed to be as uninvasive, if there is such a word, of the natural habitat as possible, so that guests were incorporated into their surroundings.

Inside the luxury is unparalleled, and I speak from experience, because I've seen some fancy places during my travels. I showered while looking out into the jungle and over the sea around my bungalow. There was power, although it was only used at certain times, while the bed and furniture would have felt at home in any Radisson penthouse. Some place to recover in!

Hilton had to leave early next morning to be with his wife at their house on Nosy Kumba, a small island between mainland Madagascar and Nosy Bé, but said in parting that I was welcome to spend another night at Tsara Bajina if I wanted to.

I gave the idea some thought, reflected that the weather next day was expected to be ideal for the crossing, and after about 10 seconds took him up on his offer.

Hilton gave me some good advice before he left. He had lived in Madagascar for a while and had actually walked a few hundred kilometres of its western coastline, an experience which had left him with a fund of war stories. He believed my main challenges would be the dangerous currents and tides as well as the southerly winds that blew predominantly in the afternoons. Stay close to the mainland, he added, and avoid three or four channels he had found which had dangerous seas.

When he had left I relaxed, very content. This stop was just what I had needed so badly. Come the morning, I'd be ready for the crossing. Seamus was already on the plane and crossing the Indian Ocean, and I'd be at Nosy Bé on schedule.

CHAPTER 25

GECKO ADVENTURES AT NOSY BÉ

I turned to see the remnants of a big foamy splash and foam
and asked what had happened; a huge skate, Seamus gabbled,
had leaped out the water and soared two metres into the air.
He simply couldn't believe it. You better believe it, I thought.
I've seen even more unbelievable sights on this trip.

I followed Hilton's advice and set off before the sun even rose above the horizon, and the early-morning winds were exactly what he had said they would be, easterlies off the Madagascar mainland. I had got some of my energy back and my hands were thoroughly plastered up; I reckoned I could average 10 km/h for the first two hours, and if I succeeded I'd have the rest of the day to do the remaining 23 km or so to Nosy Bé.

This early I couldn't see Nosy Bé at all. There was a sea-mist, and after all it was still a huge distance away. Well, give it a bit of time. I laid a southerly course by lining up some of the other islands with each other and got down to making some kilometres, checking my position on my Garmin every 45 minutes or so. For once things went just as I had planned, and at 7.30 am, after two hours at sea, I was on schedule with exactly 26 km left.

The sea around me– smooth and glassy and dark green– was as active and energetic as anything I'd seen further north. King mackerel launched themselves metres high out of the water, schools of bonito had the surface boiling as far the eye could see, turtles popped up all around me and birds made dive-bomb attacks with reckless abandon on the balls of bait fish that were trying to outrun the schools of kingfish preying on them from below. I could not have asked more of nature.

Nosy Bé drew nearer as I paddled on. I was a little tired by now, although I had so much oomph left that I could easily have paddled right past and on to the next destination. But I had a date awaiting me at Nosy Bé with a lady called *Gecko*, the catamaran on which Seamus and I were going to have a six-day holiday.

Six whole days! Time to do some filming, time to conduct some interviews, time to open some gifts from home, above all time to rest and recharge in unaccustomed luxury. I was going to be spoilt rotten!

Our meeting arrangements weren't exactly detailed. *Gecko*'s owners, Mike and Harriet João, had said they would be hanging around the north-western corner of the island from about noon, keeping an eye open for me. But I was so amazingly far ahead of schedule that I kept going past our rough-and-ready rendezvous point and turned into the first bay I found.

The French owners of the hotel in the bay promptly chased me away. I shrugged it off and went on to an adjoining bay, which turned out to be a different story altogether. The Amarina Lodge was run by a friendly Italian called Marcello, who simply couldn't believe that I had just paddled from Tsara Bajina. Had Hilton looked after me there? When I said that Hilton had, Marcello wanted to do the same and invited me to stay at his place.

I had a cool drink and charged my phone, but before I had even replaced the simcard a Malagasy guy came to stand in front of my table and said: '*Geeeeko*'. Nothing more, nothing less. I goggled at him and he stared back, saying '*Geeeeeko, geeeeeko*'.

I didn't know what the hell was going on. I knew about 100 Malagasy words, and this was definitely not one of them. Then the penny dropped when I got a clear look at his T-shirt logo, which read '*Gecko*'. Of course! '*Gecko?*' I asked, and his serious face was transformed by a huge smile.

'*Oui. Oui!*' he said '*Geeeeko!*' Our rendezvous had been made.

Since this was the end-point of my journey to Nosy Bé and an easy place to launch from again, I arranged to leave the kayak in Marcello's safekeeping till I collected it in a day or two for some filming with Seamus. Then Jasme (this was the fellow who fetched me) took me along to Mike and Harriet.

They were as eager to meet me as I was to meet them. They came from the same town as I do, Somerset West, and had fallen so deeply in love with Madagascar and its people that they had invested in their luxury catamaran – a 36-footer, if I remember correctly – and ran an almost permanent holiday business 10 months of the year. Now I was going to get an inside look at how one did this sort of thing.

It was with a feeling of sublime contentment that I sat drinking gin and tonic with Mike and Harriet while the chef cooked up a storm of his own. A pity Seamus would only arrive the next day!

Which he did, wearing his usual big grin as Jasme brought him over from the harbour jetty in a rubber duck. Our agreement to work together on the media arrangements with a documentary in mind had not included a guaranteed trip to mystical Madagascar, and so I was chuffed to have him here rather than a camera crew I didn't know from a hole in the ground. I knew that it was a sacrifice for him, because he had had to use up some of his annual leave from his day job as a news editor for the etv television channel and leave his wife at home.

Mike and Harriet had scheduled a route which would have plenty of variety, so that Seamus could film footage of me in all sorts of surroundings – on the ocean with all its colourful and dramatic life, and in historical parts of the scenery as well. Places like Russian Bay, named after the Russian settlers who had built a fort there; Hurricane Hole, the go-to place for all yachts and boats when a cyclone strikes; and the remains of a fancy Italian hotel which showed what the forces of nature could do when they felt like it.

The hotel had been on the point of opening on the northern side of Russian Bay the previous year, Mike and Harriet told us, when a violent cyclone came along and completely destroyed it in two days flat. It was an eerie feeling, picking our way through the debris of what had been luxurious five-star suites, swimming pools and restaurants. If ever there was proof that the works of man were feeble when the forces of nature were unleashed, this was it.

Harriet was a big leatherback turtle fan and explained how danger constantly stalked these great, seemingly invulnerable animals, which could grow up to a weight of half a ton. The moment of greatest peril was when a mother was ashore and laying her eggs; at that moment she was vulnerable to all sorts of natural predators ... and now that included humans as well.

I try not to be dramatic or sentimental about this sort of thing, but I don't want to imagine a world where animals like the leatherbacks don't exist any more. My life has been shaped by the interaction I've had with wild animals, both as a child and then especially on my journeys– from whales to elephants to rhinos to pythons, and now to the giant leatherback turtles.

If they go, they're gone forever. The coelacanth has hung on from ancient times mainly because till a few decades ago people didn't know it was still around, but unless somebody fights for them, a lot of other creatures will go the same way as the dodo and many others.

Another intriguing sight was an island we passed whose name translated as 'the Fifth Brother'. According to the local folklore, it was one of the original five volcanic sugarloafs just off the island of Mitsio; but then this one was banished by the gods and told never to return. The legend goes on to say that that if you touch or climb the Fifth Brother's rocky cliffs, you will die.

Albert, the boat's Malagasy skipper, insisted that this was nothing less than the truth when I scoffed at the superstition. He said he had seen a man climb onto the Fifth Brother one morning, and by nightfall he was dead. Yes! He had seen it with his own eyes.

With those very same eyes, Albert added, he had also seen a mermaid come out of the sea and stare at him. And on another occasion his brother-in-law had actually been kidnapped by a mermaid.

I was unconvinced. Was I supposed to believe this for the sake of believing it? It sounded like utter rubbish. On the other hand, we twenty-first century know-alls actually know much less than we think we do, as I have discovered on my travels, and I am always happy to change my mind if I'm proved wrong.

Seamus had some mind-blowing special wildlife moments which gave him an inkling of what I had seen and experienced so far. We were chatting out on the deck one morning when he gasped in amazement, broke off our conversation in mid-sentence and ran to the side of the boat. I turned to see the remnants of a big foamy splash and foam and asked what had happened; a huge skate, Seamus gabbled, had leaped out the water and soared two metres into the air. He simply couldn't believe it. *You better believe it,* I thought. *I've seen even more unbelievable sights on this trip.*

Another time we tracked a mind-boggling school of dolphins – or let me rephrase that, *they* tracked *us*. There must have been more than 200 of them, riding easily around *Gecko*'s bows. I would have liked to be right inside this incredible gathering, but I knew there was little chance of it happening. We would have to stop so that I could literally throw the kayak and myself overboard, and by then they would be long gone.

We gave it a try, though. The kayak and I were dropped off and Albert took *Gecko* out into deeper water, hoping to sight the dolphins again. Meanwhile I paddled frantically in *Gecko*'s wake, clocking up more than 15 km/h with my baggageless and thus much lighter kayak – pretty impressive, to be sure, but much too slow for the dolphins.

But I was wrong (and so was everybody else, I suppose). The dolphins were so finely tuned to the sounds of the sea that they must have heard *Gecko*'s engines start up again after dropping me off, although by then they were a good distance away. And so they turned back and took us all by surprise.

Without any warning they came up and started throwing themselves into the air alongside *Gecko* (and me!). I saw Seamus hanging precariously off *Gecko*'s port side, frantically shooting this very special moment with his video camera.

It didn't end there. I stayed out a bit longer while Seamus and the rest sat back and enjoyed a beer and some lunch. I had seen a few divers off a reef nearby, and since the presence of the dolphins indicated ample sea life, I popped out a Rapala to see if I could catch us some dinner, and found all sorts of interesting things happening to me; among them was a sailfish which came whizzing unexpectedly past me, and then the giant shadow of an eagle ray passing beneath the kayak.

It wasn't long before Seamus was in *Gecko*'s kayak to get a taste of the magic for himself, and even tried out an unsuccessful anti-boredom ritual I had worked out, which consisted of counting paddle-strokes for as long as I could before some interruption broke the string.

Seamus set out to beat my record, which was 350 or thereabouts, but he could only make it to just over 100 and then packed it in. Which was, perhaps, just as well – counting like that probably does more harm to your brain that anything else. At least sheep bleat when they jump over the fence in your dreams.

The interviews and filming were fitting in well with the sightseeing, eating and beer-drinking which were part of my overall recovery. The one thing that *Gecko* had not scheduled was the fishing competition that was unfolding between Seamus and myself. He took the starboard rods and I took the port ones. We were allowed to manage our own rods and reels, and choose our Rapalas.

I felt pretty confident, because I had caught tons of fish in my life, whereas Seamus was new to the game. He started out by humbly asking my advice and about which Rapalas to use, which made me even more confident, especially when I soon forged ahead, five fish to his two. Then he began to catch up and eventually passed me. I caught up with him again, and then he got ahead again. By the end of the competition the score was 11 (me) and 10.5 (him).

The reason for his half-point was that at one stage he'd hooked a big kingfish and brought it on board, only to discover that in the process a shark had nipped off everything from below the gills. What remained weighed in at over 5 kg, so before the shark snacked on it the kingfish could easily have been over 12 kg. This made it easier for us to select which fish would become dinner (all our other catches were returned to the sea).

But as it turned out, I hadn't won yet. On the way back in to the harbour Seamus damned well went and caught not one but two more sizable fish, while I managed to hook the reef. I reckoned I was not going to hear the last about Seamus's triumph for a while, and I was right.

For our last evening together I took Seamus to the mainland, to show him something of what Madagascar was like outside the glitzy tourist enclaves. That included eating too many brochettes, having a few beers and eventually landing up at a Malagasy nightclub.

In the interests of truth I must also add that while Seamus and I were tucking into the brochettes at a roadside stall we had an unexpected encounter with another species of Malagasy wildlife. A girl in her twenties came up and greeted us in French, which she followed up with an invitation to come home with her for some slap-and-tickle.

This was too good a joke opportunity to ignore, so I turned to Seamus and told him the girl wanted to provide some hospitality of the close kind. She understood this somehow, and with a big grin she put her hand on my shoulder and said: 'Man *jeu trois*, no problem. *Très bien*. No problem,' drawing a circle in the air with her index finger to emphasise that she was talking about a threesome.

Aah, the French! I thought, *they make everything sound so romantic and sincere.* But (this is also the truth) we had to disappoint her. Still, our spurning of her charms probably didn't ruin her day, since there were lots of other customers at the stall.

The night club was not just about loud music – it also had a big screen showing (to my joy) a rugby match, and (to my even greater joy) not just any rugby match: the Springboks were about to run out against the English. Terrific! Except that I then fell asleep and missed it all!

But all good things come to an end. I was a giant refreshed, and eager to hit the ocean road once more. As a parting gift Mike and Harriet arranged accommodation for me with a friend of theirs who owned a beautiful lodge in the jungles of Sakatia Island, just west of Nosy Bé.

And so I said goodbye to this very hospitable couple who had gone to such trouble and expense to make our stay a memorable one, then paddled off to say goodbye to my friendly acquaintance Marcello at the Amarina before pointing my kayak's bow towards Nosy Sakatia.

I had been beaten, bloodied and considerably bowed, but thanks to some of the good people in this world I had picked myself up from the floor, ready for the next few rounds.

CHAPTER 26

TERNS AND TURTLES ... AND THE
FIFTH BROTHER CHICKEN

The closer I got the less cut-and-dried the whole idea sounded.
When I had about 50 metres to go before landing on the
enigmatic sugar loaf I started to feel intimations of mortality.

José and Gabriella housed me at their wonderful Sakatia lodge and (among other things) fed me some brilliant spaghetti bolognaise. I loved it all. Even a cameo appearance in the shooting of one of Top Travel TV episodes fitted nicely into my preparation schedule. This was the perfect spot for really starting the dash southwards.

There was now yet another carrot – an irresistible one – dangling in front of me. If I could reach Mahajanga before Christmas, Vasti was going to try and get a flight there ... our first Christmas together in 10 years. It was going to be a tough call because it was still 400 km away, but I was feeling fit and confident that I could boost my daily average and make it on time.

Having seen some of the local terrain during my cruise in *Gecko* with Harriet and Mike, I was also confident about where I should be heading. This first open-water stretch after Nosy Sakatia had me very far out from the mainland again, 20 km or so, because I was on the way to one of the islands we had sailed past, a turtle sanctuary just north of the Fifth Brother, the island where going ashore was an act of suicide.

Something amazing happened out there. A seagull or tern (I'm not sure which now) was flying over me, heading north. I was intrigued at how far out to sea this bird was, and clearly heading even further from land. Just for fun I let out a seagull-style squawk I had been practising, in addition to Malagasy. The bird immediately tilted its head towards me.

Well, well! Was it merely a coincidence, or was I actually talking seabird language? I squawked again, and this time the bird waggled its tail-feathers and dived sharply in my direction. I watched it come down, more interested than ever, because up to now seabirds had generally ignored me.

Not this one. It headed straight for me, and about five metres from me raised its head, flared its wings open to slow down and landed on the bow of the kayak. This was a real moment, I exulted. Of course, in a minute or two the bird would take fright at something I did and fly away.

But it didn't happen. She (the bird was so beautiful it must have been a girl) made herself comfortable on the bow and didn't stir a feather, not even when I spoke to her and asked her where she was on her way to. I decided to take a short break and mix myself a cappuccino sachet – Seamus had thoughtfully brought me a new supply. She was comfortable with that, too, and set about cleaning herself.

I finished the cappuccino and got ready to start paddling again. Now, surely, she would say goodbye! Out of courtesy I explained to my new friend that she would also have to be on her way now, because she had been heading north and I was going in the opposite direction. But once again it didn't happen – this bird seemed to be keen for the company, or maybe the free ride, or both.

I began paddling, gently at first, trying not to rock the boat too much and splash her. But the sea was smooth and up on the kayak's pronounced bow she stayed nice and dry. Eventually I was paddling at full speed, keeping up a continuous conversation with the occasional humorous little squawk thrown in to make her feel really at home.

I was so engrossed in this one-sided dialogue (if there is such a thing) that it was only while taking another break an hour later that I realised I hadn't taken her picture.

I got out my camera and did the necessary. By now I was questioning her sanity for not doing what birds do, as well as my own for having a protracted conversation with a seabird. Perfect footage for the documentary. Yip, I was slowly learning.

It was all just too good to last, and it didn't. The weather decided I was having too much fun and turned on me, which meant the end of my plans to head past Russian Bay's entrance and spend the night next to the ruins of the wrecked hotel. I would have to settle for an island owned by a Malagasy friend of Harriet's that we had identified as a possible stopover place.

Having parted company with my seabird friend at last, I paddled into the southern bay, which was not as pristinely untouched as most of the north-easterly islands had been, and after I had landed I walked up what felt like a thousand steps and eventually found a few bush huts, inhabited by 10 Malagasy and about 50 lemurs.

Harriet's friend had given me a letter to the main man on the island, one Arsène, that would have probably landed me inside one of the bush huts, but somehow I had lost it. It didn't worry me – I had missed my tent amid all that luxury and would be quite content simply to be given a spot on the western side of the beach where I could erect it.

Arsène was happy to oblige and allocated a suitable spot, spelling out a few rules: where I could relieve myself, which rocks were sacred and not to be touched, where the turtle nesting-grounds were and so on. Everything was perfectly clear to me except for the bit about the nesting-ground, since my tent seemed to be slap bang in the middle of it. Oh, well, when in Madagascar do as the Malagasy do ...

I pitched my tent under the supervision of Arsène and his colleagues, shared a giant bowl of rice with them and headed for bed – I hadn't paddled for a while, so the 40 km I had covered had been more taxing than would normally have been the case. I drifted off very peacefully in the deepening dusk ... till someone bumped into my tent and started pushing at it.

'Who's that?' I asked, lifting myself onto an elbow. Nothing. 'Who's that?' I said again, louder this time.

Still no response, although the pushing seemed to ease off slightly. I decided to be brave and confront this extremely rude person who was interrupting an honest adventurer's slumbers. So I unzipped the two layers of my tent in a firm, no-nonsense way, grabbed my small metal torch for a weapon and threw back the flaps to confront the intruder.

The intruder was not intimidated by my bravura – in fact, didn't even notice me. It was a large female hawksbill turtle, busily digging an egg-laying hole no more than a metre away, her hind flippers throwing up sprays of sand that pattered down onto my tent; her large tracks in the sand showing that she had actually crawled over the foot part of the tent. Talk about minding your own business!

In the circumstances an indignant 'hey, go and dig somewhere else' obviously was not going to have any effect, so instead I ducked back inside the tent for my video camera. My filming didn't distract her either, not even when I went in really close to get some 'money' shots. She just kept on digging till the hole was about 35 or 40 cm deep – she had some difficulty along the way when she hit bedrock – and then laid a neat pile of golfball-sized eggs.

During the egg-laying I got right up to her face with its aptly named hawk's bill mouth, but she didn't bat an eyelid (not at me anyway – she was blinking, but it was to get rid of the sand she had kicked into her eyes during the digging). Slobber ran from her nose and mouth from the effort, and it was easy to see how a turtle could be killed by any bad-intentioned man or beast while she was laying.

When all her eggs had been laid she began to cover them with the same rhythm she had used during the digging, pausing now and then to rest. Halfway through she was utterly exhausted and took a long break. Eventually she was finished; she patted the sand down neatly, swung herself around on her belly-plate and dragged herself back to the water, pausing three times along the way to rest.

Then she was in the water and back to being a graceful sea-creature. The sun had dipped behind the horizon already, so I could see her clearly as she swam away, back in her world, a world of safety where she was agile and not helpless and in peril from the predators who spent their life on land.

When you see nature in action like this and you hear of the threats to the survival of some species you wonder why they have not adapted better. To my mind the answer is simple. Man has evolved too quickly, with no concern for the other creatures who share our planet. They have zero chance if we continue on our destructive path.

Falling asleep again, I had the day play over in my mind as if I were in a movie theatre. Incredible. Incredible experience and opportunity. I was the only one in this theatre and could not understand why no else had made the effort to be there.

Next stop: Fifth Brother. Visiting the ominous island was definitely in my plans as I paddled away after saying goodbye to Arsène and his colleagues – not just to have a closer look but to climb onto it, superstitions or no superstitions. *It's just a rock!* I told myself as I neared this famed and feared piece of Malagasy earth. *I'll just get onto it, take a picture and then be on my way.*

It was going to be that simple, so I imagined. No worries about the difficulty of managing the endless succession of dangerous waves breaking onto the rocks, nor the fact that most of the island consisted of cliffs 100 metres high, going straight up from the water. No problem!

But the closer I got, the less cut-and-dried the whole idea sounded. When I had about 50 metres to go before landing on the enigmatic sugar loaf I started to feel intimations of mortality. To put it more bluntly, I found myself recalling all the death-and-gloom stories I had been told, and I got scared.

What if there was just a .0000000001 per cent chance that the superstition was true? What then? Was that additional .0000000001 per cent risk worth adding to the ones I was already taking? That nagging little voice simply refused to be shut down. The bottom line was that I was, as they say in the classics, chickening out. No more, no less. I was simply too chicken to climb onto the rock because of all those stories that I had airily dismissed as rubbish and hogwash just a couple of days earlier.

I found myself wondering, as I drifted to within a metre of the rock and glided nervously by: *If I touch it with my hands, will that be the same as climbing onto it?* Not being a metaphysician, there was no answer to that, so I settled for giving the rock a few nudges with my paddle and a bit of gangster talk: 'How does that feel, huh? Let's see what you can do? Is that all you've got? You're a fake, man, a fake!' Yes, I showed that old rock, I'm telling you.

Having boosted my ego, I paddled off in a mood of semi-happiness with my feeble 'accomplishment', mixed with semi-worry about the risk – if there was one – that I had taken. It struck me that if touching it with the paddle was enough to set the curse in motion I had probably just passed part of it on to the paddle-maker back home in Cape Town, Alexa Cole.

Mentally I apologised to Alexa for possibly involving her in such dark doings, while at the same time I was unable to prevent myself from speculating about the possibility that if there *was* a curse, maybe it had been weakened by being shared ... Damn! I was really going squirrelly.

At first I didn't even see Nosy Iranja, my destination for the day, because I was goggling at the jellyfish around me – hectares of them. It was a sight both interesting and frightening. Surely a person who fell into this thick concentration could die if he was stung all over his body? The amount of neurotoxins entering his bloodstream would surely be strong enough to stop his heart, probably after first sending him into a coma.

I mean, I've been stung as a teenager in the surf at Richards Bay on the KwaZulu-Natal coast, and suffered somewhat. In addition to the pain my glands always became inflamed and I had a few dizzy spells as well. Multiply that by a few hundred ... I tried not to think about it, and I had no intention of testing my theory by falling into this sludge of jelly and poisons.

Horrible though it might be, it was an incredible sight, especially when the sun broke through and its light was refracted brightly in every single dome of the creatures around me. An aerial photo would have been worth a million bucks, I'm sure. I did take a few underwater pics, and picked up a few stings on my hand. My experience is that the palm of your hand isn't as sensitive to the poisons as the rest of you. Why? Well, why indeed?

Looking at my footage, I was astounded once again at how this underwater housing Sony gave me for the Cybershot could assess all the distances and the constantly changing light conditions to capture some really stunning pics.

The water was as flat as it had been the previous morning, but the heat was most definitely back to what I'd experienced in the last three months, and I couldn't even cool myself down with the sea water, because that was warm as well. Even the water inside the kayak had taken on a near 30-degree temperature. Needless to say, my drinking-water was lukewarm, too.

Nosy Iranja was what Hilton – who had worked there for a while, if I remember correctly, and had made some good friends – had described as another piece of paradise. One of his friends was the manager there, another South African called Theo, and Hilton had said I should simply rock up and tell Theo that he (Hilton) had said Theo must help me.

That wasn't exactly my style, and I was trying to work out a way of turning it into a more jokey approach as I got nearer, in between admiring what I saw. Nosy Iranja is a legendary island that you have unknowingly seen in many Madagascar brochures – actually two islands that are joined for half the day by a 600 metre sandbank but at high tide are separated by a strong flow of water.

Essentially the local tides and currents have worked in tandem for centuries to keep depositing enough sand to maintain the bank to create this spectacle. The smaller of the two islands hosts the luxury lodge run by Theo and the other is a protected reserve with a small village on it. An interesting fact about the bigger island is that the lighthouse (of which Madagascar has many, some of them out of service) was designed by none other than Gustav Eiffel, builder of Paris's most enduring tourism icon.

Not knowing what I discovered later on, I was hesitant about simply marching up this six-star lodge's beach to ask for help; these lodges zealously protect the privacy and wishes of their clients, and in fact Iranja even had private security men to enforce this protection.

One of them in his police-style uniform came up to me and tried to persuade me, with an emphasis that seemed to border on exerting physical restraint, that my best option was to turn around and go back to wherever I had come from. He kept saying 'No *entrée*, no *entrée*!' and I kept saying: '*S'il vous plaît, je veux Monsieur Theo.*'

This guy was good, and didn't crumble at the mention of his boss's name, but I was more determined than he was. I began a slow tired jog towards a building on the beach, but the rent-a-cop held me back, put my kayak back into the water and called for backup on his radio. Fortunately I managed to catch the recreation manager's eye in this building just before the security men really tackled me, and I told this man that I was a friend of Theo's and that he was expecting me.

Of course this was a little white lie, but only a little one – granted, Theo wasn't my friend, but he was a *friend* of a friend, and that was the best I could do in the circumstances. The recreation manager was more responsive to name-dropping than the rent-a-cop, and three minutes later I was standing in front of the great man himself and telling him that he had better help me or Hilton would disown him.

Theo really was a South African, although a long-term expatriate, and he was more than willing to help, as Hilton had predicted. The result was that he booked me into one of his bungalows for two days.

Did I really deserve a rest day at this stage? Well, no, not really. But this place was built along the same lines as Hilton's hotel. Everything a guest did – eating, sleeping, showering – was slotted seamlessly into the surrounding natural landscape. I realised that I was over-qualified to talk about humble accommodation and needed to work on my bad points – and right here at Nosy Iranja I confirmed my commitment to self-betterment.

Sony had kitted me out with a small laptop to use mainly for storing or transferring digital video and stills from my cameras, and I copied all the stills while I had the time and electricity, but decided to leave the video for one fell swoop when I got to Mahajanga. More motivation to get a move on!

Breakfast was fruit and more fruit, and although most of it was fresh only in the sense that it had just arrived from South Africa, it tasted as if it had been picked in the orchard out back. Dining in the evening was memorable. You might think that by now I had eaten enough fish to last me a lifetime, but don't you believe it — I tripled up on my Espadon Carpaccio starter as my main course

I had always believed espadon to be just another marlin, but now discovered that this was not so. Theo's guests, who came from all over the world – one man was the former owner of Jordan shoes and had lived in South Africa for two decades! – were very knowledgeable and soon put me right. Espadon was a stockier and more difficult fish to target, they told me, because it swam in extremely deep water and put up a long fight.

I was very interested in this sort of expert information, but I also had another pressing question to ask, which went something like this: 'Ah, waiter ... could you bring me another portion of espadon, if it's not too much trouble?'

I left before sunrise, so I said all my goodbyes before going to bed. When Theo's turn came he spoke very proudly of his island as a turtle sanctuary and advised me to keep an eye open for them when I left; I had told him of my experience on the island near the Fifth Brother and my hitch-hiking bird friend, and he had sensed that I loved animals, big time.

Unfortunately, though, it was too dark for me to see any turtle activity. But I couldn't wait. Thanks to that extra day at Irania I had a very long paddle ahead of me, and a famous island archipelago in my sights. The Radamas, I had been told, were considered even more beautiful and bountiful in all regards than Nosy Bé. Well, we'd see about that.

CHAPTER 27

SHARK ATTACK, HEART ATTACK

I was amazed at the damage the shark had done to the kayak's aluminium rudder. The rudder was 5 mm thick, but it was twisted; not bent, twisted! That must have taken considerably more force than would be needed simply to bend it. The shark had obviously scored a direct hit on the rudder, and with the continued force the metal had had no choice but to give way.

Everyone always asks me whether I have ever seen a shark and for a long time my answer was always: 'No, thankfully, no!' But all that changed about a kilometre before I reached the island of Kalakajoro on the fringes of the Radama archipelago (yes, it lived up to its name, the islands are stunning and have some of the best fishing in the world), where I planned to set up camp for the night.

Usually the last few kilometres of each day were strenuous and seemed unwilling to come to an end, so it's understandable that sometimes I wandered into a sort of *dwaal* – an apt Afrikaans word, meaning to wander – filled with vague visions of how nice it would be to get off my aching backside and plant my foot-soles on land again.

Perhaps 'plant' isn't the right word here. Walking wasn't a pleasure just then. The cuts under my feet that I had suffered all those months ago at Foule Point *still* hadn't healed, and almost every time I was out of the sea-water for longer than a night they became inflamed. What worried me was that the cuts seemed to be turning into holes that did not want to close up or heal. They weren't painful if left untouched, but if any pressure was applied I felt like uttering a falsetto scream.

I didn't know what to do. I didn't want to take antibiotics and I couldn't afford the time to stop off long enough to allow the cuts to get well. But maybe I would just have to afford the time soon. Apart from the cuts, my heels were beginning to fray, like a weather-beaten flag, with pieces of skin, sometimes thick ones, simply peeling off. Only one thing would cure that, and that was to get out of the sea water for longer than a day or two.

It had been another long, hot day, sticking close to shore for most of the way. The Radama archipelago has one large island and a few smaller ones all the way around it, and I had no need for company or luxury: all I needed was to find a piece of terra firma. The afternoon winds had been toying with me for days – sometimes turning themselves into head-winds, sometimes not, so every time the wind came up I had to be ready, mentally as much as physically, for a fight. And as often as not, I would just finish gearing myself for an afternoon's struggle when the wind would suddenly drop.

There was frantic activity around me in the sea just a few kilometres off the islands. Four or five times large king mackerel launched themselves entirely out of the water in an acrobatic display that resulted from their utter commitment to catching their prey. Unlike flying fish, the king mackerel didn't leap out to escape danger – it was just that they worked up such speed that they couldn't help leaving the water.

Anyway, I had decided to make the island of Kalakajoro my stop-over for the night. From what I could see it was pretty and had a

My constant companions. Hundreds of whales passed by me, some no more than a metre away. The hump of a humpbacked whale is approximately one third of the body. My kayak is 5 metres long. You do the math of this beast. Her baby rolled around on her snout, easily double the length of my vessel. Breaching whales did so at times within splashing distance. Top right is 10–15 metres away from me. Waves from the splash totally covered me and my kayak.

Sugar loafs off Nosy Bé. 'If you touch this rock you will die!' the Malagasy superstition goes.

Bottom left, Cap Sainte Marie, and the first time I gave myself a pat on the back. What I was trying to accomplish had sunk in. I like pictures that say to the viewer 'wish you were here – you can be'.

The harbour of Tamatave in sight, 5 km away. Can this be possible – 5 000 km of unventured waters, another world first, and behind my name? It felt like a dream. To have the people that mattered waiting at the end was first prize. The victory stance (right), which Seamus prophesied would definitely be the one for the end. I hold the bottle of bubbly, with Johan Loots looking on. Ambassador Monaisa got me out of prison a few times and negotiated successfully with the 'new' government to have me continue. Vasti was more part of this journey than of the Africa one – that was the way I wanted it. So many to thank ...

calm beach which just might have a fisherman or two in residence. Perfect!

I was enjoying a typical mind-wander, feet hanging casually over the side and stroking absent-mindedly over a shallow reef, with two large bottle-nosed dolphins keeping pace, when a shark's fin at least 30 cm high broke out of the water, moving at speed past the left side of the kayak, about two metres away. The fin rounded the kayak's bow and then sank away a few metres later. I sat stunned, while the dolphins shot off in different directions.

It had been a bull shark, or a tiger shark, to use its better-known name, I was sure of that – I'd seen the wavy lines on its back as well as the thickness around its head that was a sure indication of the species. And a fin of 30 cm or more meant it was near to gigantic. What the hell was going to happen now? What was I going to *do* now?

As always, my reflexes took over in the absence of any brain-function, and I grabbed my camera. This I had to have a picture of, not least for the folks back home who believed that I staggered from one shark encounter to the next, whereas I hadn't even had one.

I sat there, floating with the tide, for about three minutes, this time with my feet definitely not in the water, and waited for it to come back. That shark was interested in me … or was it? But it seemed it had decided I was not an edible item. Disappointed – and, to be honest, relieved as well – I got back into my paddling position, strapped the camera into the webbing on the deck and set off on the last few hundred metres to the beach, starting with a few extra-hard strokes to get the heavily laden kayak moving.

Once it was in motion I fell into normal paddling rhythm. One stroke … a second … a third … and then at the eighth stroke there was an almighty thud from behind me – maybe 'smash' would be a better word. My head hit the back of the kayak before I knew what was going on, and I realised I was now lying completely on my back; the paddle knocked right out of my left hand: fortunately I hadn't capsized.

And, just as fortunately, I didn't panic when I got my wits back after a few seconds of blankness. I pulled myself back up to my normal seated position and twisted around to see what had happened behind me. The water was a foamy mess, and in the spatter I could make out the contorted body of this same shark whose acquaintance I had made earlier. It seemed to be momentarily dazed. Then it gave itself a violent shake and vanished into the depths.

I was still dazed myself. Had it really happened – had a shark really rammed me, or had I had some sort of sea-nightmare? And if it *had* happened, had the shark rammed me on purpose, and was it going to come back?

Reaction started to set in now; I was panting and felt drugged and weak. But I retained enough sense to summon up the strength and co-ordination to start paddling again. Once I got to land I would be safe. So I paddled and paddled, expecting another attack at any moment.

As I dug away at the water I did something which was pretty funny in retrospect. I took out my aptly named 'Dog of War' knife and unfolded its thick, sharp blade. This knife was an impressive piece of cutlery, but I couldn't help feeling that I would still be distinctly out-gunned if the shark came visiting again. Even so, I gripped it between my teeth like a pirate so I would be ready for anything. I had got over the worst of my shock now and had decided that if that shark came back and knocked me into the water I'd be ready for him. I wasn't going to get eaten without a fight – that shark would discover that there really wasn't any such thing as a free lunch. This 'dog of war' still had a bite or two in reserve.

But the shark didn't come back, and soon I was on dry land. The beach I had seen was every bit the sanctuary I'd imagined. There were about 10 huts along its edge, and I was welcomed by a few fishermen who were repairing their nets and barely batted an eyelid at my unexpected arrival. I didn't spend much time on greetings: I wanted to see what the shark episode had done to the kayak.

I didn't find any bite-marks, which I had expected, but I was amazed at the damage the shark had done to the kayak's aluminium rudder. The rudder was 5 mm thick, but it was twisted; not bent, twisted! That must have taken considerably more force than would be needed simply to bend it. The shark had obviously scored a direct hit on the rudder, and with the continued force the metal had had no choice but to give way.

'*Requin, requin*,' the fishermen began telling one another (meaning 'shark' in French). '*Oui, oui!*' and '*deux cent kilos, peut-être deux cent cinquante*' (200 kilos, maybe 250).

What the fishermen were telling me was that they were familiar with this resident shark – they had probably had similar experiences to mine, I reckoned. They fell about laughing as I explained in a mixture of French, English and Malagasy about my encounter with their scary neighbour, and clearly accepted me into their brotherhood.

My intention had been to sleep on the beach in front of their pirogues, but they believed I'd do better at the French-run fishing lodge just around the corner from their village. I paddled around to it, with some of the younger fishermen and five or six kids trotting along the beach to show me exactly where it was.

The lodge was definitely not five-star as regards either comfort or friendliness, but then I wasn't looking for any more than a place to rest and take stock of the day's experiences. Its reed huts were tucked into the bush along the hill above the beach and creaked and groaned in the wind. The view was stunning, though, and made up for the lack of toilets and running water. If someone had asked me about what a fishing getaway should look like, this is not what I would have had in mind. But what the hell – I didn't need much, and I could have been sleeping in a shark's belly.

Next morning I found I had been robbed again, but in a very strange and somewhat ironical way. Back in Tamatave I had put three supporter stickers on the kayak's bow – a Springbok rugby badge, a Pirates soccer team badge and then, of course, the badge of my local rugby team, the Sharks. Soon after my arrival I had seen a girl aged about 10 sitting on the bow of the kayak, glancing warily around while she fiddled at something with her left hand.

I was up on the hill, too far away to shout at her, and tired, and so I persuaded myself that she was just sitting there, perfectly innocently. Well, she hadn't been. She had nicked the Sharks badge, which must have taken some effort because it was firmly glued on. How strange that my Sharks badge should have been stolen off the kayak on the very day that a real live one had scared the life out of me!

Why had the shark attacked me? If you are a fan of films like 'Jaws' you would be convinced that it was simply a bad fellow that was hooked on eating humans, but in my halting conversation with the fishermen I found out the true reason, and the lodge's French operator concurred. The shark had been attracted to the kayak, they said, because the splashing of my paddles had made sounds very similar to the ones made by schools of bait fish near the surface.

This gave me some food for thought, and in the morning I set off in a distinctly thoughtful mood.

Now, a shark is an obvious danger to a kayaker, but there are other less obvious ones, and they aren't all under the water. Flying fish, for example, which launch themselves out of the water – sometimes alone but often in large schools – and glide over the surface for up to 30 or 40 metres before going down again. The major reason why they have this flying ability is to escape from lurking predators – a very effective now-you-see-me-now-you-don't routine, I think.

But don't get in their way. A flying fish can be 45 cm long, and in a flight lasting nearly a minute can get up to 60 km/h – and they have sharp, spear-like bills that once or twice have nearly ended up sticking into me when one has launched itself in the opposite direction to a predator and I have innocently been in the way.

Which brings me to my heart attack story. People over-use the phrase, 'You nearly gave me a heart attack' when you have frightened them by accident, but I can say in all truthfulness that on this leg of my trip I was closer to suffering cardiac arrest than I had ever been.

I had just left a rocky beach where I had gone ashore for a little rest and refreshment, so I was ultra-relaxed as I got back out onto the smooth water again. Paddling is usually very different from cycling, because you constantly have to concentrate – unless, of course, the water is as smooth as a baby's bottom.

This afternoon it was baby's-bottom time, and I was soon in a very drowsy state. But then this pleasant *dwaal* session was interrupted by a cloud of hand-sized fish – a couple of hundred of them – that exploded out of the sea a few metres in front of the bow and came directly at me, probably spooked by my kayak cutting through the water towards them.

They were not flying fish, but normal ones that looked like bream, probably weighing about 300 grams apiece on average, but they were in the air and coming straight at me. The speed with which all this happened was extraordinary. Before I could duck or even register the sound of the exploding water some of them were already hitting me on the shoulder.

Now I was the one to be spooked, which was understandable, because the shark-ramming experience was still very fresh in my mind, and I have to admit that I emitted some classic terrified-individual whimperings before I got my mind back together and told myself to stop over-reacting and just carry on paddling.

Which I did, only to see another similar-sized school take to the air in front of my bow, but this lot went from right to left, splashed down and then took flight twice more as they got away from me. All I can say is that the bottom of my kayak must have looked or sounded pretty terrifying for some reason.

Or perhaps there was something dire going on underneath me

that I didn't know about, because I had constant encounters with leaping fish. At the very entrance to the harbour at Mahajanga, some days later, I was snaking my way in between a number of fishing boats when a king mackerel that must have weighed between two and three kilos shot at least five metres into the air in front of me, seemed to pause in mid-air for a moment and then turned itself casually to make a graceful re-entry into the ocean.

It was at times like these that I realised once again how fortunate I was to be able to witness the marvels of the sea at such close range ... in spite of near-heart attacks and flying assassins!

CHAPTER 28

SAVED BY THE PRAWNS

I thought I'd caught sight of the island and turned slightly more seawards to aim directly at it. But an hour later, with just about that much more time left before sunset, the horrible truth became clear: the 'island' was actually a small dhow sailing towards me, so slowly that my eyes had fooled me into thinking it was stationary.

I had left Kalakajoro later than I should have for a 45 km-plus day. The seas were mild enough to keep me confident, but it was clear from the outset as I began navigating between the islands – some small, others big – that there were serious tidal currents to contend with. At times I could feel the kayak moving laterally, a distinctly odd feeling. Fortunately my plan was to stay on the outside/western side of the archipelago, so the sideways drift suited my purpose to some degree.

I created a problem for myself when I took a stop-over on the most westerly island, Antanimora. I stopped on the southernmost point, pulled my kayak up on the rocky shore, mixed some energy juice and then quite inadvertently fell asleep in the sun and didn't wake up till an hour later. This might not sound like much of a problem, but that's what it was.

I had lost an hour's paddling time, and while I had snoozed away in the sun the tide had gone down and the water's edge was now 100 or so metres away, leaving me high, dry, sunburnt and lethargic rather than revitalised. In my post-nap drowsy state I had to make my way slowly back to water deep enough for the kayak to float, with the sharp rocks and spiky sea urchins making sure that I made haste slowly. It felt like an eternity before the water was deep enough for me to get onto the kayak again and take up my battle with the clock – I had just over half of the day's planned distance ahead of me, but only a quarter of daylight time left to cover it.

I decided to aim for a small island called Nosy Saba that Theo from Nosy Iranja had referred me to, where a man called Patrice was building a lodge. Theo and Patrice had had a couple of run-ins and I didn't expect anything much in the way of hospitality, but I needed to find the tiny island because it was the only destination I could reach in the time I had left. So there I was, 10 km out to sea, aiming with my Garmin and watching the sun setting.

But Nosy Saba just stayed away, because in addition to everything else the current had turned against me, both figuratively and literally. I didn't discover this till I stopped at one point to mix myself a lukewarm cappuccino, checked my Garmin – and found that that I was moving *backwards* at 3 km/h, normal walking speed on land!

The only way to tackle this unexpected problem was to leave off any more coffee breaks and paddle like hell. I calculated that if I could keep up a gross speed of 10 km/h I could average the 6 or 7 km/h that I would need to get me to the as yet unseen island before nightfall.

So I dug in. At one stage I got a little encouragement from seeing a big sailing dhow that was a kilometre further offshore and at times was moving slower than I was. All right, it was clearly overloaded with goods and people as well as having very little help from the wind, but I stayed just ahead of it. So perhaps I wasn't doing too badly!

Another time I thought I'd caught sight of the island and turned slightly seawards to aim directly at it. But an hour later, with just about that much more time left before sunset, the horrible truth became clear: the 'island' was actually a small dhow sailing *towards* me, so slowly that my eyes had fooled me into thinking it was stationary.

It was a bad moment, but Nosy Saba was still there on the GPS screen, and to my desperate eyes it looked closer than before. Wishful thinking, perhaps, but just then it was all I had to cling to. And I mean 'all', because the sun-glare now made it nearly impossible to scan the horizon properly. I literally kept going on faith.

It was another sharp reminder of what it meant to be a solo adventurer. Going it alone means you don't have people ready to plan your daily route, reassure you about your progress and then, if everything goes pear-shaped, whip you out of the water. Nope, you're all by yourself, at the mercy of your own and nature's devices.

Facing my predicament seemed to calm me down, and as the sun dipped its lower half behind the dark horizon I didn't feel any panic, just took out my camera and shot one of the prettiest sunsets I'd ever seen, one where I was, as I like to say, 'right inside the picture', which gave it so much more meaning.

And then, as if by magic, Nosy Saba appeared out of the fading sun-glare. Now I realised why I had not spotted the island earlier – it was very flat, with nothing higher than a few pine-type trees lining one side. Just as the sun set completely I saw a powerful torch flashing from between the trees, and I was sure the people there had spotted me and were guiding me in to the safest landing area.

I had been heading for the nearest piece of island, but now I changed direction towards the flashing light, overcome with relief that I was expected – a wonderful feeling after a long and stressful day. A little later I steered the kayak in next to three or four small ski-boats and pulled it ashore.

Somewhat to my surprise, no one was waiting for me as I dragged the kayak to above the high-water mark. I looked around and called out 'hello' a few times, got no response and went to look for some signs of life. How strange that the islanders should guide me in and then ignore me!

A few hundred metres further, after wandering past the almost-finished lodge building, I found a brightly lit building that looked as if it was destined to be a dining hall. I walked in, still soaking wet, and found myself face to face with a white man. I gave him a friendly greeting and asked to speak to Patrice. He stared at me, not saying a word. Thinking he had misunderstood, I asked him again, and then he replied: 'Who are you to ask?'

Not exactly a friendly response, but I kept my cool. I told him who I was, that I had been told about this great lodge that was about to open and (without mentioning names) that the guys from Tsara Banjina and Nosy Iranja had referred me to him, hinting that I would be looked after if I asked for help. As an afterthought, I asked half-jokingly whether he was the man who had flashed the torch to help me come in.

Patrice (because this was him, as it turned out) responded to my question in a pretty disheartening way: Why, he asked, would he want to help me get to shore? I was taken aback, to say the least. Why would he want to treat me like this? What was he going to do, tell me to get the hell off his island?

At that moment, fortunately, one those super-friendly Malagasy guys that I kept on meeting arrived on the scene and led me to a small office next to the hall and introduced me to the general manager. His name was Laurent, and what a different human being he was. He didn't even mind that I muddied up his fancy office floor.

Laurent said he was happy to help me out – 'But first we eat!' He would feed me, he said, if I was willing to be a test subject for the hotel's new staff – kitchen workers, waiters, cleaners and so on. I had no trouble agreeing to be his guinea-pig. It isn't often that you pay for your accommodation simply by allowing yourself to be pampered. It had turned out to be a good day, after all.

Thanks to the decent food and rest I enjoyed at Nosy Saba (not to mention the opportunity to recharge the batteries of my various bits and pieces of electronic gear) I set myself a stiff target for the next leg – 40 to 50 kilometres across the mouth of the Bay of Narinda. My first stop would be Nosy Lava, about 25 km away, a big island almost directly in line with my course.

For some obscure reason I had been unable to e-mail my newspaper column back to Cape Town via Laurent's satellite internet connection, and so I planned to got ashore at Nosy Lava and try again, if they had an internet connection. If not, I would do it over my satellite phone – sure, that way would be crazily expensive, but I had a good story to tell and in any case I didn't want to let the long-suffering editors down again, although luckily they knew that sending pieces regularly from the back of beyond was sometimes difficult, if not impossible.

Nosy Lava was easily discernable as I set out on a sea which was almost boiling with life; huge schools of bait fish swirled around below me and the predator fish were so busy attacking them that every now and then one would shoot out of the water.

Nosy Lava, incidentally, was locally famous for being the former home of one of Madagascar's largest prisons, a sort of Indian Ocean Alcatraz. Or perhaps it was more like the French Devil's Island in the Pacific, because most of the population, I was told, were freed convicts or their descendants.

I landed on the island's rocky west coast and this time left the kayak nearer the water so that I wouldn't end up being stranded by the tide again. I had decided while paddling that satellite phone dictation was going to be the way to send my column, although the token payment I received would probably only cover the first few minutes. I got hold of Seamus, who was at work and very busy but managed to squeeze in half an hour to take down the 800 words I dictated – which wasn't as easy as it sounds, because there was a lot of back-and-forthing to make sure everything was accurate.

While I was doing this, a large stilt-legged bird – a grey stork, I think – kept approaching closer and closer to me. I think it was genuinely inquisitive: at times it cocked its head as if trying to eavesdrop. It was good to have an interaction with nature on dry land, for a change.

The heat was horrendous, and taking a dip didn't help – the water was probably warmer than the air above it. It got so hot that after I had finished with Seamus I crawled in under a small ledge in the rock to cool down. What I had not planned to do was to enjoy the relative coolness so much that I fell asleep again; when I woke up about an hour later I realised how fortunate I was that my kayak had not been carried away by the tide from where I had recklessly left it to save myself some effort.

That wasn't the worst of it: while I had been sawing logs under the ledge the wind had picked up to such an extent that I realised I would have to spend the night where I was, and with considerable self-disgust set about looking for a place to pitch my tent. But once again help came from an unexpected source.

As I stood looking grimly out at my invisible destination, which I would now not be able to reach till some time the next day, I heard a splash to my left and spotted a snorkel bobbing up and down in the rocky shallows nearby. I wasted no time in dragging my kayak into the water and going out to make the acquaintance of the snorkel's owner. He turned out to be a French tourist who explained that he had sailed there with a friend, and that they were staying in huts just over the hill – nowhere near the prison, he hastened to add with a grin.

This was good news. I found the huts and negotiated a token fee with the owner to sleep there. And that was how the big day I had planned turned into a much smaller one. I knew that I would have to make up for it tomorrow and the next day, because I was beginning slowly to fall behind schedule.

I spent a pleasant evening with the two Frenchmen. They were both retired policemen, relatively young at 58 and in brilliant shape. They were living proof of something I had often seen: people who enjoy the outdoors are at an immediate advantage when it comes to staying fit, healthy and in shape. Forget the technical explanations – that's just how it works out.

A little further down the coast I made the acquaintance of a company that gladdens the hearts of countless food-loving Frenchmen: UNIMA, a prawn-farming organisation that supplies most of France with its stocks of the delicious little crustaceans.

I had put in a marathon 55 km that day as part of my catching-up project, and as I paddled towards a small turn in the coastline that I had selected as my end-point I felt the first symptoms of what promised to be a blinding migraine setting in. I couldn't understand it. I had eaten well, I wasn't having caffeine withdrawal and although 55 km was a very long haul, it wasn't *that* long.

But there it was. A migraine strikes at will, and from experience I knew this one was going to be a real paralyser. To make matters worse, I had just caught a huge 17-kilo kingfish which had been simply unable to resist my Rapala after it had been in the water no longer than 10 minutes. The kingfish was inconsiderate enough to put up a tremendous fight that lasted a good hour.

So, migraine in head and kingfish in tow, I rounded the little point where I intended to spend the night and to my delight sighted a small boat moored near a building ... a gift from God in my current state.

When I staggered ashore I discovered that the boat and building belonged to UNIMA, and the manager, a friendly Malagasy guy named Thierry, was more than willing to exchange the huge fish I had caught for a night under cover. As he smilingly put it, out here in the wilderness, all he and his staff ate was prawns. Now I could eat their prawns while they ate my fish. Whoever said bartering was out of date?

Thierry not only fed me prawns and put me up, he also made sure that the company doctor was available next morning to nurse my migraine, which had subsided but not yet vanished altogether. It would have been better, perhaps, if I had stayed over for another day, but I couldn't afford the time till I got to Mahajanga except in a case of dire emergency, which this was not. So after a sandwich, a heartfelt 'thank you' and an appropriate farewell I was on the water again.

Hilton at Tsara Banjina had told me a lot about my next stop – Anjajavy, Madagascar's first and most famous five-star eco-lodge, about 20 km away. I arrived there laden with gifts from the sea, because on the way I simply couldn't stop catching fish – first a small five-kilo kingfish, which I let go, then a mackerel of three or four kilos that I kept for dinner or a gift, then a massive kingfish that must have weighed something like 13 kilos.

This one I also let go, just like the first, as an act of contrition for killing that monstrous kingfish off Antalaha and then not eating it. I believed it was a good start towards making up with Mother Nature, over whose capacious bosom I was currently crawling.

Anjajavy looked exactly like Hilton's word-picture of it. First of all there was its stunning setting, in a cove created by dramatic rock formations on both sides of the beach, with beautiful A-frame bungalows spread along the rear. I strolled up the long wooden staircase that led off the sand onto a raised area with a lovely pool and dining area.

There I met the manageress, Natalie, and later Daniel, who was slightly higher up in the hierarchy, I suppose, because his mother owned the lodge. Daniel had often visited South Africa, he told me;

he lived part of the year in the United States with his mother and part of it here, and he was very hospitable. He insisted I have lunch with him, and since it was obviously too late to set off again afterwards, offered me a bed for the night in the staff house. I was glad to accept, because I wasn't feeling 100 per cent; although I had been taking plenty of paracetamol and Vitamin C, in fact I was feeling very run-down.

I still felt unwell when I got up early next morning. But there was no question of lingering: I had to keep moving, even if it was for only a few kilometres. Anyway, while saying my farewells to Daniel and Natalie I heard a strange remark that left me smiling all day. Daniel could see I wasn't well and asked if I was all right. I replied that I wasn't, and hinted that I probably needed to rest and recover a little more.

'Hmmmm,' Daniel pondered, 'I don't think that would be possible. I have told all the guests here that you are an adventurer, and, well, I just don't think that is what the people want to see: an adventurer not going out. They are all expecting to see you leave today.'

Now I don't think he meant it the way it sounds, but I had to smile at the fact that there were actually guests there who would be disappointed in not seeing an adventurer doing what he was supposed to do, namely carry on adventuring, right under their eyes. Classic!

Lovely new rock formations greeted me as I paddled away. The water was dirtyish, but there were plenty of fish – I caught and released a kingfish and a mackerel, but I kept another kingfish of about eight kilos. My day's target was a 40 km paddle down to another UNIMA station, and I got there easily enough. This prawn farm was a big one, spread out over a huge expanse of land just inside the bay I was about to cross, with some of the ponds several hundred metres long.

Once again I got a friendly welcome and the offer of a bed for the night. The accommodation they offered me wasn't luxurious, but it was more than enough for my needs, and I was grateful for it; I was still unwell and could feel a gradual physical deterioration setting in a little further with every passing day. But my routine had to remain the same: turn in early, rise just as early. That was the only way I was going to stay on schedule.

Another enduring memory of that farm that I took away with me involves some of the local wildlife, although not of a kind that I felt like making a close acquaintance with. This plant was in a wilderness area, and three times I had to dodge snakes at least a metre long *inside* their camp. No matter what people tell me about this snake or that not being lethal, I'm still petrified by them. These particular ones had bright contrasting patterns on their backs, and according to the staff there, were very common in that part of the world. So what!

The prawn farmers said goodbye with great excitement but also with trepidation. Ahead of me lay the long, narrow Bay of Mahajamba, and they didn't believe it was humanly possible for someone to cross it in a kayak; recently, they said, a ski-boat had capsized in the bay with the loss of all on board. I took this at face value because I had heard many similar ones already.

It did remind me, though, of a story Mr Thierry had told me. The prawn farm was well-known among the local communities of fishermen, he said, and when emergencies struck they were often asked to help get sick or injured people to hospitals. One such call awoke him in the middle of the night: sea cucumber fishermen/divers had been out on a deep reef off the coast near the mouth of Mahajamba Bay mouth and were taking a good catch when suddenly a shark attacked one man and bit off the entire calf-muscle of one of his legs.

They managed to get him on to the support boat within minutes and applied an ultra-tight tourniquet. The man was semi-conscious now and in a stable condition, so Mr Thierry had one of his skippers load the man and his friends into the larger of their ski-boats and race down to Mahajanga for help – not that he had much hope for the guy after seeing his injury, since there was nothing left of his leg but one long bone.

Well, the boat got to Mahajanga a few hours later and fortunately a doctor was available when they arrived. The problem was that this doctor had zero experience. From what I understood Mr Thierry to say, releasing a tourniquet after a lengthy time of constriction is virtually a sentence of immediate death because it results in an arterial spasm that will reduce a patient's chances to nil within seconds, even if the best resuscitation equipment is available. This doctor asked a few questions, got the patient into an operating theatre and did just that, and it was all over in one deep breath for this poor brave man of the sea.

It makes you think twice about criticising your local private hospital in South Africa for asking you to fill in the same admission form every time you go there; at least you know the doctor will have experience and knowledge that extend beyond the pages of a textbook.

I stayed very near the coastline as I headed towards the bay's 16 km mouth, and only chose a course for the dreaded crossing when I could clearly make out the white cliffs on the other side. I kept a sharp eye out when I set off on the crossing, because I knew four large rivers emptied into the bay, one of them the Mahajamba River, and I could expect to run across some debris and silt.

There was debris and silt all right, but on a scale that shocked me. I had only seen the result of deforestation of this magnitude once before, in Mozambique. The water was red-brown and soupy; I knew that from here the bay ran inland for 28 km and was 10 km wide in places, and that the loss of this amount of silt – essentially quality top soil – would be considered a catastrophe almost anywhere in the world. Unbelievable, simply unbelievable. It looked as if the earth's very life-blood was pouring into the sea.

But I had other things to contend with. The sea was waging a war with a strong current, and now I understood why boats could sink here. Yet in all truth I wasn't worried about my own safety; I was too concerned with looking ahead, from just beyond my bow to 300 metres further, to see where this ghastly red sludge came to an end. And I wondered who, meaning which NGO, was supposed to be trying to educate both the government and thus the locals about what the deforestation was doing, not just to their land but to their future.

It is difficult to digest this. I believe people in glass houses shouldn't throw stones. The West has screwed up its environment but now wants to tell the rest of us how to save ours. The other side of the argument, one which I'm in favour of, is to let the idiots who couldn't look after their most precious riches, but are wise enough to admit their mistakes, come to share what the developed countries believe were their turning-points in balancing development with preservation.

Essentially it's a debate that asks some tough questions of those in the industrial and developed world. Yep, let's save the planet and cut carbon emissions and so on, but they should lead the way, not the reverse. Damn, it's a confusing argument, and for me as an African, an emotional one. My world that was naturally preserved for millions of years is way more precious than your 1 000-year-old building.

In any case, as you will have guessed, I made it safely over the deadly bay, and after putting in a good whack I turned in at a suitable landing place near a little village of six huts where I would be able to get hold of water. Not a person there spoke a word of English or French, or at least any word of either that mattered. What mattered was my fish catch of the day, which I shared with them. Then I pitched my tent and went to sleep thinking of Vasti and the possibility of a visit from her.

CHAPTER 29

GOOD AND BAD THINGS
AT MAHAJANGA

*I realised another difference between my Africa cycle trip and
this one. Then I had had the luxury of knowing that if I had
any unsavoury experiences in a country and subsequently
became proverbially 'gatvol' of the place where I was, the next
border and a new beginning were never far off. Here there
were no borders and no new beginnings. If I got gatvol, all I
could do was accept my situation and move on.*

My priority now was to reach Mahajanga as soon as possible,
because I wanted to see if it could be arranged for Vasti to join me
there for Christmas. Believe it or not, it would be our first together
in the entire 10 years of our companionship, and apart from the
pure joy of being with her I badly needed her presence for other
reasons.

I was at a low ebb spiritually as well as physically, and the boost
she would give to my spirits might also, I thought, play a vital role
in my physical recovery. I was in bad shape; every day started and
ended with multitudes of medicine, vitamins and headache and

fever stuff that seemed to hold the wolves of sickness at bay – but only just.

The way I planned it, I would reach Mahajanga and find out if Vasti could make it at Christmas. If she could I'd make the necessary arrangements for her stay and then keep on going down the coast as far as I could before she arrived, stash my kayak somewhere safe and, with any luck, manage to hitch a ride back to Mahajanga on a local sailboat to meet her.

So I pushed myself hard, and perhaps a little recklessly. One sleep north of Mahajanga I went through a dangerous stretch of water that, although I did not fully comprehend it till later, was definitely another place where a small kayak should not venture, especially when the sea was so choppy and filthy. On the last day's paddle, however, the sea was calm and not too dirty, although definitely not crystal clear, and I put out a Rapala lure. Then I reconsidered my situation and hauled it in again.

I was trying to make good time; if I hooked a fish now it would cost me an hour's worth of paddling time to bring it in, and then I would not get anywhere near Mahajanga by nightfall. My Garmin showed that there was a village called Antsanitia just 20 km north of Mahajanga itself. If I could make it there I would have covered another brilliant distance of 55 km. So I put everything else out of my mind, even the thoughts of Mahajanga and Vasti's possible visit, so that I could concentrate my flagging efforts.

My first sight of Antsanitia was a giant A-frame shape, visible from quite a distance, which was clearly not a natural structure. It became more and more confusing to my slightly addled mind as I drew closer, because it seemed to keep changing shape. Actually getting up to it was an arduous business, especially considering my enfeebled condition. Sand banks kept appearing, and each time this happened I had to make a judgement call as to whether to cut inside it and save time, or go around it. But every time I tried the inside option the water-level would turn out to be too low and I would end up dragging the kayak for a few hundred exhausting metres.

But I persevered (well, I couldn't do anything else, could I?) and the last dragging session brought me to a lagoon at the foot of a high cliff – and right below, the strange shape-shifting building. Then I saw why it had seemed to change shape whenever I changed direction – it was actually a cluster of bungalows, with people sitting at tables outside, eating and drinking and probably all wondering who the hell I was.

I left my kayak alongside the other craft anchored on the beach, one of them a small catamaran, and climbed a long wooden staircase in search of the owner or manager. He turned out to be a smiling Frenchman named Stephan, and before I had even finished explaining who I was and where I had come from, he said: 'Ah! You stay with us? *Oui*? Yes?'

Without waiting for a reply he whistled up some of this staff to carry the kayak up the embankment, and before I could get a word in edgeways it was parked next to one of the bungalows. I was getting worried now that I was operating under false pretences, and explained that I didn't have much money and couldn't afford to stay there.

His reply was simply: 'You pay little, maybe just for your food and beer? No?'

Hell, yes! Lady Luck had smiled on me once again and dropped me in the lap of a man who was not only kind-hearted and realised I needed help but also a keen traveller who wanted to hear all about my adventures.

It turned out that the lady wasn't just smiling, but positively beaming. I had an urgent need of Mahajanga's cell and internet reception, and Stephan and his wife, who ran the lodge on behalf of its owner, regularly travelled the 25 km stretch into Mahajanga. Even better, the next trip was scheduled for the following morning. Perfect!

I ate well, laid my ailing carcass down in the bungalow and next morning undertook the bumpy trip to town with Stephan. Now I could contact Vasti and, so I fervently hoped, arrange with her to come over. To my joy the answer was 'yes'. Vasti would arrive a few days before Christmas and leave just after New Year. I was blown away – it was much more than I had expected. Now I had to start planning to make sure her stay was as enjoyable as I could make it, so that night I sat down with Stephan to discuss the matter.

I was considerably worried about this, because I had now discovered that Antsanitia was the cream of the accommodation crop in the entire Mahajanga region, and what I could afford for Vasti's stay was very modest, to say the least. I knew Vasti wouldn't mind staying in the rough and scruffy places which were my customary abodes on this trip, but I wanted better than that for her – the only problem being that hole in my pocket.

Stephan, bless his heart, didn't promptly show me the door, as many hoteliers would have done. We could have the same deal as he'd given me, he said, but unfortunately we would have to pay a token fee for our room. Done! I don't think he realised what a great Christmas present he had given us.

Mahajanga was only about 20 km by sea, and it was a really pleasant paddle. I passed the time with any number of fishermen who were floating around to try their luck or sailing off somewhere, while fish launched themselves out the water as they hunted their smaller co-residents, and gulls and albatrosses dived and circled above.

On arrival I started looking around for accommodation that suited my shrunken bank account. This turned out to be a cute beach house managed by a lovely Malagasy lady, who rented me a room for about $10 US. This was slightly expensive in my books, but it included secure storage for my kayak and my belongings. Then I took a wander through the town.

One thing I always steer away from on my journeys is thinking about what time of year it is and what I am missing that is going on back home. But now, strolling around Mahajanga, I couldn't help feeling a tug at my heartstrings as I passed an old, battered but still gracious double-storeyed French-style house that had Christmas ball decorations and lights all over its road-facing balcony. They were as kitsch as anything, but I'm not ashamed to say that I stopped for a moment to admire them and empathise with the atmosphere that this family was trying to create. In truth I did more than empathise – I was downright envious.

This is not to say that the citizens of Mahajanga exhibited any noticeable Christmas vibe – it was just business as usual. I couldn't understand it. Didn't the people here want an excuse to generate a holiday spirit, particularly the best one of them all? About the only signs of it were the Christmas hats some of the foreign-owned restaurants handed out to their distinctly reluctant staff to wear.

To my mind people are free to refrain from buying Christmas trees or to use religion, culture and so forth as excuses for not celebrating the birth of Jesus, but I don't see why this should also mean side-stepping the vibe that this time of year brings out. In South Africa we are such a diverse bunch of people that we enjoy everybody's holidays.

I love it when my Muslim friends celebrate Eid; after all, having actually endured (and shared) their hunger-driven mood-swings and grumpiness during the month of fasting I believe I deserve a share of the Eid vibe, not to mention its customary treats. Same goes for my Jewish friends over their Rosh Hashanah or New Year. Although I may not totally see the deeper importance of their celebrations, I can't help but get swept into the vibe the holiday brings to them and their families.

On the other hand, safely at home at a future Christmas I'll probably yearn for Mahajanga with its 100 per cent humidity, warm seas and warm beer. But for now I would have loved to be back home indulging in such perverse pleasures as traffic jams on Camps Bay

Road, crazed shopping activity in the malls, with stores that have been playing the same Christmas carols since October.

My original travel plans now underwent drastic modification. I was in much worse shape than I had imagined, and my resistance was now so low that I had barely settled in before my unhealed feet finally laid me low with a serious infection – high temperature, fever and all. And as if that was not bad enough, thieves stole some vital and expensive items out of the kayak while I lay ill.

I forced myself to stay positive and remain focused on all the good things that had come my way. After all, the items that had been stolen could be replaced, albeit at some cost. That worked till the thieves struck again and carried off my video camera and all its batteries. I gave myself another lecture on the same lines as the earlier one: *It's only a material item. Right?* But this time myself replied: *No! Actually it's not that simple!* The fact was that although the camera itself was a worldly thing that could be replaced, the footage in it was not. It was a unique record of unique things that had happened to me. What it amounted to was that a piece of my life had been stolen.

The cameras that Sony had supplied me with were the latest technology available. All the high-definition video images I captured went directly onto the camera's built-in hard drive, to be downloaded onto a personal computer as soon as possible. I had made the downloading a priority to ensure that none of my irreplaceable footage was lost, but I had deferred the latest download, and all the footage I had taken since Nosy Bé was still in the camera's hard drive when it was stolen.

I was beyond furious, lame with disappointment, and the attitude of the staff at the guesthouse where I was staying, and who had been supposed to make sure my belongings were secure, didn't help either. When I had arrived they had all been positively over-eager to help me, but now all were suddenly aloof and uninterested in my problems. Some even made the bizarre accusation that I had made up the story of a theft so that I could lay some sort of claim for compensation.

Can you beat that? It was at times like this that I realised how alone I was in my strange quest in this strange country. But then I spent a day calming down and thinking about it, and went back to the manager with a proposal: I would offer a reward to whoever returned my camera, no questions asked. Then I settled down to holding thumbs. Even if I didn't get the camera back, I needed that footage!

That was also when I realised another difference between my Africa cycle trip and this one. Then I had had the luxury (the value of which I did not grasp at the time) of knowing that if I had any unsavoury experiences in a country and subsequently became pro-verbially *'gatvol'* of the place where I was, the next border and a new beginning were never far off. Here there were no borders and no new beginnings. If I got *gatvol*, all I could do was accept my situation and move on.

And in my usual reconciliatory mood (voodoo being slightly too complicated for me) I wished the new owner of that top-of-the-range Sony endless accidental formatting of irreplaceable footage he had just taken.

But you have to take the bad with the good, particularly when you have no choice in the matter. I recovered from my infection and fever, having wised up to the importance of actually completing an antibiotics course rather than stopping as soon as I felt better. And then I had something else to smile about: Vasti arrived with a bag full of presents and messages. It would be a merry Christmas and (I hoped, hanging on to my thumbs) a happy New Year.

Vasti and I were able to share an incredible place – the Lac Sacré, or Sacred Lake, near Antsanitia, just south of Mahajanga. This *'fady'* lake had been praised to the skies by so many locals that we just had to see the place for ourselves. As usual, I was sceptical of the numerous superstitious stories that were fed to me regarding this supposedly magical place, but magical is what it turned out for Vasti and me!

Although I still didn't believe the fables that accompanied the place, I was in awe of it all the same. White-green in colour, about 30 metres wide and two metres deep, it was home to big fish that followed us as we walked around the water's edge. I simply couldn't help breaking the *fady* rules and taking some underwater pictures of these friendly fin exponents. Amazingly, they're a mixture of saltwater and freshwater fish which now are all surviving in purely fresh water; exactly what they were I don't know, but to a South African they looked like carp and eels at first glance.

Some of the carp-style fish in this little lake were huge. If a 'Vaalie' dam fisherman from Pretoria caught one of these on his bait of choice – a ball of *pap* (stiff porridge) – he'd be put on the cover of his local newspaper. But over there he'd probably be strung up from the nearest palm tree, because the lake is very sacred, and revered by all the local population. I discovered this when I asked if I could swim in the lake, and was told: 'Yes ... but you cannot get out again, as you will not be safe from the people.' I wonder if they would have strung up my camera as well if anyone had seen me taking those pictures?

The legend of the lake went something like this: the king of this part of the country, at the time when Madagascar was still ruled by a bunch of regional kings, lost a war against the ruler of Antananarivo and had to flee to this waterless area of the Mahajanga area. His soldiers and people were dying of thirst, but they were saved by a brave warrior, who was wandering around with his herd of zebu cattle in search of drinking water.

When one of the zebu walked over a certain area of land a strong fountain of fresh water began to gush out of the dry ground. The spring not only revived the king's army and his people, but gave them so much new spirit that they got their land back. Now, hundreds of years later, the water flowed as strongly as ever.

And we also met a French couple at the Antsanitia resort who raised my spirits considerably. The girl told me one thing that stuck like flypaper. After hearing of my adventures before Mahajanga and the subsequent robberies, she challenged me with this remark: 'If you want to be a modern-day adventurer, you need to be a true *warrior*. Things that take place during a quest are irrelevant to a warrior; the end-result is the only goal.'

Quite right, I thought. *I am a warrior! Roll on, New Year! I'm ready for you!*

CHAPTER 30

TURMOIL ON LAND AND SEA

Even two kilometres out to sea huge trees, torn roots and all out of the ground, were drifting past me, a surreal sight – but the strangest thing of all was that the water was fresh, without even a hint of salinity, even though I was a good way out into the Mozambique Channel. Exhausted and thirsty as I was in the oppressive heat, I wasn't tempted to drink any of it: it was about the same colour as a kindergarten's paintbrush-washing tray.

The early days of the New Year were an itchy time for me. I wanted to get going again, but I couldn't leave Mahajanga right away. The good news was that Sony had approved the replacement of my stolen video cameras and accessories, which was a huge relief. The bad news was that the thieves had not responded to my reward offer, and the loss of my footage really hurt.

I was still suffering from periodical spells of negative thoughts – to put it politely – about the theft, but I was definitely less depressed about my loss than before, and was looking at the bigger picture. Namely, that at the end of this trip I would still be a successful adventurer, while they would still be what they had always been – just ordinary thieves.

So *bonne chance, mes amis*, I thought, *dirty rats that you are!*

I started realising that I had been in Mahajanga far too long when I noticed that someone knew or recognised me wherever I went – in fact, I had become part of Mahajanga's cast of local characters. I was such a familiar sight that the locals had even given me a nickname! Were they already pointing me out to strangers as well?

Cries of '*Jesosy, Jesosy, Jesosy!*' followed me when I walked down a street, politely trying to answer each greeting with a smile or a wave. '*Jesosy*' is the Malagasy word for 'Jesus' and I have to admit that I could see the reason for it. By now my beard was bold and thick, while my hair hung down to the traditional biblical length. I couldn't help thinking that my chances of winning an audition for a part in some epic about the bad old days in Judea were at their peak.

Actually it was rather nice to be welcomed by name, although, to be honest, I wished they had picked something a little less ecclesiastical – even 'Caveman' would have done!

Departure time started getting nearer when the replacement cameras and equipment arrived from Sony. But before I could get myself back on the water, I had to go through a couple more misadventures without getting anywhere near the sea, more proof that I am capable of unwittingly getting into trouble no matter where I am.

On a Sunday I headed into town to draw some cash at an ATM, which I managed, although not without some spiritual trauma. I spoke to the machine, the machine spoke to me and the cash stuck its head out of its little slot. But I didn't grab it fast enough and the ATM swallowed it again.

I did better on my next try, but I knew I would have to wait a few weeks before the card company would give me a refund on that first swallowed lot. Eish! Anyway, I walked away, cash in pocket, and to get out of the pelting rain I ducked in under a metal bus-stop shelter with advertising all over it, just like the ones we have at home.

While I stood there, deep in thought about the other things I planned to do, a taxi-bus stopped across the road to collect a passenger, and I noticed that it was headed for the exact area where my kayak was being stored. I made a split-second decision to go and check on my battered but faithful companion, ran across the road and jumped into the front seat of the bus.

I hadn't even shuffled my wet frame into a comfortable position when I heard the crunching sound of exploding timber, looked up and saw a huge 10-metre tree which had been hanging over the street come crashing down, smashing the left-hand side of the bus stop under which I had just been standing!

I was so surprised that for a moment I felt as if I were in the middle of a dream. Then the screams of a couple of children in the shelter woke me up. I jumped out of the bus, and together with some other passengers sprinted through the water to help. Fortunately the people in the shelter weren't badly hurt, and we helped them into taxis bound for the local hospital as quickly as possible.

This served as a warning that the notorious Madagascan rainy season everyone had been warning me about had now arrived, and that it would have a definite effect on the way I tackled the rest of my trip. I believed, though, that if I stuck to very early starts I would be able to get most of my daily paddling done before being faced with the strong winds that, I was assured, usually followed the heavy early-morning downpours.

Madagascar was certainly complicated when it came to the weather. Go a few hundred kilometres north or south, east or west, and you find yourself in a different world. Now I was heading directly into cyclone season, but I didn't feel too concerned: I wasn't anywhere near the northern coast, which in my humble opinion was easily the most dangerous zone.

On the other hand, a cyclone is not something to fool with, no matter which coast it descends on. And when you had two of them arriving simultaneously – which is what happened now – it was like a couple of gatecrashers who roll up uninvited, eat more than anyone else, drink your best wines, break expensive glasses, cause disharmony among your real friends ... and then, to top it all, won't go away.

As far as I was concerned, that was definitely the case with Eric and Fanele, the terrible twins of the year's cyclone season. Fanele in particular overstayed her welcome, keeping me bunkered down for a week, waiting in vain for a gap in the weather that would allow me to hit the water again. Eric appeared to be a decent enough chap, as cyclones go, but Fanele not only stuck around well past going-home time but got completely out of control, her peak performance being winds of nearly 200 km/h and 18-foot waves. Time to call the police!

Frustration aside, it gave me some first-hand experience of what Malagasy people have to endure every year. I had always thought that in this part of the world the cyclone season included a couple of severe rainstorms and, on the odd occasion, some gale-force wind and flooding. How wrong I was – and these two weren't even considered critically serious, even though one was classed as a Grade 3!

Growing up on the KwaZulu-Natal north coast, I experienced the brunt of Demoina in 1987. I was too young then to really comprehend the ravages of nature on our people and infrastructure – I was too focused on the excitement of being ferried to school and back across temporary bridges. Yet this was what Madagascar's people went through, year in and year out! South Africans are definitely spoilt as far as the weather is concerned.

It was a hairy business at times when I finally set off for the halfway mark, Maintirano. Even two kilometres out to sea huge trees, torn roots and all out of the ground, were drifting past me, a surreal sight – but the strangest thing of all was that the water was fresh, without even a hint of salinity, even though I was a good way out into the Mozambique Channel. Exhausted and thirsty as I was in the oppressive heat, I wasn't tempted to drink any of it: it was about the same colour as a kindergarten's paintbrush-washing tray.

My greatest immediate concern was safely crossing large bays and river mouths, because every day brought a new challenge as I dealt with the turbulence created by moving tides, currents and the additional millions of litres of rainwater now trying to escape gravity. At times so much floating debris – mainly logs and foliage – had been washed down that I couldn't put my paddle properly into the water.

The turmoil caused by Eric and Fanele mirrored the political turmoil which had broken out in Madagascar. Andry Rajoelina, Antananarivo's mayor and also leader of the political opposition, had stirred up the disgruntled Malagasy when he called President Marc Ravalomanana a corrupt dictator. The result was a wave of riots that saw radio and television stations burnt to the ground, shops looted and at least 34 people killed.

I didn't know anything about this till I reached the remote town of Soalala in the Bay of Baly on 26 January. Apparently rumours had been rife that South Africa was sending mercenaries to reinstate the president, and I was a gift from the gods to the policemen who detained me, demanding to see my papers. Some mercenary I was, coming to overthrow the country with an arsenal consisting of a paddle, a pocket-knife, a video camera and a battered Rapala lure!). I decided they had not ever met an actual mercenary. The matter was quickly sorted out, but I had a suspicion it would happen again, and I was right.

In general I like police and believe they follow a thankless but honourable profession. But that tends to go a bit sour at times like this. In the next several weeks the political chaos rebounded on me because it made Malagasy policemen more aggressive and suspicious of anything unfamiliar, and I was to have several more run-ins with them, because I was about as unfamiliar as could be.

In the far-flung parts of Madagascar life went on pretty much as usual, but from then on I just didn't feel 100 per cent safe when I called in at the bigger towns; there was an underlying tension that was clearly putting a strain on the people.

The next 10 days were tough and lonely. This was partly due to the fact that I was avoiding human contact when I could because I didn't want any more of my equipment stolen (I could hardly go along to Sony and ask them to replace the second video camera they'd given me!), but mainly because the coastline had changed quite drastically and become inhospitable.

I paddled past kilometre after kilometre of desert shoreline, punctuated here and there by towering cliffs, followed by more desert. Often this meant paddling an extra two hours at the end of a long day just to find some suitable place to come ashore. Along this part of the coast the tide runs out for several kilometres, and so although there was no shortage of river-mouths I'd sometimes have to walk a kilometre inland to find a hut where I could get some water. The only conceivable advantage of this was that it might put me out of reach of the next tropical storm (unnamed as yet) that was brewing in the Indian Ocean.

The fish also stopped biting, and in addition to muscle-weariness, thirst and loneliness I began to be plagued by hunger-pangs as well. I remember telling Seamus during one of our satphone conversations that I was paddling from 6.00 am to 6.00 pm and just then hadn't had anything to eat for two days except a chocolate bar and a piece of stale bread.

I did have one memorable meal, though – memorable for all the wrong reasons – at a deserted beach when I was about 10 days from Maintirano. The only other person there was a pleasant character whom I shall call Marc, who introduced himself by saying: 'I'm a businessman.' Exactly what kind of businessman I only found out later.

Marc was actually a poacher of turtles – in fact, he was currently on his latest hunt – and as we sat and ate together on the deserted stretch of beach and watched the sun set over the Mozambique Channel he explained to me just how well-structured his 'industry' was, with ultra-organised transport routes ferrying the poached turtles to eager customers in Thailand.

I was shocked, since poaching turtles is a definite no-no where I come from. But Marc seemed to have no qualms about his chosen line of business. As far as I could understand, given the language problem, he believed he was not endangering the survival of one of the world's near-extinct animals.

I couldn't process all this at once. He was not a criminal in the sense of someone who would knock you on the head and steal your possessions while you were sleeping. Personally he was a nice guy who worked hard – after all, he was willing to walk (yes, walk) more than 100 km through remote, unpopulated forests – with one goal in mind, which was to feed his family back in Mahajanga.

A man with energy and caring determination really deserved to succeed at what he was doing ... but what he and others like him were doing was helping to bring about the ultimate disappearance of a threatened species.

But his upbringing had not allowed him access to the sort of information about conservation that people in the developed world have at their fingertips, as many in the developed world have had. To him it was just a harmless job because, like me, he saw value in someone who was willing to work hard for his daily bread.

I suppose one could say that Marc was a wrongdoer, but that the actual criminals were his clients and their middlemen, who, unlike Marc, certainly knew better, not to say the authorities who had provided him with such a poor education and had not made it possible for him to delve into the huge amount of information which is more readily accessible now to the ordinary man than it has ever been before.

But however you apportion the blame, the bottom line remains that turtles, those almost prehistoric sea-creatures, are vanishing from the world's oceans.

In spite of everything I was still on track to complete my journey in May. In the meantime, though, my immediate aim was to get to Maintirano. As readers of *Around Africa on my Bicycle* will know, I see my journeys consisting of two distinct parts: one half going away from home; the other half heading back. So reaching the half-way mark would be a great moment, and I spent the next few days paddling away in a veritable fever of anticipation.

And then I was there, landing at the village of Maintirano. I was in horrendous condition. I had heat-rash all over my body, my feet were swollen and infected from mosquito-bites, the tendons in my shoulders were inflamed, my lower back was knotted by cramps, my lips were blistered by the sun and I was suffering from the worst sun-blindness I'd ever experienced. Not to mention the fact that I had not had a proper meal for three days.

But I had made it. The sun didn't stop in its course and no heavenly choir appeared to serenade me, and my only 'welcome' was from swarms of mosquitoes in such numbers that it felt as if I were breathing them (and I certainly chewed some in unwary moments). All the same, suddenly my dream of circumnavigating this huge island wasn't a dream any more, but a concrete reality. I had paddled over 2 400 kilometres, and now I was on the downhill run, so to speak.

There was more to it than that, though. From the early planning stages onward this trip had been something of a seesaw ride. I believe in positive thinking, and I'd maintained that motivation most of the time, but sometimes I had wondered if I had taken on too much.

The week before I left, I remember, I couldn't sleep. And it wasn't just from excitement. It was from fear. I remember asking myself whether my enthusiasm for solo and obviously dangerous adventure had clouded any logical decision-making abilities in me.

As my departure-time came ever nearer I found myself mentally replaying the predictions of all the prophets of doom who had shaken their heads about my ambitious project, and although I managed to push all those predictions onto the back-burner, the fact remains that as I paddled out of Tamatave's harbour on the first 20 km of the journey I was nauseous with fear. Physical fear? Possibly. Fear of failure? Probably.

Doubt: it's an ugly thing that can defeat you as surely as a bullet in the heart.

Well, it hadn't so far. I had travelled more than two thousand kilometres along Madagascar's stunning coastline, and now I was on the downhill run, so to speak. I had seen and experienced things few other men will ever see or experience: whales at arm's length from me, giant turtles laying their eggs next to my tent, a shark ramming my kayak, parasites eating pieces of me – and then, of course, all the fine people I'd met along the way – Malagasy of all walks of life, French, South African and other expatriates. I had experienced the kindness and hospitality of people so poor that they had very little to share ... and yet shared it willingly.

Just as I did on the Africa trip, I couldn't stop pulling out my map every now and then to trace the route I had covered so far and gloat a little. Somehow the distance I still had to cover seemed a lot shorter. The despair I had felt after my mishaps in Mahajanga was dead and buried. I was bursting with excitement at the prospect of getting to the finishing line. Just keep going! That was the secret. That had always been the secret. Just keep going.

The next stretch, heading down to the town of Tuléar, would be as tough and lonely as the one I'd just completed. But that's the way of an adventurer.

CHAPTER 31

NIGHT SHIFT FROM HELL

*The wind had turned and was now a strong southerly,
blowing directly into my face and slowing me down to about
4 km/h, a mere crawl. I did the only thing I could, which
was to keep my head down, grimly digging the paddle blades
into the black water all around me on this endless journey. I
seemed to be a modern-day Flying Dutchman, condemned to
paddle down the Madagascan coast for all eternity.*

Rules, as someone once said, are made to be broken. It would be rash to take this rather sweeping statement literally, but there can be no doubt that sometimes the ends justify the means ... my journey to the town of Morandava being a case in question.

The undeniable fact was that I had to get there on time, so that I could meet up with Seamus, my long-suffering expedition manager, who was not only slowly going crazy keeping me on track but was also responsible for all the video footage – both by and of me – for that premium documentary we intended to make.

Seamus had made it clear that we had precious little time to shoot, and had insisted that I make Morandava town that coming Monday. I had assured him I would, even though the day before I had lost valuable time while meandering through a confusing maze of river mangroves. But that was neither here nor there: it was Morandava on Monday or bust. As it turned out, it was nearly bust.

That Monday morning I beat the sun to work and was on the water at 5.30 am, with, according to my calculation, about 45 km to go. I felt a bit bereft without the services of my trusty Garmin, but it had suddenly succumbed to moisture penetration (and who could blame it, after what I had put it through?). Seamus was bringing a replacement, so I would have to rely on my map. On the other hand, my predecessors in the Madagascar adventure game hadn't even had a half-way decent map, so what was I moaning about?

The first 20 km seemed to fly by, and I happily marked off each of the bays I passed after identifying them on the map. At this rate it felt as if I could expect to lay eyes on Morandava at any time, just beyond the next point. But by late morning, having passed about 10 points of land, I began getting a sinking feeling.

Was my map telling me the truth, or had it, unbeknown to me, actually been compiled by Mickey Mouse? I yearned for my ailing Garmin. By now my body was tiring after the fierce effort I had put into it so far, but I could also feel myself growing mentally weary. Something was definitely wrong – why did it have to happen on such a vitally important day?

But there was nothing to do except keep paddling and focus on hope rather than belief. I paddled and paddled and paddled and paddled, and then after 13 hours of unrelenting effort eventually reached a crossroads as real as the one you find on land. To be precise, the sun was setting and I was faced with a momentous decision: Was I going to keep paddling or find somewhere to overnight?

If I did go on, I would be breaking the one immutable rule that I had set myself. Paddling by day was dangerous enough; paddling at night was asking for serious trouble, not excluding an unpleasant death by drowning or unseen predator.

Well, to me there was only one answer. I would have to ditch my supposedly iron-clad rule and just keep going, come what may. Strangely enough, though, what really kept me going was the vision of a big, steaming plate of spaghetti bolognaise that made even the muscle cramps after all those hours crunched up on the kayak more bearable.

And I knew it would be there if only I could make it to Morandava. You see, the owner of the Chez Maggie hotel was a friend of Hilary Bradt (of Bradt guidebook fame), and had promised to spoil us while Seamus was there. And the spoiling was scheduled to begin that night, not the next day.

It was a nerve-racking business. Around me was a darkness so intense that I couldn't even see the bow of my kayak, or watch the behaviour of the sea, so that waves continually pitched over me without any warning. In spite of all my efforts, too, my thoughts kept on turning to what might be lurking in the deep, dark waters under the kayak's hull.

But I paddled on – if not for survival or Seamus, then certainly for that plate of spaghetti. The eggheads are still arguing about what the Holy Grail actually was – a drinking-cup or a person – but I'd bet nobody ever envisaged it as consisting of a platter of Italian pasta.

It became excruciatingly hard work for my ever more tired body. To make it worse, the wind had turned and was now a strong southerly, blowing directly into my face and slowing me down to about 4 km/h, a mere crawl. I did the only thing I could, which was to keep my head down, grimly digging the paddle blades into the black water all around me on this endless journey. I seemed to be a modern-day Flying Dutchman, condemned to paddle down the Madagascan coast for all eternity.

And then around 8.00 pm I spotted cell phone masts ahead of me in the murk. At first I couldn't believe that I wasn't hallucinating, but they were there all right, about 10 km away. From somewhere I summoned up a final surge of energy, egged on by the sight of Morandava's twinkling lights when I got nearer.

Finally I was there. I had to make a few crash landings in the dark to find out exactly where I was, but by 10.00 pm I was staggering (literally) towards Chez Maggie's front door with a couple of late-night beach strollers helping to carry the kayak. It had taken 16 and a half hours, but I had arrived and would be able to satisfy both my needs and my wants.

It was just a pity ... after all my back-breaking efforts, the people at Chez Maggie informed me that Seamus hadn't yet arrived because his flight had been delayed.

The spaghetti was good, though.

CHAPTER 32

AD HOC SHOPPING IN TULÉAR

I didn't harbour any permanent bad feelings, but leaving the town behind represented the end to a difficult time which was now, thankfully, a thing of the past. While I was there I wasn't as comfortable and in love with the country as I had been before. Now I was back at sea again, and the real Riaan was re-emerging.

The coup, regime change or simple mayhem – call it what you will – that gripped Madagascar as I made my painful way down towards its southern tip couldn't have come at a worse time for me. I mean, here I was, ready to immerse myself in the island's natural wonders, and instead I found myself caught up in the political turmoil, even if only on its periphery.

Fortunately I had left Mahajanga just as the first riots and looting in the major towns began, which gave me a relatively carefree month in the most isolated and news-free region of the country. The only sign that all was not well was the lack of tourists wherever I landed.

This was particularly evident as I neared Tuléar. Some of the prettiest places you could hope to find, which normally have a substantial number of foreigners enjoying the spectacular diving sites, were empty or almost empty. This was bad for the operators, no doubt, but it cut much deeper, because in many cases it represented a huge chunk of some outlying village's living. Looking at it from that perspective, it was possible to comprehend the extent of the damage the unrest was doing to Madagascar.

The national agony was particularly evident when I arrived at Tuléar. The tension was almost palpable, and everyone seemed to have a different opinion about what was going on.

People in the tourism industry will tell you that something like this is just a temporary slowdown, but the fact is – as we know in South Africa – perceptions tend to outlive the facts by a good margin. Malagasy people had long had a well-deserved reputation for being a friendly, laid-back lot, but that image was badly hurt by the violence and destruction, and as I walked around Tuléar I became convinced that only fools would laugh it off as a short-lived phenomenon.

Madagascar tourism, I ruminated, needed a better strategy than that. But first the country needed to right the political situation. The fact was that in 2006 a few million people voted Marc Ravalomanana back into power, and they would probably go on supporting him rather than a new president who had been put in place by the military.

And then Madagascar – all of it, government and marketing bodies included – would have to convince the world that it had a clear and precise strategy for delivering on the promises that had been made to the masses. Africa has an unfortunate history of liberation which is not followed by the fulfilment of promises.

These thoughts were fuelled by sheer disappointment. I had sincerely believed that Madagascar had managed to avoid the simmering instability of most of the rest of Africa, and I had been completely wrong. The symptoms had been there, and I had not noticed them, or perhaps didn't want to. But all that was Madagascar's problem, not mine, and I had to be selfish now, because I still had a long way to go and not all that much time to do it in.

Two days after my arrival I disliked Tuléar even more than I had after first landing there. I am 100 per cent willing to accept adventure in whatever form it presents herself. That's who I am. But when I find my life at stake through the wickedness of man – who, after all, is supposed to be exalted above the beasts of the field by his ability to think – I begin to wonder what is really worth offering my life up for.

I say this because one night I was walking back from a restaurant with two new acquaintances when we were held up at gunpoint and robbed of our bags, which in my case held not only the new Garmin Seamus had brought me but also all my documents from the government and – worst of all – my daily journal, the absolute backbone of everything we planned to do after I had returned home. All my records had gone.

But Lady Luck, having taken away with one hand, gave back with the other. A couple of days later another victim spotted the mugger in the town market, seized him and took him to the police, who soon persuaded him to tell them where he lived. Some of the goods were discovered – not my papers or Garmin, but (joy of joys!) they did find my journal lying next to his bed.

Getting my Madagascan documents replaced was something that really worried me, because I had heard that all government institutions were semi-crippled by the uncertainty caused by the political turmoil. But to my delight I found that at least one arm of government was anything but – I got copies of all my documents in just two or three days.

Some of my faith in human kindness was also restored when DHL South Africa, on hearing of the mugging, promptly offered their services in getting the most vital of the lost items to me in record time – the most badly needed one being a replacement

323

Garmin, which was now even more important than before. The terrain ahead included 200 km stretches of sheer cliffs, and the only way to find safe landing-places was by using the GPS. It was a great kindness and a great relief, because I had expected that the courier charge would be about $400 US.

And it was heart-warming to find myself on the receiving end of hundreds of e-mails from people commiserating about the robbery. They helped to remind me of why I was there and what I hoped to achieve. My return message to all of them was: Thank you. I needed that. Riaan Manser is back. It'll take way more than that to stop me.

Getting over the mugging took some time. *I'm not in it for this*, I found myself silently repeating for days after the attack, recalling the time when I was held hostage by the Liberian rebels on my Africa cycle trip.

Life-threatening situations like these make you think more honestly and take stock about where you are in your life right then. Was I making maximum use of the threescore years and ten allocated to me? What had I accomplished in the past year ... or the past month ... or the past week ... even the past day?

Many people believe the journeys I undertake are my ultimate dreams coming to fruition, but that's not so. My ultimate dream is to have children one day, to take my son to rugby matches, to watch my daughter in a school play, to sit with my wife and plan how we are going to give our children more than we had as children. Beyond the sleepless nights with crying babies and the inevitable teenage rebellion years I can see my dream turning out to be at least half of the vision I hope and dream for. That would be good enough.

After my dismal start a lot of good and/or interesting things happened to me in quick succession.

The new president of Madagascar, Andry Rajoelina, arrived with a cavalcade to reassure people in the region that their lives would improve with him at the helm. I hoped he could pull it off, or Madagascar might well end up running a close second to Zimbabwe in the 'hero to zero' race. I got my new documents and DHL rushed my replacement equipment to me. Then, to crown it all, I met an Australian who was making a significant investment in the future by manufacturing diesel fuel from the seeds of the jatropha plant.

He was globe-trotter extraordinaire Adam Broadhurst, CEO of a company called GEM (standing for Green Energy Madagascar). He told me he employed an unbelievable 8 500 people to care for the jatropha crops he had planted from scratch.

The jatropha tree is not exactly a household word, but according to Adam it will be the fuel of the future. It grows quickly, needs no pampering – it is hardier than a cactus – and yields an unparalleled amount of oil from its seed-pods.

Personally I think humans are realising that they have been too self-centred for their own good in the last 50 years. Maybe we as a race will show real intelligence in the next decade and actually do what most scientists believe to be impossible by reversing the destruction we have caused on our planet.

I paddled away from Tuléar without regret. I didn't harbour any permanent bad feelings, but leaving the town behind represented the end to a difficult time which was now, thankfully, a thing of the past. While I was there I wasn't as comfortable and in love with the country as I had been before. Now I was back at sea again, and the real Riaan was re-emerging.

A few hours' paddling took me over the Tropic of Capricorn. It was no great occasion, but it had special meaning for me. On my Africa trip I twice crossed the equator and also my favourite, the Greenwich Meridian. Each time I made a private mental fuss about it, because each crossing represented significant progress towards my goal, and the same thing applied here.

As I travelled downwards from the Tropic of Capricorn I considered what lay ahead and knew that I would have to adjust to new circumstances. The days of doing 50–60 km in one stretch were over, I calculated. Down in the south the sea was in a constant bad temper, with winds of over 30 km/h only adding to the agitation and further hindering my abilities; and with few sheltered bays and beaches I could expect to be dodging rocks at nearly every landing.

So I would be willing to creep cautiously along if that was what the cliff-bound region with its angry sea required. Not the sort of talk one would expect from an adventurer? Well, I still had a fair chunk of my threescore and ten left to use up, and you don't get old by being careless. Any experienced mariner will tell you that a healthy respect for the sea and its immense power is paramount to survival out there. The sea never tires. It hasn't for thousands of years, and won't unless something catastrophic happens; and most of all, it does not suffer fools gladly.

So I had everything that I needed. I had only 450 km more to go. I had enough fear of the sea, but not too much. My kayak was perfect for rough water; I was healthy (if slightly worn down by now) and on top of all this I had some wonderful technology supporting me in the form of my GPS. All in all, I was a hell of a lot better off than my predecessors of 350 years ago.

CHAPTER 33

SEAS DOWN SOUTH

The sea was acting up to such an extent, five-metre swells and all, that it was plainly impossible to launch my little five-metre kayak. So there I sat for five days with a growing feeling that the sea was not testing me but taunting me with its mighty power to remind me of the humble place I occupied on the food chain when I ventured away from land.

My little world changed dramatically as I worked my way southward from Tuléar. I found myself battling seas that brought back unpleasant memories of the conditions I faced coming up the east coast at the start of my trip – huge six-metre swells chased by permanent head winds of over 25 km/h ... soon, strangely enough, it seemed like years since I could safely budget 5 km in a day.

What it actually came down to was that my entire rhythm and routine had been turned upside-down. Previously I would wake up just before sunrise, pack my tent and baggage away and then set off on what I had worked out would be the first stage of a three-stage day. Early mornings were usually favourable, and so in the first four or five hours I would try to get about 60 per cent of the budgeted distance out of the way. This would allow me to beach somewhere at lunch-time, drink some energy juice (luke-warm!) and possibly have a nap of about 20 or 30 minutes. The afternoon would then, depending on the conditions, see me complete the remaining distance an hour before sunset. If conditions became too difficult I would negotiate a settlement plan with myself: I would calculate the total distance I had hoped to do that day and work out what sort of negative effect it would have on the next day's budgeted distance if I didn't make today's target. The second part of the calculation concerned the way I planned to cover the remainder of the day's kilometre-budget in the current adverse sea state: pushing on with all I had in me to complete it as soon as possible, or go '*mora mora*' (slowly, slowly), the risk being that I might reach my destination much later – although, it was to be hoped, before sunset.

This system worked with varying degrees of success. Sometimes I wouldn't manage the full distance, and occasionally I'd end up still paddling long after the sun had already set – this latter, incidentally, being a non-negotiable no-no for most sea paddlers, including myself (except in shit-or-bust circumstances).

Well, that was then. What I found now was that I would have a paddling window of only three or four hours in which to comfort-ably cover a reasonable distance. This change was not my choice, but was dictated to me by the head-winds combined with the huge swell; throw a head-on current into the mix and, in spite of the most extreme effort I would be reversing back up the coast, even though my bow was pointing south.

So now I pushed on throughout the day if the conditions al-lowed it. Stopping off for a midday snooze had become next to im-possible, because the cliffs sometimes ran almost uninterruptedly for 100 km, and negotiating a landing on an unprotected beach was something I only wanted to have to do once a day. That said, the coast was stunning in its beauty, and I often stopped for a moment to marvel at what lay before my eyes and remind myself about where I was on the planet.

This new form of travel naturally upset my timetable, and the delay caused by my troubles at Tuléar didn't help either, so at this stage it looked as if I wouldn't reach Tamatave till near the end of June. I felt bad about that: Vasti's birthday was coming up, and I had had firm plans to meet up with her somewhere so that we could spend it together.

By now, of course, I was a veteran *fady*-listener, but when I reached a fishermen's village called Beheloka the old wives' tales took on a new twist that I really had not expected in this day and age.

'Yes, the sea you will have to worry about,' I was told by some Antananarivo residents I happened to meet at Beheloka, 'but your real worry should be the cannibal villages en route. There are many in the deep south of Madagascar.'

This was too much. Did they think they could fool a seasoned adventurer?

'Nah,' I scoffed. 'Cannibals don't exist any more – that's no more than dramatised folklore that's still doing the rounds now, isn't it?'

This may have sounded pretty adventurer-like, but to be honest, part of my bravado was an attempt to convince myself. My philosophy was 'seeing is believing', but of course the problem with this was that once you had seen something for yourself you were usually in too deep to do anything about getting yourself out of it.

I had heard, and from one personal experience I can confirm it, that the Dezo tribe down south were a far tougher bunch than any other Malagasy I had met, but I didn't think that this extended to their wanting to eat me. And as far as I could see, 99 per cent of the Malagasy lived in fear of *fady* and assorted fairy-tales.

I had picked up a variety of both by this stage of my trip: if an aye-aye lemur enters a village at night, someone in that village will die; if a woman sees a turtle being slaughtered she will either become barren or bring bad luck to her family, or both; and so on. One *fady* that affected me directly was the belief that if a white man touched a child on the head the youngster would go crazy or suffer some prolonged illness.

The fairy-tale that perplexed me the most, though – and which I had heard from a number of people – was the one about seeing a real, live, genuine mermaid. Each time I heard the story it was told so convincingly that even my rock-like scepticism wavered a bit at the edges.

OK, as a gland-crazy kid I saw the movie 'Splash' and for the next year I went surfing with the fervent hope that Darryl Hannah would pop out of the water within conversational distance of me. Needless to say, Ms Hannah didn't make an appearance anywhere in my vicinity. But show me a photo or other convincing evidence and I'd be willing to change my mind and join public-spirited groups like the Save the Loch Ness Monster Society, if one exists.

About half-way between Tuléar and Madagascar's fast-approaching southernmost point, Cap Sainte Marie, I had a few days of particularly tough paddling which amounted to running a daily gauntlet. I would set off at sunrise, knowing that no matter what the sea was like later in the day, I would have no option but to press on to my planned destination, because the swell would be pounding the rocky shore with such enthusiasm that there would be no question of finding another good spot – there simply weren't any, and the ones that did exist were not all that good either.

Take my approach to the small town of Itampolo. The morning had started well but soon turned bad, with a southerly wind blowing in my face from 7.00 am onwards. Painful experience had taught me that an early-morning southerly meant only one thing: much stronger wind later on. I had planned to do 45 km that day, but by 9.00 am I was almost ready to risk a rock landing rather than continue to inch forward at three or four kilometres an hour.

Then I had a stroke of luck: the wind dropped for about four hours, which gave me the break I so desperately needed. I made maximum progress while the good times lasted and finally reached my safe landing place after 13 hours on the water. All part of the fun, I guess.

I still had that cannibal story in the back of mind (this is no reflection on the worthy burghers of Itampolo or anywhere else I visited, who, if they had big black missionary-sized pots, kept them well out of sight), and I decided that when I made friends at villages further along this part of the route I would always walk away backwards when I left. I wasn't paranoid or anything, but I saw no reason to let anyone see my hindquarters invitingly bouncing away inside my wetsuit bottoms.

Having avoided becoming somebody's gourmet lunch, if in fact there was a menu somewhere which would have been glad to feature me, I found myself within a hop and skip, so to speak, of Cap Sainte Marie, only to be marooned at the village of Lavanono because the sea was acting up to such an extent, five-metre swells and all, that it was plainly impossible to launch my little five-metre kayak. So there I sat for five days with a growing feeling that the sea was not testing me but taunting me with its mighty power to remind me of the humble place I occupied on the food chain when I ventured away from land.

The long wait gave me time to service the kayak – they are tough little beasts, but from time to time they need some serious and devoted TLC – and fortunately for me Lavanono is not only a pretty little place but also a legendary surfing spot, with rides of up to a kilometre on good days. Proof of that is the really stunning surfing pics the owner of the little hotel there, Gigi, has put up.

Unlike many hoteliers, Gigi had his head screwed on the right way. He was first and foremost a conservationist, and after that his main concern was safety. That meant he was not in favour of huge bus-loads of dreadlocked surfers invading the village, even though this would obviously generate a much larger cash inflow for him.

Firstly, he pointed out, the village couldn't handle 50 rip-roaring surfers at a time, and secondly there was no medical care available if you happened to make too close an acquaintance with the jagged, razor-sharp reef, and Lavanono was so remote that you could forget about an emergency evacuation. This last made me think a bit about various places to which I had ventured so far on this journey – I had certainly been to some which were far more isolated than Lavanono.

Eish! I suppose sometimes I need to go bald-headed at a thing, rash, not to say foolhardy, though it might be. If I weren't willing to do this, then my trip around Madagascar, for example, might well have been permanently parked on the 'never been done before' list.

Gigi was obviously a good man. It was a pity that he hadn't been around (or had maybe been unable to stop) a shocking act of eco-vandalism back in the early 1990s, when a bunch of Japanese expats calmly blew chunks out of the reef with dynamite to provide easier access to the beach for the fishermen's pirogues. Or that was the pretext, anyway.

As a matter of interest, Lavanono gave me a piquant little reminder of South Africa that, homesick though I was, I could have done without. When I was growing up in Zululand, part of my upbringing was to run through the vicious thorns known in Afrikaans as '*dubbeltjies*'. This doubtful pastime was a sort of homage, so to speak, to King Shaka, who had insisted that his soldiers fight barefoot and would toughen them up by making them run through fields full of these thorns.

Well, on my first morning at Lavanono I went to have a look at the village ... barefoot. So there I was, confidently waltzing along the sandy track from the beach in search of a cup of coffee ... and, with ever greater frequency, pausing to extract the thorns that had embedded themselves in foot-soles which had become invitingly soft after eight months of constant immersion.

The further I went, the worse it got, and soon I had attracted a vocal but supportive audience. Now, a good adventurer should also try to be a good showman, and so I soldiered on. But it was like walking over hot coals, and eventually even my built-in stubbornness failed me. By now I was in the thickest area of the thorns, and it felt as if I were walking over hot coals. This time my stubbornness did not see me through.

Trying to balance on the one foot while pulling the *dubbeltjies* out of the other became not only impossible but an exercise in futility, because as soon as I put a newly de-thorned foot down to attend to its colleague it would pick up a new batch of *dubbeltjies*. I must have looked totally ridiculous, because the crowd's sympathetic chatter turned into heartless laughter.

How it would all have ended I don't know, but then one of the village elders took pity on me, came over and without a word handed me his sandals so that I could escape from the consequences of my foolishness. Did I mention that he walked over to me barefoot and returned the same way? Yep, one of King Shaka's boys for sure.

The seas finally calmed down, and I left Lavanono with some regret, because it really was a delightful place, but at the same time I was eager to get on with the rest of my journey ... and, let me be the first to admit, with a little fear in my heart, because I would be rounding Cap Sainte Marie, which has claimed many ships in both past and modern times, whose bones you can sometimes see not far beneath you.

CHAPTER 34

AROUND THE CAPE –
AND INTO THE CLINK

*A cynic would say: 'It's not over till it's over, chum,' and he
would be perfectly right. Those final 14 days made damn sure
that I didn't cruise along in a haze of homecoming happiness –
Madagascar had taken me on board, and it wasn't going to
cut me loose just like that.*

Cap Sainte Marie is an awesome – and awe-inspiring – place. The
limestone mountain drops straight down into the ocean, and rank
after rank of huge waves crash endlessly onto its foot like great
hungry sea-monsters. It was truly one of the most stunning things
I had seen on this nine-month voyage, and I felt somewhat outside
of myself as I bobbed around at the mercy of the five-metre swells.

It was also something of a spiritual moment, and I found myself
taking stock of how far I'd actually come. I felt like a million bucks
as I craned my neck upwards to admire the towering orange-yellow
cliffs and boulders rising above me. Memories of the other three
compass points I had passed on my journey around Madagascar –
east, north and west – flooded back, and once again I was hit square

on by that invisible beam of motivation and inspiration that had brought me through so much.

It was an out-of-body experience all right. I made a video diary entry there but can't remember what I said in it, except that I told the camera to go to Google Earth and see where I found myself at that precise moment. *They won't believe that I'm out here all alone*, I thought, *totally unaided and on the smallest sea-going vessel used by man.*

I'm not a man who blows his trumpet when he's achieved something, but I was proud of this accomplishment. I had endured hardship and risks such as few men or women have to face in their daily lives, and I had been richly rewarded – not in terms of money or adulation, but in the intangible things that make life meaningful. I could have garnered millions of adoring fans with much less effort by getting myself into a Big Brother house, but what a trumpery thing it would have been in comparison with this.

But as the Bible says, the humble shall be exalted and the mighty laid low. After the exaltation of passing Cap Sainte Marie I was soon laid very low indeed. A couple of days further up the coast I arrived at another place I never want to see again, by the name of Ambovombe, and there I was welcomed by being slung into a police cell with no one for company but assorted rats, fleas and bats.

As usual I blundered into this quite innocently. My first big mistake was landing at an unappetising village of about 20 huts near Ambovombe on a Saturday afternoon, when the top hierarchy of civil governance – to wit, the mayor and his senior policeman – were smashed out of their minds. Whether they were celebrating something or routinely got sloshed every Saturday afternoon there I can't say (the place didn't look as if it saw much excitement), but when you run into a boozed-up minor bureaucrat with time on his hands it usually means trouble – and so it was this time.

The trouble started when the mayor and his top cop demanded to see my passport. Now the robbery at Tuléar came back to haunt me. Among the things stolen from me and never recovered were copies of my passport, and the police there had given me a document explaining the whole thing in some detail. But this wasn't good enough for His Dishonour and his minion, so they arrested me on the spot and took me to Ambovombe, where I was tossed unceremoniously into a filthy police cell. The charge: terrorism and/or mercenary activity.

Needless to say, I was flabbergasted, because I was in even worse shape than I had been last time I was seized on this charge up the coast. In spite of all its current woes, Madagascar was surely in no danger from a solitary weather-beaten man with swollen feet and strapped-up wrists in an overloaded kayak.

But there it was. The Ambovombe police were no more open to argument than my original captors, and weren't at all interested in the fact that (a) I had been in Madagascar for going on 10 months and the ship of state was still afloat, although listing slightly to port through no fault of mine, or (b) an assurance from the South African Embassy that I was strictly legit and in fact helping to spread the good word about Madagascar to all the potential tourists out there.

I think Tourism Madagascar will excuse me for not writing anything positive about Ambovombe. It's a little difficult to work up any enthusiasm after spending time in a lightless cell and having bats crawl over you while rats scurry around your bare feet. Oh, yes, and the fleas jumping around in your pants and shirt at the same time to catch a quick snack.

Anyway, after two nights in positively the worst accommodation I have ever inhabited (and that is saying something), the tireless efforts of the South African Embassy and Tourism Madagascar finally got the jail doors open, so that I could make tracks out of Ambovombe, which I did at top speed.

My next big stop was Fort Dauphin, a couple of days up the coast, and on the way I had a very special moment when I made the acquaintance – fortunately a peaceful one – of a hammerhead shark. I was an hour into my paddling day, making my way through slightly murky water about 2.5 km out to sea when this large grey shark just popped out of the water about two metres from me and swimming in the same direction, only a little slower.

At first I couldn't make out what sort of shark it was, but when I stopped paddling and just glided alongside it (there was now scarcely more than a metre between us) I could see its eyes clearly on the edge of its hammer-shaped head and the lines of differing shades of grey running along its body.

It was feeding, I think, and not at all concerned by my presence, and it was only when I tried to take a photo and accidentally banged against my camera with my graphite Orka paddle that it took any notice of me and veered calmly away. Wow! Was I scared, bearing in mind my previous shark encounter? Actually I wasn't. 'Energised' would be a better word.

I was really looking forward to reaching Fort Dauphin, where I would be able to link up with some of the many South Africans working there and – touch wood – be able to see the Bulls beat the Chiefs at Loftus Versfeld stadium. I was missing watching rugby big time: just another thing you take for granted at home ... like a warm bed that's not at ground level and not shared with the local wildlife, in a room which has windows and lacks a sign outside saying PRISON. After this trip, I swore, I'd never take anything for granted again!

On the outskirts of Fort Dauphin (or so I thought) I found myself temporarily assuming yet another role in addition to that of mad paddler, shark bait and jailbird. I made the acquaintance of a pleasant fellow named Luc, who told me, when I asked him about a safe place to land, to go 'just around the rocks, that's where you'll find the South Africans'.

Well, I'd like to thank Luc for his directions, even though they were 100 per cent incorrect, so that 'around the rocks' didn't bring me to either the South Africans or a safe landing-place. But his bum advice did provide me with an unforeseen and unforgettable extra chapter in my Madagascar adventure.

Filled with misplaced faith in Luc's directions I paddled forth. But neither of his promises materialised. I pushed past one jutting outcrop of rocks after the other till sunset was literally minutes away before admitting to myself that I wasn't going to meet up with my fellow countrymen just yet, and that I would have to land at the first place that looked half-way safe.

I made a rather rough landing between two clumps of jagged rocks, dragged the kayak up onto the excuse for a beach – a little 300-metre stretch of sand with rocks on either side – hastily set up camp and fell asleep totally exhausted just as the final spray of sunlight disappeared. I had a peaceful night's rest, but that was the only good news when I woke up next morning. I was now sandwiched into the cliff with no access to the sea.

The surf I had successfully negotiated the previous evening had tripled in size, to the point where it was ludicrous to think that I would manage to get out to sea again. Behind me, stretching as far as I could see in either direction, was a vertical cliff at least 60 metres high. Apart from a few choice but futile curses, which I didn't waste much breath on, the only thing to say as I picked up my kit was 'What now?' while mentally kicking myself for not seeing what I was getting myself into.

What now indeed. For a while I stood there and did the only thing I could think of, which was to keep glancing to left and right and then up at the jagged and very intimidating cliff above me, hoping for a miracle. The miracle didn't come, and so I sat on the beach and spent a long and lonely 12 hours twiddling my thumbs.

But when evening came the surf stayed as menacing as it had been all day, so eventually I unpacked my sleeping bag again. Maybe it would be better in the early morning, with the surf going down enough for me to escape from my little prison (which at least didn't have rats and bats).

But next morning the surf was even higher! Then three diminutive Malagasy fishermen who had seen me marooned on the little beach came clambering down the cliff to see if they could help, and I had an idea. Would they, I asked them, help me to get my kayak up the cliff face? Yes, sure, they said, adding that they knew where there was a good place from which to launch the kayak once we had got it up the cliff.

So we got to work. When I think about it now, it was really a crazy idea that could have killed one or all of us, or at the least seen my kayak smashed beyond repair, but the fishermen were so convinced of success that I was swept away by their enthusiasm. Even then, before I had fully grasped the risks involved, my heart was in my throat for the entire perilous and painstaking three hours it took us to get to the top. But we made it, and thanks to those three nameless but heroic fishermen with their characteristic Malagasy friendliness – and thanks to Luc too – I have a story that I never expected to be telling.

I finally made it on 31 May to Fort Dauphin, where I was welcomed by a group of hospitable South Africans who supplied me with some much-needed TLC and as many plates of spaghetti bolognaise as I could stomach ... and as a bonus, Seamus was there too. I imagine that, like me, he found it hard to believe that his 10 months of hard work, nail-biting and hair-raising emergencies were almost at an end.

Two weeks to go! When I looked at my map I could scarcely believe it – it seemed I had been paddling forever. I was long past the 80 per cent mark, and another couple of centimetres (translation: 400 km, give or take) would see me paddling around the Tamatave breakwater, in view of the beach from which I had launched the kayak, all naive and enthusiastic, 10 whole months ago.

At this stage a cynic would say: 'It's not over till it's over, chum,' and he would be perfectly right. Those final 14 days made damn sure that I didn't cruise along in a haze of homecoming happiness – Madagascar had taken me on board, and it wasn't going to cut me loose just like that.

For instance, there was the kingfish saga. Imagine a 5 kg kingfish alive and kicking on the end of my Rapala while a hook on the other end was deeply embedded in my finger – talk about 'No Food for Lazy Man'! I also had two serious shore-break crashes, snapping an all-important steel rudder cable during one of them.

As a bonus, the wind pumped straight into my face day after day, and tendonitis came visiting again – but this time I didn't have the luxury of a rest day because the return date was now cast in concrete and the deposit on the brass band had been paid, so to speak: 8 July – the day I would finish this world first.

The story of the hook in the finger would make anybody cringe. The razor-sharp barb had set so deeply into the tip of my left ring finger that brute force could not dislodge it (this was when I really understood how good these Rapala hooks actually were – I just wished I could have discovered it in a less painful way!).

I had no option except to force the hook in even deeper and twist it till its point emerged on the other side. Then I clamped it closed with my pliers and, at the cost of plenty more pain, pulled the hook out the way it had come in. Sheesh! I tried to dull the pain by telling myself that at least I'd got another story to tell – I even took a photo of my mangled finger. It didn't help, though. Then I heard myself saying: *Come on, Riaan, you've had enough adventure now. Come on man, just get home now!* That didn't help for the pain either, but it certainly got me going again.

Then there were those two rough landings. After 10 months I had become pretty good at spotting decent-looking places to land, so I was now pretty confident when I started my run through the surf. But sometimes that confidence was misplaced, because my kayak alone weighed 70 kg, and so tended to gain momentum slowly at first. Since a surf-landing requires that you get going – fast – at just the right moment, you sometimes get stuck in a position where you don't plan to be, and that's what happened here. The second hard landing, the one where the steel cable snapped (and to do that takes brute force) had me over the falls on a six-foot-plus cruncher. It felt as if I was on the Cobra Roller-Coaster at the Ratanga Junction amusement park.

And, of course, through all this the wind was doing its malign thing. Wind blowing from directly in front in rough seas is a paddler's worst nightmare, particularly when said paddler is suffering from tendonitis. At its worst it lamed my entire arm, and I was taking anti-inflammatories every day in spite of my principled aversion to over-medicating. Oh, yes, and then there was the pinched nerve in my back ...

Come on body, hold out for just a few more days! I can just about hear that brass band striking up!

On that final stretch I got a present from Madagascar's colonial past which is a blessing to this day, decades after the tricolor was hauled down for the last time: the Canal des Pangalanes, surely one of the greatest – and least-known – of the world's major artificial waterways and, at the time of its construction, the longest in the world.

It is a network of canals linking natural rivers and lakes that runs for 665 km from Farafangana northwards right up to Tamatave itself, and after my sufferings at sea its tranquil waters and easily accessible landing-places were like a holiday. I didn't use it all the way, but it certainly eased my final dash to Tamatave, although I had a final brush with yet another bunch of suspicious cops at Manakara on 23 June.

There the entire local police force descended on a bungalow where I was overnighting and interrogated its owner on suspicion of harbouring a mercenary. They also had a good look through my papers before conceding that I was clearly no more than a somewhat broken-down kayaker. I really do believe that Madagascar's tourism image would be improved if someone in government could brief the long arm of the law about the finer points of spotting hired gunmen.

I finally paddled into Tamatave's harbour at precisely 3.20 pm local time on 8 July – a month later than I had planned. But I got there. That was what counted, that and the sight of Vasti's dear face after I had beached the kayak for the last time, 5 000 km and 11 months after setting off from that very spot.

Madagascar hadn't finally relaxed its grip on me yet, however. Our Air Malagasy flight home to Johannesburg's OR Tambo Airport was delayed by three hours, and when we arrived our luggage somehow got misplaced … only ours out of the whole passenger list, please note.

I looked calm, but inside me it was another matter. For almost a year I had been in sole control of my life (well, almost, weather excluded), but today, one of the most important of my journey, I was not. The fact was that on this trip I had slowly been going *'bossies'* – bush-crazy – much more than on the Africa cycle journey.

Well, I would just have to get used to it again. That's the way it is with all adventurers.

The crowd, which included friends, strangers, sponsors and media people – print journalists, Reuters, the South African Broadcasting Corporation, etc – had waited patiently for me, but now they crowded around. The reporters were onto me like a shot and I got swept away to be interrogated, with everyone wanting a first-hand version of Madagascar's highs and lows.

Still, I managed to chat with some interesting people, many of whom I'd never met before, and to autograph their copies of my Africa book as well as various children's T-shirts. I felt like a genuine C-grade rock star!

But Cape Town was calling loudly. I wanted to get to our home at Betty's Bay, I wanted to see the things I'd missed so much, I wanted to commune with Russell, our pet pig. He was a mere pink piglet when I left, but now he was a year old, and I wanted to see if he was developing into a fine upstanding figure of a porker. In a nutshell, there's no place like home, no matter how great your interest in the distant places.

CHAPTER 35

A FINAL WORD BY
SEAMUS REYNOLDS

Seamus Reynolds, who suffered and rejoiced through every kilometre of that trip with me, deserves a final word. He says some good things about me, which I am not saying are necessarily accurate. But the words below, written when I was still 750 km from Tamatave, provide a different perspective on the trip – from the outside looking in, rather than the other way around, which is the view I had.

ONE OF THE GREATEST OF ALL TIME ...

'I am thinking that Riaan's achievement is already ranking against some of the greatest feats of endurance, like reaching the South Pole and sailing alone around the world. If he makes it all the way round Madagascar, it will even challenge the iconic first scaling of Everest by Hillary and should go down in the annals of adventure as one of the greatest of all time.'

When I received the above email, on behalf of Riaan, I first thought it was stretching things somewhat. But the more one considers the magnitude of kayaking around Madagascar, alone and unaided, the clearer it becomes as to exactly the enormity of the threshold Riaan Manser is standing on.

As Riaan's expedition manager I have been the closest witness to this epic journey but until I visited him in Fort Dauphin recently, I honestly had no comprehension of the physical danger he encounters on a daily basis.

Sitting around a kitchen table this last week we trawled through folder after folder of digital videos and photographs; at one point I could feel Riaan hovering over my shoulder when I replayed a particular clip at least five times. I was watching some of the ugliest, most brutal waves I have ever seen – ten foot barrels of frothing white foam thundering into slabs of barnacled rock.

'Can you believe I came in through that?' Riaan chirped with a hint of bravado.

Why, was my next question, but he beat me to it. 'I obviously can't sleep on my kayak at sea, so I have no choice. It was the easiest section I could find.'

It was then that the email fell into place. This was, after all, written by Johan Loots, the legendary adventure kayaker who designed Riaan's kayak; a man who openly admits he thought Riaan's Madagascar idea was completely nuts.

I handed Riaan a printed copy and saw his head nod as he read the following paragraph, realising that at least there was someone out there who thoroughly understands the hardships he endures in his bid to be recognised as a world-class solo adventurer.

> *'It's time the media pays serious attention to this adventure. It has not had the fanfare of another Holgate safari, nor the adulatory coverage of a balloon trip by Branson, but all the more reason why it's so incredible.*
>
> *'From the very beginning Manser has had to face the hardships of the real, solo adventurer; the preparation, the searching for a suitable craft, the shipping and visa problems and then the cyclones, surf, storms, distances, tropical disease, muggings and even a coup d'état! Done on a shoestring with hardly a whimper, the achievement is already, quite frankly, nothing short of sensational.'*